ŚRĪMAD-BHĀGAVATAM

Ninth Canto

"Liberation"

(Part Three—Chapters 17–24)

With the Original Sanskrit Text,
Its Roman Transliteration, Synonyms,
Translation and Elaborate Purports

by

His Divine Grace
A.C. Bhaktivedanta Swami Prabhupāda
Founder-*Ācārya* of the International Society for Krishna Consciousness

THE BHAKTIVEDANTA BOOK TRUST
New York · Los Angeles · London · Bombay

Readers interested in the subject matter of this book
are invited by the International Society for Krishna Consciousness
to correspond with its Secretary.

International Society for Krishna Consciousness
3764 Watseka Avenue
Los Angeles, California 90034

First Printing, 1977: 20,000 copies

Library of Congress Cataloging in Publication Data (Revised)

Puranas. Bhāgavatapurāna.
Śrīmad-Bhāgavatam.

Includes bibliographical references and indexes.
CONTENTS: Canto 1. Creation. 3 v.—Canto 2. The cosmic manifestation. 2 v.—Canto 3. The status quo. 4 v.—Canto 4. The creation of the Fourth Order. 4 v.—Canto 5. The creative impetus. 2 v.
1. Chaitanya, 1486-1534. I. Bhaktivedanta Swami, A. C., 1896- II. Title.
BL1135.P7A22 1972 73-169353
ISBN 0-912776-96-x

ALL GLORY TO ŚRĪ GURU AND GAURĀṄGA

ŚRĪMAD BHĀGAVATAM

of

KṚṢṆA-DVAIPĀYANA VYĀSA

यन्मायाचेष्टितं पुंसः स्थित्युत्पत्त्यप्ययाय हि ।
अनुग्रहस्तन्निवृत्तेरात्मलाभाय चेष्यते ॥५८॥

yan māyā-ceṣṭitaṁ puṁsaḥ
sthity-utpatty-apyayāya hi
anugrahas tan-nivṛtter
ātma-lābhāya ceṣyate (p. 239)

BOOKS by
His Divine Grace A. C. Bhaktivedanta Swami Prabhupāda

Bhagavad-gītā As It Is
Śrīmad-Bhāgavatam, Cantos 1–9 (27 Vols.)
Śrī Caitanya-caritāmṛta (17 Vols.)
Teachings of Lord Caitanya
The Nectar of Devotion
The Nectar of Instruction
Śrī Īśopaniṣad
Easy Journey to Other Planets
Kṛṣṇa Consciousness: The Topmost Yoga System
Kṛṣṇa, the Supreme Personality of Godhead (3 Vols.)
Perfect Questions, Perfect Answers
Dialectic Spiritualism—A Vedic View of Western Philosophy
Transcendental Teachings of Prahlād Mahārāja
Kṛṣṇa, the Reservoir of Pleasure
Life Comes from Life
The Perfection of Yoga
Beyond Birth and Death
On the Way to Kṛṣṇa
Geetār-gan (Bengali)
Rāja-vidyā: The King of Knowledge
Elevation to Kṛṣṇa Consciousness
Kṛṣṇa Consciousness: The Matchless Gift
Back to Godhead Magazine (Founder)

A complete catalog is available upon request

The Bhaktivedanta Book Trust
3764 Watseka Avenue
Los Angeles, California 90034

Table of Contents

CHAPTER TWENTY-FOUR

Kṛṣṇa, the Supreme Personality of Godhead

Preface

We must know the present need of human society. And what is that need? Human society is no longer bounded by geographical limits to particular countries or communities. Human society is broader than in the Middle Ages, and the world tendency is toward one state or one human society. The ideals of spiritual communism, according to *Śrīmad-Bhāgavatam*, are based more or less on the oneness of the entire human society, nay, of the entire energy of living beings. The need is felt by great thinkers to make this a successful ideology. *Śrīmad-Bhāgavatam* will fill this need in human society. It begins, therefore, with the aphorism of Vedānta philosophy *janmādy asya yataḥ* to establish the ideal of a common cause.

Human society, at the present moment, is not in the darkness of oblivion. It has made rapid progress in the field of material comforts, education and economic development throughout the entire world. But there is a pinprick somewhere in the social body at large, and therefore there are large-scale quarrels, even over less important issues. There is need of a clue as to how humanity can become one in peace, friendship and prosperity with a common cause. *Śrīmad-Bhāgavatam* will fill this need, for it is a cultural presentation for the re-spiritualization of the entire human society.

Śrīmad-Bhāgavatam should be introduced also in the schools and colleges, for it is recommended by the great student-devotee Prahlāda Mahārāja in order to change the demoniac face of society.

kaumāra ācaret prājño
dharmān bhāgavatān iha
durlabhaṁ mānuṣaṁ janma
tad apy adhruvam arthadam
(*Bhāg.* 7.6.1)

Disparity in human society is due to lack of principles in a godless civilization. There is God, or the Almighty One, from whom everything emanates, by whom everything is maintained and in whom everything is merged to rest. Material science has tried to find the ultimate source of creation very insufficiently, but it is a fact that there is one ultimate source of everything that be. This ultimate source is explained rationally and authoritatively in the beautiful *Bhāgavatam* or *Śrīmad-Bhāgavatam.*

Śrīmad-Bhāgavatam is the transcendental science not only for knowing the ultimate source of everything but also for knowing our relation with Him and our duty towards perfection of the human society on the basis of this perfect knowledge. It is powerful reading matter in the Sanskrit language, and it is now rendered into English elaborately so that simply by a careful reading one will know God perfectly well, so much so that the reader will be sufficiently educated to defend himself from the onslaught of atheists. Over and above this, the reader will be able to convert others to accepting God as a concrete principle.

Śrīmad-Bhāgavatam begins with the definition of the ultimate source. It is a bona fide commentary on the *Vedānta-sūtra* by the same author, Śrīla Vyāsadeva, and gradually it develops into nine cantos up to the highest state of God realization. The only qualification one needs to study this great book of transcendental knowledge is to proceed step by step cautiously and not jump forward haphazardly like with an ordinary book. It should be gone through chapter by chapter, one after another. The reading matter is so arranged with its original Sanskrit text, its English transliteration, synonyms, translation and purports so that one is sure to become a God-realized soul at the end of finishing the first nine cantos.

The Tenth Canto is distinct from the first nine cantos because it deals directly with the transcendental activities of the Personality of Godhead Śrī Kṛṣṇa. One will be unable to captuie the effects of the Tenth Canto without going through the first nine cantos. The book is complete in twelve cantos, each independent, but it is good for all to read them in small installments one after another.

I must admit my frailties in presenting *Śrīmad-Bhāgavatam*, but still I am hopeful of its good reception by the thinkers and leaders of society on the strength of the following statement of *Śrīmad-Bhāgavatam* (1.5.11):

tad-vāg-visargo janatāgha-viplavo
yasmin prati-ślokam abaddhavaty api

nāmāny anantasya yaśo 'ṅkitāni yac
chṛṇvanti gāyanti gṛṇanti sādhavaḥ

"On the other hand, that literature which is full with descriptions of the transcendental glories of the name, fame, form and pastimes of the unlimited Supreme Lord is a transcendental creation meant to bring about a revolution in the impious life of a misdirected civilization. Such transcendental literatures, even though irregularly composed, are heard, sung and accepted by purified men who are thoroughly honest."

Oṁ tat sat

A. C. Bhaktivedanta Swami

Introduction

"This *Bhāgavata Purāṇa* is as brilliant as the sun, and it has arisen just after the departure of Lord Kṛṣṇa to His own abode, accompanied by religion, knowledge, etc. Persons who have lost their vision due to the dense darkness of ignorance in the age of Kali shall get light from this *Purāṇa*." (*Śrīmad-Bhāgavatam* 1.3.43)

The timeless wisdom of India is expressed in the *Vedas*, ancient Sanskrit texts that touch upon all fields of human knowledge. Originally preserved through oral tradition, the *Vedas* were first put into writing five thousand years ago by Śrīla Vyāsadeva, the "literary incarnation of God." After compiling the *Vedas*, Vyāsadeva set forth their essence in the aphorisms known as *Vedānta-sūtras*. *Śrīmad-Bhāgavatam* is Vyāsadeva's commentary on his own *Vedānta-sūtras*. It was written in the maturity of his spiritual life under the direction of Nārada Muni, his spiritual master. Referred to as "the ripened fruit of the tree of Vedic literature," *Śrīmad-Bhāgavatam* is the most complete and authoritative exposition of Vedic knowledge.

After compiling the *Bhāgavatam*, Vyāsa impressed the synopsis of it upon his son, the sage Śukadeva Gosvāmī. Śukadeva Gosvāmī subsequently recited the entire *Bhāgavatam* to Mahārāja Parīkṣit in an assembly of learned saints on the bank of the Ganges at Hastināpura (now Delhi). Mahārāja Parīkṣit was the emperor of the world and was a great *rājarṣi* (saintly king). Having received a warning that he would die within a week, he renounced his entire kingdom and retired to the bank of the Ganges to fast until death and receive spiritual enlightenment. The *Bhāgavatam* begins with Emperor Parīkṣit's sober inquiry to Śukadeva Gosvāmī: "You are the spiritual master of great saints and devotees. I am therefore begging you to show the way of perfection for all persons, and especially for one who is about to die. Please let me know what a man should hear, chant, remember and worship, and also what he should not do. Please explain all this to me."

Śukadeva Gosvāmī's answer to this question, and numerous other questions posed by Mahārāja Parīkṣit, concerning everything from the nature of the self to the origin of the universe, held the assembled sages in rapt attention continuously for the seven days leading to the King's death. The sage Sūta Gosvāmī, who was present on the bank of the Ganges when Śukadeva Gosvāmī first recited *Śrīmad-Bhāgavatam,* later repeated the *Bhāgavatam* before a gathering of sages in the forest of Naimiṣāraṇya. Those sages, concerned about the spiritual welfare of the people in general, had gathered to perform a long, continuous chain of sacrifices to counteract the degrading influence of the incipient age of Kali. In response to the sages' request that he speak the essence of Vedic wisdom, Sūta Gosvāmī repeated from memory the entire eighteen thousand verses of *Śrīmad-Bhāgavatam,* as spoken by Śukadeva Gosvāmī to Mahārāja Parīkṣit.

The reader of *Śrīmad-Bhāgavatam* hears Sūta Gosvāmī relate the questions of Mahārāja Parīkṣit and the answers of Śukadeva Gosvāmī. Also, Sūta Gosvāmī sometimes responds directly to questions put by Śaunaka Ṛṣi, the spokesman for the sages gathered at Naimiṣāraṇya. One therefore simultaneously hears two dialogues: one between Mahārāja Parīkṣit and Śukadeva Gosvāmī on the bank of the Ganges, and another at Naimiṣāraṇya between Sūta Gosvāmī and the sages at Naimiṣāraṇya Forest, headed by Śaunaka Ṛṣi. Furthermore, while instructing King Parīkṣit, Śukadeva Gosvāmī often relates historical episodes and gives accounts of lengthy philosophical discussions between such great souls as the saint Maitreya and his disciple Vidura. With this understanding of the history of the *Bhāgavatam,* the reader will easily be able to follow its intermingling of dialogues and events from various sources. Since philosophical wisdom, not chronological order, is most important in the text, one need only be attentive to the subject matter of *Śrīmad-Bhāgavatam* to appreciate fully its profound message.

The translator of this edition compares the *Bhāgavatam* to sugar candy—wherever you taste it, you will find it equally sweet and relishable. Therefore, to taste the sweetness of the *Bhāgavatam,* one may begin by reading any of its volumes. After such an introductory taste, however, the serious reader is best advised to go back to Volume One of the First Canto and then proceed through the *Bhāgavatam,* volume after volume, in its natural order.

This edition of the *Bhāgavatam* is the first complete English translation of this important text with an elaborate commentary, and it is the first widely available to the English-speaking public. It is the product of the scholarly and devotional effort of His Divine Grace A. C. Bhaktivedanta Swami Prabhupāda, the world's most distinguished teacher of Indian religious and philosophical thought. His consummate Sanskrit scholarship and intimate familiarity with Vedic culture and thought as well as the modern way of life combine to reveal to the West a magnificent exposition of this important classic.

Readers will find this work of value for many reasons. For those interested in the classical roots of Indian civilization, it serves as a vast reservoir of detailed information on virtually every one of its aspects. For students of comparative philosophy and religion, the *Bhāgavatam* offers a penetrating view into the meaning of India's profound spiritual heritage. To sociologists and anthropologists, the *Bhāgavatam* reveals the practical workings of a peaceful and scientifically organized Vedic culture, whose institutions were integrated on the basis of a highly developed spiritual world view. Students of literature will discover the *Bhāgavatam* to be a masterpiece of majestic poetry. For students of psychology, the text provides important perspectives on the nature of consciousness, human behavior and the philosophical study of identity. Finally, to those seeking spiritual insight, the *Bhāgavatam* offers simple and practical guidance for attainment of the highest self-knowledge and realization of the Absolute Truth. The entire multivolume text, presented by the Bhaktivedanta Book Trust, promises to occupy a significant place in the intellectual, cultural and spiritual life of modern man for a long time to come.

The Publishers

His Divine Grace
A. C. Bhaktivedanta Swami Prabhupāda
Founder-Ācārya of the International Society for Krishna Consciousness

PLATE ONE

One day Vṛṣaparvā's daughter Śarmiṣṭhā, who was innocent but angry by nature, was walking in the palace garden with Śukrācārya's daughter Devayānī and thousands of other friends. The garden was full of lotuses, sweetly singing birds and bumblebees, and trees laden with flowers and fruits. When the young, lotus-eyed girls came to the bank of a reservoir of water, they wanted to enjoy by bathing. Thus they left their clothing on the bank and began sporting, throwing water on one another. While sporting in the water, the girls suddenly saw Lord Śiva passing by, seated on the back of his bull with his wife, Pārvatī. Ashamed because they were naked, the girls quickly got out of the water and covered themselves with their garments. Śarmiṣṭhā unknowingly put Devayānī's dress on her own body, thus angering Devayānī, who then spoke as follows: "Oh, just see the activities of this servant-maid, Śarmiṣṭhā! Disregarding all etiquette, she has put on my dress, just like a dog snatching clarified butter meant for use in a sacrifice!" *(pp. 19–21)*

PLATE TWO

The princess Śarmiṣṭhā once approached King Yayāti at the appropriate time for conception. In a secluded place, she requested the King, the husband of her friend Devayānī, to enable her to have a son also. Aware of the principles of religion, which state that a warrior or king must fulfill the sexual desire of any woman who approaches him, King Yayāti agreed to Śarmiṣṭhā's request. Although he remembered that Devayānī's father, Śukrācārya, had warned him against the act, King Yayāti considered this union the desire of the Supreme and had sex with Śarmiṣṭhā. When the proud Devayānī understood from outside sources that Śarmiṣṭhā was pregnant by her husband, she became frenzied with anger. Thus she departed for her father's house. King Yayāti, who was very lusty, followed his wife, caught her and tried to appease her by speaking pleasing words and massaging her feet, but he could not satisfy her by any means. When Śukrācārya learned of the situation, he became extremely angry. He furiously addressed the King: "You untruthful fool, lusting after women! You have done a great wrong. I therefore curse you to be attacked and disfigured by old age and invalidity!" *(pp. 35–38)*

PLATE THREE

Once, after the exalted King Rantideva spent forty-eight days fasting, not even drinking water, excellent food made with ghee was brought to him, but when he was about to eat it, a *brāhmaṇa* guest appeared. Rantideva, therefore, did not eat the food, but instead immediately offered a portion of it to the *brāhmaṇa.* When the *brāhmaṇa* left and Rantideva was just about to eat the remnants of the food, a *śūdra* appeared. Rantideva therefore divided the remnants between the *śūdra* and himself. Again, when he was just about to eat the remnants of the food, another guest appeared. Rantideva therefore gave the rest of the food to the new guest and was about to content himself with drinking some water to quench his thirst, but this also was precluded, for a thirsty guest came and Rantideva gave him the water. This was all ordained by the Supreme Personality of Godhead just to glorify King Rantideva—to show how tolerant a devotee is and how readily he foregoes his own satisfaction for the benefit of others. *(pp. 123–129)*

PLATE FOUR

After Śrīla Vyāsadeva and his wife (the daughter of Jābāli) had performed penances together for many years, he placed his seed in her womb. The child remained in the womb of his mother for twelve years, and when the father asked the son to come out, the son replied that he would not come out unless he were completely liberated from the influence of *māyā* (illusion). Vyāsadeva then assured the child that he would not be influenced by *māyā*, but the child did not believe his father, for the father was still attached to his wife and children. Vyāsadeva then went to Dvārakā and informed Lord Kṛṣṇa, the Personality of Godhead, about his problem. At Vyāsadeva's request, Lord Kṛṣṇa then went to Vyāsadeva's cottage, where he assured the child in the womb that he would not be influenced by *māyā*. Thus assured, the child came out, but he immediately went away and became the great *parivrājakācārya* (wandering saint) Śukadeva Gosvāmī. *(p. 140)*

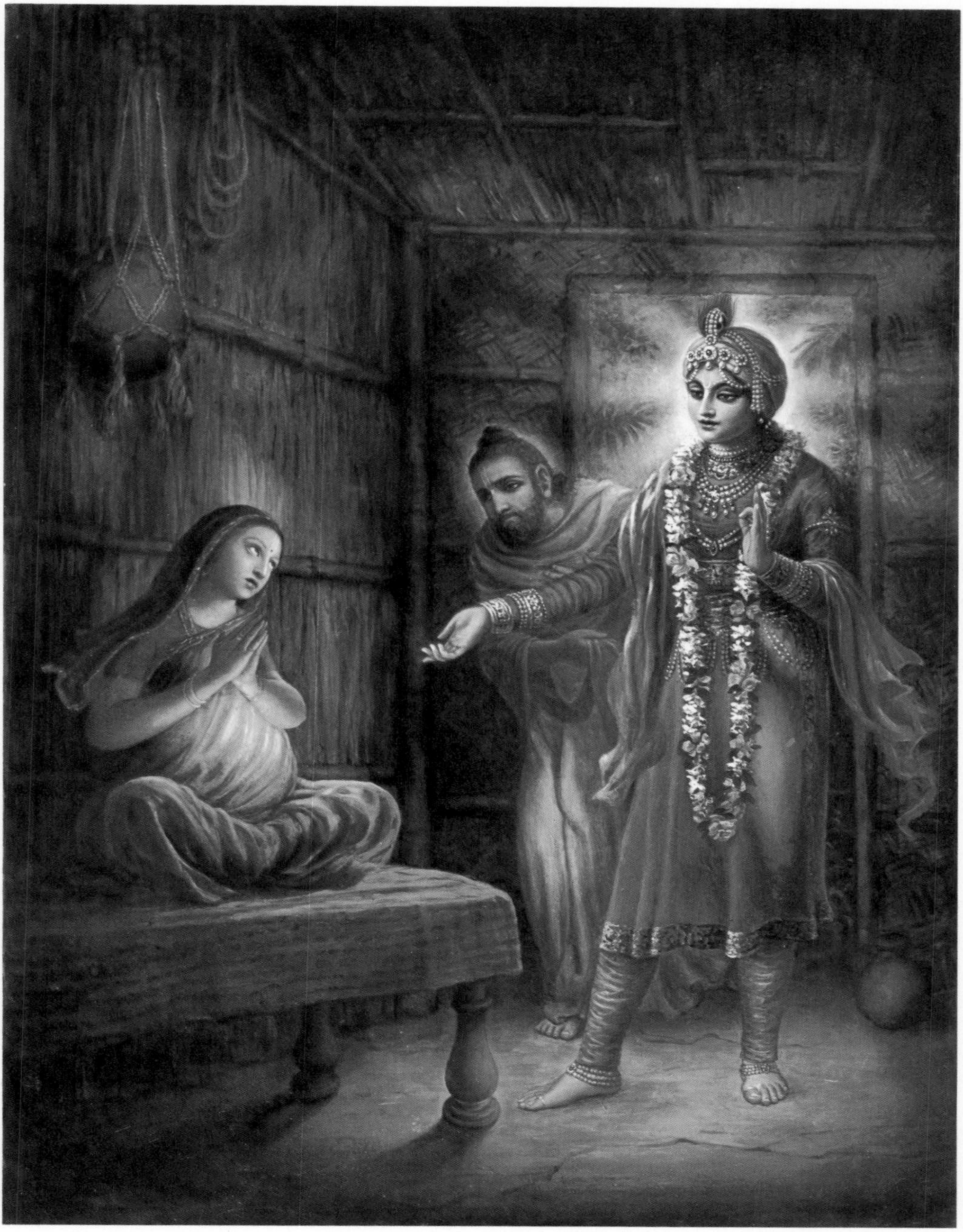

PLATE FIVE

Once when the powerful *yogī* Durvāsā was a guest at the house of Kuntī's father, Kuntī satisfied Durvāsā by rendering service. Therefore she received a mystic power by which she could call any demigod. To examine the potency of this mystic power, the pious Kuntī called for the sun-god, who immediately appeared before her, much to her surprise. She told the sun-god, "I was simply examining the effectiveness of this mystic power. I am sorry I have called you unnecessarily. Please return and excuse me." The sun-god said, "O beautiful Kuntī, your meeting with a demigod cannot be fruitless. Therefore, let me place my seed in your womb so that you may bear a son. I shall arrange to keep your virginity intact, since you are still an unmarried girl." After saying this, the sun-god discharged his semen into the womb of Kuntī and then returned to the celestial kingdom. Immediately thereafter, Kuntī gave birth to a child, who was like a second sun-god. *(pp. 222–224)*

PLATE SIX

The Supreme Personality of Godhead, Kṛṣṇa, the Supersoul in the hearts of all living entities, descends in His original form as a human being in the dynasty of Yadu. By His pleasing smiles, His affectionate behavior, His instructions and His uncommon pastimes like raising Govardhana Hill, Lord Kṛṣṇa pleases all of human society. Although the Lord's form exactly resembles that of a human being, His form is different from ours, for it is completely spiritual and thus attractive to everyone. Kṛṣṇa's body is the essence of loveliness, and, as the only abode of beauty, fame and opulence, it is self-perfect and ever-fresh. One of the *gopīs* once playfully warned her friend about the power of Kṛṣṇa's attraction: "My dear friend, if you are at all attached to your worldly friends, do not look at the smiling face of Lord Govinda as He stands on the bank of the Yamunā at Keśī-ghāṭa. Casting sidelong glances, He places His flute to His lips, which seem like newly blossomed twigs. His transcendental body, bending in three places, appears very bright in the moonlight." *(p. 248)*

PLATE SEVEN

Kṛṣṇa's face, which is like an eternal festival of beauty, is decorated with ornaments, such as earrings resembling sharks. His ears are beautiful, His cheeks brilliant, and His smiling attractive to everyone. The inhabitants of Vṛndāvana, such as the cowherd boys, the cows, the calves, the *gopīs* and Kṛṣṇa's father and mother, enjoyed seeing Kṛṣṇa's beautiful features so much that they could never be fully satisfied. Thus they became angry at the creator for the disturbance caused by the momentary blinking of their eyes. The *gopīs* especially were very much afflicted by Kṛṣṇa's absence. When He left Vṛndāvana village for the pasturing grounds, where He tended the cows and calves, the *gopīs* saw Kṛṣṇa walking on the path and thought that His lotus feet (which the *gopīs* dared not place on their breasts because they thought their breasts too hard) were being pierced by broken chips of stone. Just by thinking in this way, the *gopīs* were affected, and they cried at home. *(pp. 249–250)*

CHAPTER SEVENTEEN

The Dynasties of the Sons of Purūravā

Āyu, the eldest son of Purūravā, had five sons. This chapter describes the dynasties of four of them, beginning with Kṣatravṛddha.

Āyu, the son of Purūravā, had five sons—Nahuṣa, Kṣatravṛddha, Rajī, Rābha and Anenā. The son of Kṣatravṛddha was Suhotra, who had three sons, named Kāśya, Kuśa and Gṛtsamada. The son of Gṛtsamada was Śunaka, and his son was Śaunaka. The son of Kāśya was Kāśi. From Kāśi came the sons and grandsons known as Rāṣṭra, Dīrghatama and then Dhanvantari, who was the inaugurator of medical science and was a *śaktyāveśa* incarnation of the Supreme Personality of Godhead, Vāsudeva. The descendants of Dhanvantari were Ketumān, Bhīmaratha, Divodāsa and Dyumān, who was also known as Pratardana, Śatrujit, Vatsa, Ṛtadhvaja and Kuvalayāśva. The son of Dyumān was Alarka, who reigned over the kingdom for many, many years. Following in the dynasty of Alarka were Santati, Sunītha, Niketana, Dharmaketu, Satyaketu, Dhṛṣṭaketu, Sukumāra, Vītihotra, Bharga and Bhārgabhūmi. All of them belonged to the dynasty of Kāśi, the descendant of Kṣatravṛddha.

The son of Rābha was Rabhasa, and his son was Gambhīra. Gambhīra's son was Akriya, and from Akriya came Brahmavit. The son of Anenā was Śuddha, and his son was Śuci. The son of Śuci was Citrakṛt, whose son was Śāntaraja. Rajī had five hundred sons, all of extraordinary strength. Rajī was personally very powerful and was given the kingdom of heaven by Lord Indra. Later, after Rajī's death, when the sons of Rajī refused to return the kingdom to Indra, by Bṛhaspati's arrangement they became unintelligent, and Lord Indra conquered them.

The grandson of Kṣatravṛddha named Kuśa gave birth to a son named Prati. From Prati came Sañjaya; from Sañjaya, Jaya; from Jaya, Kṛta; and from Kṛta, Haryabala. The son of Haryabala was Sahadeva; the son of Sahadeva, Hīna; the son of Hīna, Jayasena; the son of Jayasena, Saṅkṛti; and the son of Saṅkṛti, Jaya.

TEXTS 1–3

श्रीबादरायणिरुवाच
यः पुरूरवसः पुत्र आयुस्तस्याभवन् सुताः ।
नहुषः क्षत्रवृद्धश्च रजी राभश्च वीर्यवान् ॥ १ ॥
अनेना इति राजेन्द्र शृणु क्षत्रवृधोऽन्वयम् ।
क्षत्रवृद्धसुतस्यासन् सुहोत्रस्यात्मजास्त्रयः ॥ २ ॥
काश्यः कुशो गृत्समद इति गृत्समदादभूत् ।
शुनकः शौनको यस्य बह्वृचप्रवरो मुनिः ॥ ३ ॥

śrī-bādarāyaṇir uvāca
yaḥ purūravasaḥ putra
āyus tasyābhavan sutāḥ
nahuṣaḥ kṣatravṛddhaś ca
rajī rābhaś ca vīryavān

anenā iti rājendra
śṛṇu kṣatravṛdho 'nvayam
kṣatravṛddha-sutasyāsan
suhotrasyātmajās trayaḥ

kāśyaḥ kuśo gṛtsamada
iti gṛtsamadād abhūt
śunakaḥ śaunako yasya
bahvṛca-pravaro muniḥ

śrī-bādarāyaṇiḥ uvāca—Śrī Śukadeva Gosvāmī said; *yaḥ*—one who; *purūravasaḥ*—of Purūravā; *putraḥ*—son; *āyuḥ*—his name was Āyu; *tasya*—of him; *abhavan*—there were; *sutāḥ*—sons; *nahuṣaḥ*—Nahuṣa; *kṣatravṛddhaḥ ca*—and Kṣatravṛddha; *rajī*—Rajī; *rābhaḥ*—Rābha; *ca*—also; *vīryavān*—very powerful; *anenāḥ*—Anenā; *iti*—thus; *rāja-indra*—O Mahārāja Parīkṣit; *śṛṇu*—just hear from me; *kṣatravṛdhaḥ*—of Kṣatravṛddha; *anvayam*—the dynasty; *kṣatravṛddha*—of Kṣatra-vṛddha; *sutasya*—of the son; *āsan*—there were; *suhotrasya*—of Suhotra; *ātmajāḥ*—sons; *trayaḥ*—three; *kāśyaḥ*—Kāśya; *kuśaḥ*—Kuśa; *gṛtsamadaḥ*—Gṛtsamada; *iti*—thus; *gṛtsamadāt*—from Gṛtsamada; *abhūt*—there was; *śunakaḥ*—Śunaka; *śaunakaḥ*—Śaunaka; *yasya*—of whom (Śunaka); *bahu-ṛca-pravaraḥ*—the best of those conversant with the *Ṛg Veda; muniḥ*—a great saintly person.

TRANSLATION

Śukadeva Gosvāmī said: From Purūravā came a son named Āyu, whose very powerful sons were Nahuṣa, Kṣatravṛddha, Rajī, Rābha and Anenā. O Mahārāja Parīkṣit, now hear about the dynasty of Kṣatravṛddha. Kṣatravṛddha's son was Suhotra, who had three sons, named Kāśya, Kuśa and Gṛtsamada. From Gṛtsamada came Śunaka, and from him came Śaunaka, the great saint, the best of those conversant with the Ṛg Veda.

TEXT 4

काश्यस्य काशिस्तत्पुत्रो राष्ट्रो दीर्घतमःपिता ।
धन्वन्तरिर्दीर्घतमस आयुर्वेदप्रवर्तकः ।
यज्ञभुग् वासुदेवांशः स्मृतमात्रार्तिनाशनः ॥ ४ ॥

kāśyasya kāśis tat-putro
rāṣṭro dīrghatamaḥ-pitā
dhanvantarir dīrghatamasa
āyur-veda-pravartakaḥ
yajña-bhug vāsudevāṁśaḥ
smṛta-mātrārti-nāśanaḥ

kāśyasya—of Kāśya; *kāśiḥ*—Kāśi; *tat-putraḥ*—his son; *rāṣṭraḥ*—Rāṣṭra; *dīrghatamaḥ-pitā*—he became the father of Dīrghatama; *dhanvantariḥ*—Dhanvantari; *dīrghatamasaḥ*—from Dīrghatama; *āyuḥ-veda-pravartakaḥ*—the inaugurator of medical science, *Āyur Veda; yajña-bhuk*—the enjoyer of the results of sacrifice; *vāsudeva-aṁśaḥ*—incarnation of Lord Vāsudeva; *smṛta-mātra*—if he is remembered; *ārti-nāśanaḥ*—it immediately vanquishes all kinds of disease.

TRANSLATION

The son of Kāśya was Kāśi, and his son was Rāṣṭra, the father of Dīrghatama. Dīrghatama had a son named Dhanvantari, who was

the inaugurator of the medical science and an incarnation of Lord Vāsudeva, the enjoyer of the results of sacrifices. One who remembers the name of Dhanvantari can be released from all disease.

TEXT 5

तत्पुत्रः केतुमानस्य जज्ञे भीमरथस्ततः ।
दिवोदासो द्युमांस्तस्मात् प्रतर्दन इति स्मृतः ॥ ५ ॥

tat-putraḥ ketumān asya
jajñe bhīmarathas tataḥ
divodāso dyumāṁs tasmāt
pratardana iti smṛtaḥ

tat-putraḥ—his son (the son of Dhanvantari); *ketumān*—Ketumān; *asya*—his; *jajñe*—took birth; *bhīmarathaḥ*—a son named Bhīmaratha; *tataḥ*—from him; *divodāsaḥ*—a son named Divodāsa; *dyumān*—Dyumān; *tasmāt*—from him; *pratardanaḥ*—Pratardana; *iti*—thus; *smṛtaḥ*—known.

TRANSLATION

The son of Dhanvantari was Ketumān, and his son was Bhīmaratha. The son of Bhīmaratha was Divodāsa, and the son of Divodāsa was Dyumān, also known as Pratardana.

TEXT 6

स एव शत्रुजिद् वत्स ऋतध्वज इतीरितः ।
तथा कुवलयाश्वेति प्रोक्तोऽलर्कादयस्ततः ॥ ६ ॥

sa eva śatrujid vatsa
ṛtadhvaja itīritaḥ
tathā kuvalayāśveti
prokto 'larkādayas tataḥ

saḥ—that Dyumān; *eva*—indeed; *śatrujit*—Śatrujit; *vatsaḥ*—Vatsa; *ṛtadhvajaḥ*—Ṛtadhvaja; *iti*—like that; *īritaḥ*—known; *tathā*—as well as; *kuvalayāśva*—Kuvalayāśva; *iti*—thus; *proktaḥ*—well known; *alarka-ādayaḥ*—Alarka and other sons; *tataḥ*—from him.

TRANSLATION

Dyumān was also known as Śatrujit, Vatsa, Ṛtadhvaja and Kuvalayāśva. From him were born Alarka and other sons.

TEXT 7

षष्टिंवर्षसहस्राणि षष्टिंवर्षशतानि च ।
नालर्कादपरो राजन् बुभुजे मेदिनीं युवा ॥ ७ ॥

ṣaṣṭiṁ varṣa-sahasrāṇi
ṣaṣṭiṁ varṣa-śatāni ca
nālarkād aparo rājan
bubhuje medinīṁ yuvā

ṣaṣṭim—sixty; *varṣa-sahasrāṇi*—such thousands of years; *ṣaṣṭim*—sixty; *varṣa-śatāni*—hundreds of years; *ca*—also; *na*—not; *alarkāt*—except for Alarka; *aparaḥ*—anyone else; *rājan*—O King Parīkṣit; *bubhuje*—enjoyed; *medinīm*—the surface of the world; *yuvā*—as a young man.

TRANSLATION

Alarka, the son of Dyumān, reigned over the earth for sixty-six thousand years, my dear King Parīkṣit. No one other than him has reigned over the earth for so long as a young man.

TEXT 8

अलर्कात् सन्ततिस्तस्मात् सुनीथोऽथ निकेतनः ।
धर्मकेतुः सुतस्तस्मात् सत्यकेतुरजायत ॥ ८ ॥

alarkāt santatis tasmāt
sunītho 'tha niketanaḥ
dharmaketuḥ sutas tasmāt
satyaketur ajāyata

alarkāt—from Alarka; *santatiḥ*—a son known as Santati; *tasmāt*—from him; *sunīthaḥ*—Sunītha; *atha*—from him; *niketanaḥ*—a son named Niketana; *dharmaketuḥ*—Dharmaketu; *sutaḥ*—a son; *tasmāt*—and from Dharmaketu; *satyaketuḥ*—Satyaketu; *ajāyata*—was born.

TRANSLATION

From Alarka came a son named Santati, and his son was Sunītha. The son of Sunītha was Niketana, the son of Niketana was Dharmaketu, and the son of Dharmaketu was Satyaketu.

TEXT 9

धृष्टकेतुस्ततस्तस्मात् सुकुमारः क्षितीश्वरः ।
वीतिहोत्रोऽस्य भर्गोऽतो भार्गभूमिरभून्नृप ॥ ९ ॥

dhṛṣṭaketus tatas tasmāt
sukumāraḥ kṣitīśvaraḥ
vītihotro 'sya bhargo 'to
bhārgabhūmir abhūn nṛpa

dhṛṣṭaketuḥ—Dhṛṣṭaketu; *tataḥ*—thereafter; *tasmāt*—from Dhṛṣṭaketu; *sukumāraḥ*—a son named Sukumāra; *kṣiti-īśvaraḥ*—the emperor of the entire world; *vītihotraḥ*—a son named Vītihotra; *asya*—his son; *bhargaḥ*—Bharga; *ataḥ*—from him; *bhārgabhūmiḥ*—a son named Bhārgabhūmi; *abhūt*—generated; *nṛpa*—O King.

TRANSLATION

O King Parīkṣit, from Satyaketu came a son named Dhṛṣṭaketu, and from Dhṛṣṭaketu came Sukumāra, the emperor of the entire world. From Sukumāra came a son named Vītihotra; from Vītihotra, Bharga; and from Bharga, Bhārgabhūmi.

TEXT 10

इतीमे काशयो भूपाः क्षत्रवृद्धान्वयायिनः ।
राभस्य रभसः पुत्रो गम्भीरश्चाक्रियस्ततः ॥१०॥

itīme kāśayo bhūpāḥ
kṣatravṛddhānvayāyinaḥ

rābhasya rabhasaḥ putro
gambhīraś cākriyas tataḥ

iti—thus; *ime*—all of them; *kāśayaḥ*—born in the dynasty of Kāśi; *bhūpāḥ*—kings; *kṣatravṛddha-anvaya-āyinaḥ*—also within the dynasty of Kṣatravṛddha; *rābhasya*—from Rābha; *rabhasaḥ*—Rabhasa; *putraḥ*—a son; *gambhīraḥ*—Gambhīra; *ca*—also; *akriyaḥ*—Akriya; *tataḥ*—from him.

TRANSLATION

O Mahārāja Parīkṣit, all of these kings were descendants of Kāśi, and they could also be called descendants of Kṣatravṛddha. The son of Rābha was Rabhasa, from Rabhasa came Gambhīra, and from Gambhīra came a son named Akriya.

TEXT 11

तद्गोत्रं ब्रह्मविज् जज्ञे शृणु वंशमनेनसः ।
शुद्धस्ततः शुचिस्तस्माच्चित्रकृद् धर्मसारथिः ॥११॥

tad-gotraṁ brahmavij jajñe
śṛṇu vaṁśam anenasaḥ
śuddhas tataḥ śucis tasmāc
citrakṛd dharmasārathiḥ

tat-gotram—the descendant of Akriya; *brahmavit*—Brahmavit; *jajñe*—took birth; *śṛṇu*—just hear from me; *vaṁśam*—descendants; *anenasaḥ*—of Anenā; *śuddhaḥ*—a son known as Śuddha; *tataḥ*—from him; *śuciḥ*—Śuci; *tasmāt*—from him; *citrakṛt*—Citrakṛt; *dharma-sārathiḥ*—Dharmasārathi.

TRANSLATION

The son of Akriya was known as Brahmavit, O King. Now hear about the descendants of Anenā. From Anenā came a son named Śuddha, and his son was Śuci. The son of Śuci was Dharmasārathi, also called Citrakṛt.

TEXT 12

ततः शान्तरजो जज्ञे कृतकृत्यः स आत्मवान् ।
रजेः पञ्चशतान्यासन् पुत्राणाममितौजसाम् ॥१२॥

tataḥ śāntarajo jajñe
kṛta-kṛtyaḥ sa ātmavān
rajeḥ pañca-śatāny āsan
putrāṇām amitaujasām

tataḥ—from Citrakṛt; *śāntarajaḥ*—a son named Śāntaraja; *jajñe*—was born; *kṛta-kṛtyaḥ*—performed all kinds of ritualistic ceremonies; *saḥ*—he; *ātmavān*—a self-realized soul; *rajeḥ*—of Rajī; *pañca-śatāni*—five hundred; *āsan*—there were; *putrāṇām*—sons; *amita-ojasām*—very, very powerful.

TRANSLATION

From Citrakṛt was born a son named Śāntaraja, a self-realized soul who performed all kinds of Vedic ritualistic ceremonies and therefore did not beget any progeny. The sons of Rajī were five hundred, all very powerful.

TEXT 13

देवैरभ्यर्थितो दैत्यान् हत्वेन्द्रायाददाद् दिवम् ।
इन्द्रस्तस्मै पुनर्दत्त्वा गृहीत्वा चरणौ रजेः ।
आत्मानमर्पयामास प्रह्रादाद्यरिशङ्कितः ॥१३॥

devair abhyarthito daityān
hatvendrāyādadād divam
indras tasmai punar dattvā
gṛhītvā caraṇau rajeḥ
ātmānam arpayām āsa
prahrādādy-ari-śaṅkitaḥ

devaiḥ—by the demigods; *abhyarthitaḥ*—being requested; *daityān*—the demons; *hatvā*—killing; *indrāya*—to Indra, the King of heaven; *adadāt*—delivered; *divam*—the kingdom of heaven; *indraḥ*—the King of heaven; *tasmai*—unto him, Rajī; *punaḥ*—again; *dattvā*—returning; *gṛhītvā*—capturing; *caraṇau*—the feet; *rajeḥ* —of Rajī; *ātmānam*—the self; *arpayām āsa*—surrendered; *prahrāda-ādi*—Prahlāda and others; *ari-śaṅkitaḥ*—being afraid of such enemies.

TRANSLATION

On the request of the demigods, Rajī killed the demons and thus returned the kingdom of heaven to Lord Indra. But Indra, fearing such demons as Prahlāda, returned the kingdom of heaven to Rajī and surrendered himself at Rajī's lotus feet.

TEXT 14

पितर्युपरते पुत्रा याचमानाय नो ददुः ।
त्रिविष्टपं महेन्द्राय यज्ञभागान् समाददुः ॥१४॥

pitary uparate putrā
yācamānāya no daduḥ
triviṣṭapaṁ mahendrāya
yajña-bhāgān samādaduḥ

pitari—when their father; *uparate*—passed away; *putrāḥ*—the sons; *yācamānāya*—although requesting from them; *no*—not; *daduḥ*—returned; *triviṣṭapam*—the heavenly kingdom; *mahendrāya*—unto Mahendra; *yajña-bhāgān*—the shares of ritualistic ceremonies; *samādaduḥ*—gave.

TRANSLATION

Upon Rajī's death, Indra begged Rajī's sons for the return of the heavenly planet. They did not return it, however, although they agreed to return Indra's shares in ritualistic ceremonies.

PURPORT

Rajī conquered the kingdom of heaven, and therefore when Indra, the heavenly king, begged Rajī's sons to return it, they refused. Because they had not taken the heavenly kingdom from Indra but had inherited it from their father, they considered it their paternal property. Why then should they return it to the demigods?

TEXT 15

गुरुणा हूयमानेऽग्नौ बलभित् तनयान् रजेः ।
अवधीद् भ्रंशितान् मार्गान्न कश्चिदवशेषितः ॥१५॥

guruṇā hūyamāne 'gnau
balabhit tanayān rajeḥ
avadhīd bhraṁśitān mārgān
na kaścid avaśeṣitaḥ

guruṇā—by the spiritual master (Bṛhaspati); *hūyamāne agnau*—while oblations were being offered in the fire of sacrifice; *balabhit*—Indra; *tanayān*—the sons; *rajeḥ*—of Rajī; *avadhīt*—killed; *bhraṁśitān*—fallen; *mārgāt*—from the moral principles; *na*—not; *kaścit*—anyone; *avaśeṣitaḥ*—remained alive.

TRANSLATION

Thereafter, Bṛhaspati, the spiritual master of the demigods, offered oblations in the fire so that the sons of Rajī would fall from moral principles. When they fell, Lord Indra killed them easily because of their degradation. Not a single one of them remained alive.

TEXT 16

कुशात् प्रतिः क्षात्रवृद्धात् सञ्जयस्तत्सुतो जयः ।
ततः कृतः कृतस्यापि जज्ञे हर्यबलो नृपः ॥१६॥

kuśāt pratiḥ kṣātravṛddhāt
sañjayas tat-suto jayaḥ
tataḥ kṛtaḥ kṛtasyāpi
jajñe haryabalo nṛpaḥ

kuśāt—from Kuśa; *pratiḥ*—a son named Prati; *kṣātravṛddhāt*—the grandson of Kṣatravṛddha; *sañjayaḥ*—a son named Sañjaya; *tat-sutaḥ*—his son; *jayaḥ*—Jaya; *tataḥ*—from him; *kṛtaḥ*—Kṛta; *kṛtasya*—from Kṛta; *api*—as well as; *jajñe*—was born; *haryabalaḥ*—Haryabala; *nṛpaḥ*—the king.

TRANSLATION

From Kuśa, the grandson of Kṣatravṛddha, was born a son named Prati. The son of Prati was Sañjaya, and the son of Sañjaya was Jaya. From Jaya, Kṛta was born, and from Kṛta, King Haryabala.

TEXT 17

सहदेवस्ततो हीनो जयसेनस्तु तत्सुतः ।
सङ्कृतिस्तस्य च जयः क्षत्रधर्मा महारथः ।
क्षत्रवृद्धान्वया भूपा इमेश्रृण्वथनाहुषान् ॥१७॥

sahadevas tato hīno
jayasenas tu tat-sutaḥ
saṅkṛtis tasya ca jayaḥ
kṣatra-dharmā mahā-rathaḥ
kṣatravṛddhānvayā bhūpā
ime śṛṇv atha nāhuṣān

sahadevaḥ—Sahadeva; *tataḥ*—from Sahadeva; *hīnaḥ*—a son named Hīna; *jayasenaḥ*—Jayasena; *tu*—also; *tat-sutaḥ*—the son of Hīna; *saṅkṛtiḥ*—Saṅkṛti; *tasya*—of Saṅkṛti; *ca*—also; *jayaḥ*—a son named Jaya; *kṣatra-dharmā*—expert in the duties of a *kṣatriya; mahā-rathaḥ*—a greatly powerful fighter; *kṣatravṛddha-anvayāḥ*—in the dynasty of Kṣatravṛddha; *bhūpāḥ*—kings; *ime*—all these; *śṛṇu*—hear from me; *atha*—now; *nāhuṣān*—the descendants of Nahuṣa.

TRANSLATION

From Haryabala came a son named Sahadeva, and from Sahadeva came Hīna. The son of Hīna was Jayasena, and the son of Jayasena was Saṅkṛti. The son of Saṅkṛti was the powerful and expert fighter named Jaya. These kings were the members of the Kṣatravṛddha dynasty. Now let me describe to you the dynasty of Nahuṣa.

Thus end the Bhaktivedanta purports of the Ninth Canto, Seventeenth Chapter, of the Śrīmad-Bhāgavatam, *entitled "The Dynasties of the Sons of Purūravā."*

CHAPTER EIGHTEEN

King Yayāti Regains His Youth

This chapter gives the history of King Yayāti, the son of Nahuṣa. Among Yayāti's five sons, the youngest son, Pūru, accepted Yayāti's invalidity.

When Nahuṣa, who had six sons, was cursed to become a python, his eldest son, Yati, took *sannyāsa*, and therefore the next son, Yayāti, was enthroned as king. By providence, Yayāti married the daughter of Śukrācārya. Śukrācārya was a *brāhmaṇa* and Yayāti a *kṣatriya*, but Yayāti married her nonetheless. Śukrācārya's daughter, named Devayānī, had a girl friend named Śarmiṣṭhā, who was the daughter of Vṛṣaparvā. King Yayāti married Śarmiṣṭhā also. The history of this marriage is as follows. Once Śarmiṣṭhā was sporting in the water with thousands of her girl friends, and Devayānī was also there. When the young girls saw Lord Śiva, seated on his bull with Umā, they immediately dressed themselves, but Śarmiṣṭhā mistakenly put on Devayānī's clothes. Devayānī, being very angry, rebuked Śarmiṣṭhā, who also became very angry and responded by rebuking Devayānī and throwing her into a well. By chance, King Yayāti came to that well to drink water, and he found Devayānī and rescued her. Thus Devayānī accepted Mahārāja Yayāti as her husband. Thereafter, Devayānī, crying loudly, told her father about Śarmiṣṭhā's behavior. Upon hearing of this incident, Śukrācārya was very angry and wanted to chastise Vṛṣaparvā, Śarmiṣṭhā's father. Vṛṣaparvā, however, satisfied Śukrācārya by offering Śarmiṣṭhā as Devayānī's maidservant. Thus Śarmiṣṭhā, as the maidservant of Devayānī, also went to the house of Devayānī's husband. When Śarmiṣṭhā found her friend Devayānī with a son she also desired to have a son. Therefore, at the proper time for conception, she also requested Mahārāja Yayāti for sex. When Śarmiṣṭhā became pregnant also, Devayānī was very envious. In great anger, she immediately left for her father's house and told her father everything. Śukrācārya again became angry and cursed Mahārāja Yayāti to become old, but when Yayāti begged

Śukrācārya to be merciful to him, Śukrācārya gave him the benediction that he could transfer his old age and invalidity to some young man. Yayāti exchanged his old age for the youth of his youngest son, Pūru, and thus he was able to enjoy with young girls.

TEXT 1

श्रीशुक उवाच
यतिर्ययातिः संयातिरायतिर्वियतिः कृतिः ।
षडिमे नहुषस्यासन्निन्द्रियाणीव देहिनः ॥ १ ॥

śrī-śuka uvāca
yatir yayātiḥ saṁyātir
āyatir viyatiḥ kṛtiḥ
ṣaḍ ime nahuṣasyāsann
indriyāṇīva dehinaḥ

śrī-śukaḥ uvāca—Śrī Śukadeva Gosvāmī said; *yatiḥ*—Yati; *yayātiḥ*—Yayāti; *saṁyātiḥ*—Saṁyāti; *āyatiḥ*—Āyati; *viyatiḥ*—Viyati; *kṛtiḥ*—Kṛti; *ṣaṭ*—six; *ime*—all of them; *nahuṣasya*—of King Nahuṣa; *āsan*—were; *indriyāṇi*—the (six) senses; *iva*—like; *dehinaḥ*—of an embodied soul.

TRANSLATION

Śukadeva Gosvāmī said: O King Parīkṣit, as the embodied soul has six senses, King Nahuṣa had six sons, named Yati, Yayāti, Saṁyāti, Āyati, Viyati and Kṛti.

TEXT 2

राज्यं नैच्छद् यतिः पित्रा दत्तं तत्परिणामवित् ।
यत्र प्रविष्टः पुरुष आत्मानं नावबुध्यते ॥ २ ॥

rājyaṁ naicchad yatiḥ pitrā
dattaṁ tat-pariṇāmavit
yatra praviṣṭaḥ puruṣa
ātmānaṁ nāvabudhyate

rājyam—the kingdom; *na aicchat*—did not accept; *yatiḥ*—the eldest son, Yati; *pitrā*—by his father; *dattam*—offered; *tat-pariṇāma-vit*—knowing the result of becoming powerful as a king; *yatra*—wherein; *praviṣṭaḥ*—having entered; *puruṣaḥ*—such a person; *ātmānam*—self-realization; *na*—not; *avabudhyate*—will take seriously and understand.

TRANSLATION

When one enters the post of king or head of the government, one cannot understand the meaning of self-realization. Knowing this, Yati, the eldest son of Nahuṣa, did not accept the power to rule, although it was offered by his father.

PURPORT

Self-realization is the prime objective of human civilization, and it is regarded seriously by those who are situated in the mode of goodness and have developed the brahminical qualities. *Kṣatriyas* are generally endowed with material qualities conducive to gaining material wealth and enjoying sense gratification, but those who are spiritually advanced are not interested in material opulence. Indeed, they accept only the bare necessities for a life of spiritual advancement in self-realization. It is specifically mentioned here that if one enters political life, especially in the modern day, one looses the chance for human perfection. Nonetheless, one can attain the highest perfection if one hears *Śrīmad-Bhāgavatam.* This hearing is described as *nityaṁ bhāgavata-sevayā.* Mahārāja Parīkṣit was involved in politics, but because at the end of his life he heard *Śrīmad-Bhāgavatam* from Śukadeva Gosvāmī, he attained perfection very easily. Śrī Caitanya Mahāprabhu has therefore suggested:

sthāne sthitāḥ śruti-gatāṁ tanu-vāṅ-manobhir
ye prāyaśo 'jita jito 'py asi tais tri-lokyām
(*Bhāg.* 10.14.3)

Regardless of whether one is in the mode of passion, ignorance or goodness, if one regularly hears *Śrīmad-Bhāgavatam* from the self-realized soul, one is freed from the bondage of material involvement.

TEXT 3

पितरि भ्रंशिते स्थानादिन्द्राण्या धर्षणाद् द्विजैः ।
प्रापितेऽजगरत्वं वै ययातिरभवन्नृपः ॥ ३ ॥

pitari bhraṁśite sthānād
indrāṇyā dharṣaṇād dvijaiḥ
prāpite 'jagaratvaṁ vai
yayātir abhavan nṛpaḥ

pitari—when his father; *bhraṁśite*—was caused to fall down; *sthānāt*—from the heavenly planets; *indrāṇyāḥ*—of Śacī, the wife of Indra; *dharṣaṇāt*—from offending; *dvijaiḥ*—by them (upon her lodging a complaint with the *brāhmaṇas*); *prāpite*—being degraded to; *ajagaratvam*—the life of a snake; *vai*—indeed; *yayātiḥ*—the son named Yayāti; *abhavat*—became; *nṛpaḥ*—the king.

TRANSLATION

Because Nahuṣa, the father of Yayāti, molested Indra's wife, Śacī, who then complained to Agastya and other brāhmaṇas, these saintly brāhmaṇas cursed Nahuṣa to fall from the heavenly planets and be degraded to the status of a python. Consequently, Yayāti became the king.

TEXT 4

चतसृष्वादिशद् दिक्षु भ्रातॄन् भ्राता यवीयसः ।
कृतदारो जुगोपोर्वीं काव्यस्य वृषपर्वणः ॥ ४ ॥

catasṛṣv ādiśad dikṣu
bhrātṝn bhrātā yavīyasaḥ
kṛta-dāro jugoporvīṁ
kāvyasya vṛṣaparvaṇaḥ

catasṛṣu—over the four; *ādiśat*—allowed to rule; *dikṣu*—directions; *bhrātṝn*—four brothers; *bhrātā*—Yayāti; *yavīyasaḥ*—young; *kṛta-dāraḥ*—married; *jugopa*—ruled; *ūrvīm*—the world; *kāvyasya*—the daughter of Śukrācārya; *vṛṣaparvaṇaḥ*—the daughter of Vṛṣaparvā.

TRANSLATION

King Yayāti had four younger brothers, whom he allowed to rule the four directions. Yayāti himself married Devayānī, the daughter of Śukrācārya, and Śarmiṣṭhā, the daughter of Vṛṣaparvā, and ruled the entire earth.

TEXT 5

श्रीराजोवाच
ब्रह्मर्षिर्भगवान् काव्यः क्षत्रबन्धुश्च नाहुषः ।
राजन्यविप्रयोः कस्माद् विवाहः प्रतिलोमकः ॥ ५ ॥

śrī-rājovāca
brahmarṣir bhagavān kāvyaḥ
kṣatra-bandhuś ca nāhuṣaḥ
rājanya-viprayoḥ kasmād
vivāhaḥ pratilomakaḥ

śrī-rājā uvāca—Mahārāja Parīkṣit inquired; *brahma-ṛṣiḥ*—the best of the *brāhmaṇas; bhagavān*—very powerful; *kāvyaḥ*—Śukrācārya; *kṣatra-bandhuḥ*—belonged to the *kṣatriya* class; *ca*—also; *nāhuṣaḥ*—King Yayāti; *rājanya-viprayoḥ*—of a *brāhmaṇa* and a *kṣatriya; kasmāt*—how; *vivāhaḥ*—a marital relationship; *pratilomakaḥ*—against the customary regulative principles.

TRANSLATION

Mahārāja Parīkṣit said: Śukrācārya was a very powerful brāhmaṇa, and Mahārāja Yayāti was a kṣatriya. Therefore I am curious to know how there occurred this pratiloma marriage between a kṣatriya and a brāhmaṇa.

PURPORT

According to the Vedic system, marriages between *kṣatriyas* and *kṣatriyas* or between *brāhmaṇas* and *brāhmaṇas* are the general custom. If marriages sometimes take place between different classes, these marriages are of two types, namely *anuloma* and *pratiloma. Anuloma,* marriage between a *brāhmaṇa* and the daughter of a *kṣatriya,* is permissible, but *pratiloma,* marriage between a *kṣatriya* and the daughter of a *brāhmaṇa,* is not generally allowed. Therefore Mahārāja Parīkṣit was curious about how Śukrācārya, a powerful *brāhmaṇa,* could accept the principle of *pratiloma.* Mahārāja Parīkṣit was eager to know the cause for this uncommon marriage.

TEXTS 6–7

श्रीशुक उवाच

एकदा दानवेन्द्रस्य शर्मिष्ठा नाम कन्यका ।
सखीसहस्रसंयुक्ता गुरुपुत्र्या च भामिनी ॥ ६ ॥
देवयान्या पुरोद्याने पुष्पितद्रुमसङ्कुले ।
व्यचरत् कलगीतालिनलिनीपुलिनेऽबला ॥ ७ ॥

śrī-śuka uvāca
ekadā dānavendrasya
śarmiṣṭhā nāma kanyakā
sakhī-sahasra-saṁyuktā
guru-putryā ca bhāminī

devayānyā purodyāne
puṣpita-druma-saṅkule
vyacarat kala-gītāli-
nalinī-puline 'balā

śrī-śukaḥ uvāca—Śrī Śukadeva Gosvāmī said; *ekadā*—once upon a time; *dānava-indrasya*—of Vṛṣaparvā; *śarmiṣṭhā*—Śarmiṣṭhā; *nāma*—by name; *kanyakā*—a daughter; *sakhī-sahasra-saṁyuktā*—accompanied by thousands of friends; *guru-putryā*—with the daughter of the *guru,* Śukrācārya; *ca*—also; *bhāminī*—very easily irritated; *devayānyā*—with Devayānī; *pura-udyāne*—within the palace garden; *puṣpita*—full of flowers; *druma*—with nice trees; *saṅkule*—congested; *vyacarat*—was walking; *kala-gīta*—with very sweet sounds; *ali*—with bumblebees; *nalinī*—with lotuses; *puline*—in such a garden; *abalā*—innocent.

TRANSLATION

Śukadeva Gosvāmī said: One day Vṛṣaparvā's daughter Śarmiṣṭhā, who was innocent but angry by nature, was walking with Devayānī, the daughter of Śukrācārya, and with thousands of friends, in the palace garden. The garden was full of lotuses and trees of flowers and fruits and was inhabited by sweetly singing birds and bumblebees.

TEXT 8

ता जलाशयमासाद्य कन्याः कमललोचनाः ।
तीरे न्यस्य दुकूलानि विजह्रुः सिञ्चतीर्मिथः ॥ ८ ॥

tā jalāśayam āsādya
kanyāḥ kamala-locanāḥ
tīre nyasya dukūlāni
vijahruḥ siñcatīr mithaḥ

tāḥ—they; *jala-āśayam*—to the lakeside; *āsādya*—coming; *kanyāḥ*—all the girls; *kamala-locanāḥ*—with eyes like lotus petals; *tīre*—on the bank; *nyasya*—giving up; *dukūlāni*—their dresses; *vijahruḥ*—began to sport; *siñcatīḥ*—throwing water; *mithaḥ*—on one another.

TRANSLATION

When the young, lotus-eyed girls came to the bank of a reservoir of water, they wanted to enjoy by bathing. Thus they left their clothing on the bank and began sporting, throwing water on one another.

TEXT 9

वीक्ष्य व्रजन्तं गिरिशं सह देव्या वृषस्थितम् ।
सहसोत्तीर्य वासांसि पर्यधुर्व्रीडिताः स्त्रियः ॥ ९ ॥

vīkṣya vrajantaṁ giriśaṁ
saha devyā vṛṣa-sthitam
sahasottīrya vāsāṁsi
paryadhur vrīḍitāḥ striyaḥ

vīkṣya—seeing; *vrajantam*—passing by; *giriśam*—Lord Śiva; *saha*—with; *devyā*—Pārvatī, the wife of Lord Śiva; *vṛṣa-sthitam*—seated upon his bull; *sahasā*—quickly; *uttīrya*—getting out of the water; *vāsāṁsi*—garments; *paryadhuḥ*—put on the body; *vrīḍitāḥ*—being ashamed; *striyaḥ*—the young girls.

TRANSLATION

While sporting in the water, the girls suddenly saw Lord Śiva passing by, seated on the back of his bull with his wife, Pārvatī. Ashamed because they were naked, the girls quickly got out of the water and covered themselves with their garments.

TEXT 10

शर्मिष्ठाजानती वासो गुरुपुत्र्याः समव्ययत् ।
स्वीयं मत्वा प्रकुपिता देवयानीदमब्रवीत् ॥१०॥

śarmiṣṭhājānatī vāso
guru-putryāḥ samavyayat
svīyaṁ matvā prakupitā
devayānīdam abravīt

śarmiṣṭhā—the daughter of Vṛṣaparvā; *ajānatī*—without knowledge; *vāsaḥ*—the dress; *guru-putryāḥ*—of Devayānī, the daughter of the *guru; samavyayat*—put on the body; *svīyam*—her own; *matvā*—thinking; *prakupitā*—irritated and angry; *devayānī*—the daughter of Śukrācārya; *idam*—this; *abravīt*—said.

TRANSLATION

Śarmiṣṭhā unknowingly put Devayānī's dress on her own body, thus angering Devayānī, who then spoke as follows.

TEXT 11

अहो निरीक्ष्यतामस्या दास्याः कर्म ह्यसाम्प्रतम् ।
अस्मद्धार्यं धृतवती शुनीव हविरध्वरे ॥११॥

aho nirīkṣyatām asyā
dāsyāḥ karma hy asāmpratam
asmad-dhāryaṁ dhṛtavatī
śunīva havir adhvare

aho—alas; *nirīkṣyatām*—just see; *asyāḥ*—of her (Śarmiṣṭhā); *dāsyāḥ*—just like our servant; *karma*—activities; *hi*—indeed; *asāmpratam*—without any etiquette; *asmat-dhāryam*—the garment meant for me; *dhṛtavatī*—she has put on; *śunī iva*—like a dog; *haviḥ*—clarified butter; *adhvare*—meant for offering in the sacrifice.

TRANSLATION

Oh, just see the activities of this servant-maid Śarmiṣṭhā! Disregarding all etiquette, she has put on my dress, just like a dog snatching clarified butter meant for use in a sacrifice.

TEXTS 12–14

यैरिदं तपसा सृष्टं मुखं पुंसः परस्य ये ।
धार्यते यैरिह ज्योतिः शिवः पन्थाः प्रदर्शितः ॥१२॥
यान् वन्दन्त्युपतिष्ठन्ते लोकनाथाः सुरेश्वराः ।
भगवानपि विश्वात्मा पावनः श्रीनिकेतनः ॥१३॥
वयं तत्रापि भृगवः शिष्योऽस्या नः पितासुरः ।
अस्मद्धार्यं धृतवती शूद्रो वेदमिवासती ॥१४॥

yair idaṁ tapasā sṛṣṭaṁ
mukhaṁ puṁsaḥ parasya ye
dhāryate yair iha jyotiḥ
śivaḥ panthāḥ pradarśitaḥ

yān vandanty upatiṣṭhante
loka-nāthāḥ sureśvarāḥ
bhagavān api viśvātmā
pāvanaḥ śrī-niketanaḥ

vayaṁ tatrāpi bhṛgavaḥ
śiṣyo 'syā naḥ pitāsuraḥ
asmad-dhāryaṁ dhṛtavatī
śūdro vedam ivāsatī

yaiḥ—by which persons; *idam*—this entire universe; *tapasā*—by austerity; *sṛṣṭam*—was created; *mukham*—the face; *puṁsaḥ*—of the Supreme Person; *parasya*—transcendental; *ye*—those who (are); *dhāryate*—is always born; *yaiḥ*—by which persons; *iha*—here; *jyotiḥ*—the *brahmajyoti,* the effulgence of the Supreme Lord; *śivaḥ*—auspicious; *panthāḥ*—way; *pradarśitaḥ*—is directed; *yān*—to whom; *vandanti*—offer prayers; *upatiṣṭhante*—honor and follow; *loka-nāthāḥ*—the directors of the various planets; *sura-īśvarāḥ*—the demigods; *bhagavān*—the Supreme Personality of Godhead; *api*—even; *viśva-ātmā*—the Supersoul; *pāvanaḥ*—the purifier; *śrī-niketanaḥ*—the husband of the goddess of fortune; *vayam*—we (are); *tatra api*—even greater than other *brāhmaṇas; bhṛgavaḥ*—descendants of Bhṛgu; *śiṣyaḥ*—disciple; *asyāḥ*—of her; *naḥ*—our; *pitā*—father; *asuraḥ*—belong to the demoniac group; *asmat-dhāryam*—meant to be worn by us; *dhṛtavatī*—she has put on; *śūdraḥ*—a non-*brāhmaṇa* worker; *vedam*—the *Vedas; iva*—like; *asatī*—unchaste.

TRANSLATION

We are among the qualified brāhmaṇas, who are accepted as the face of the Supreme Personality of Godhead. The brāhmaṇas have created the entire universe by their austerity, and they always keep the Absolute Truth within the core of their hearts. They have directed the path of good fortune, the path of Vedic civilization, and because they are the only worshipable objects within this world, they are offered prayers and worshiped even by the great demigods, the directors of the various planets, and even by the Supreme Personality of Godhead, the Supersoul, the supreme purifier, the husband of the goddess of fortune. And we are even more respectable because we are in the dynasty of Bhṛgu. Yet although this woman's father, being among the demons, is our disciple, she has put on my dress, exactly like a śūdra taking charge of Vedic knowledge.

TEXT 15

एवं क्षिपन्तीं शर्मिष्ठा गुरुपुत्रीमभाषत ।
रुषा श्वसन्त्युरङ्गीव धर्षिता दष्टदच्छदा ॥१५॥

evaṁ kṣipantīṁ śarmiṣṭhā
guru-putrīm abhāṣata
ruṣā śvasanty uraṅgīva
dharṣitā daṣṭa-dacchadā

evam—thus; *kṣipantīm*—chastising; *śarmiṣṭhā*—the daughter of Vṛṣaparvā; *guru-putrīm*—unto the daughter of the *guru,* Śukrācārya; *abhāṣata*—said; *ruṣā*—being very angry; *śvasantī*—breathing very heavily; *uraṅgī iva*—like a serpent; *dharṣitā*—offended, trampled; *daṣṭa-dat-chadā*—biting her lip with her teeth.

TRANSLATION

Śukadeva Gosvāmī said: When thus rebuked in cruel words, Śarmiṣṭhā was very angry. Breathing heavily like a serpent and biting her lower lip with her teeth, she spoke to the daughter of Śukrācārya as follows.

TEXT 16

आत्मवृत्तमविज्ञाय कत्थसे बहु भिक्षुकि ।
किं न प्रतीक्षसेऽस्माकं गृहान् बलिभुजो यथा ॥१६॥

ātma-vṛttam avijñāya
katthase bahu bhikṣuki
kiṁ na pratīkṣase 'smākaṁ
gṛhān balibhujo yathā

ātma-vṛttam—one's own position; *avijñāya*—without understanding; *katthase*—you are talking madly; *bahu*—so much; *bhikṣuki*—beggar; *kim*—whether; *na*—not; *pratīkṣase*—you wait; *asmākam*—our; *gṛhān*—at the house; *balibhujaḥ*—crows; *yathā*—like.

TRANSLATION

You beggar, since you don't understand your position, why should you unnecessarily talk so much? Don't all of you wait at our house, depending on us for your livelihood like crows?

PURPORT

Crows have no independent life; they fully depend on the remnants of foodstuffs thrown by householders into the garbage tank. Therefore, because a *brāhmaṇa* depends on his disciples, when Śarmiṣṭhā was heavily rebuked by Devayānī she charged Devayānī with belonging to a family of crowlike beggars. It is the nature of women to fight verbally at even a slight provocation. As we see from this incident, this has been their nature for a long, long time.

TEXT 17

एवंविधैः सुपरुषैः क्षिप्त्वाचार्यसुतां सतीम् ।
शर्मिष्ठा प्राक्षिपत् कूपे वासश्चादाय मन्युना ॥१७॥

evaṁ-vidhaiḥ suparuṣaiḥ
kṣiptvācārya-sutāṁ satīm
śarmiṣṭhā prākṣipat kūpe
vāsaś cādāya manyunā

evam-vidhaiḥ—such; *su-paruṣaiḥ*—by unkind words; *kṣiptvā*—after chastising; *ācārya-sutām*—the daughter of Śukrācārya; *satīm*—Devayānī; *śarmiṣṭhā*—Śarmiṣṭhā; *prākṣipat*—threw (her); *kūpe*—into a well; *vāsaḥ*—the garments; *ca*—and; *ādāya*—taking away; *manyunā*—because of anger.

TRANSLATION

Using such unkind words, Śarmiṣṭhā rebuked Devayānī, the daughter of Śukrācārya. In anger, she took away Devayānī's garments and threw Devayānī into a well.

TEXT 18

तस्यां गतायां स्वगृहं ययातिर्मृगयां चरन् ।
प्राप्तो यदृच्छया कूपे जलार्थी तां ददर्श ह ॥१८॥

tasyāṁ gatāyāṁ sva-gṛhaṁ
yayātir mṛgayāṁ caran
prāpto yadṛcchayā kūpe
jalārthī tāṁ dadarśa ha

tasyām—when she; *gatāyām*—went; *sva-gṛham*—to her home; *yayātiḥ*—King Yayāti; *mṛgayām*—hunting; *caran*—wandering; *prāptaḥ*—arrived; *yadṛcchayā*—by chance; *kūpe*—in the well; *jala-arthī*—desiring to drink water; *tām*—her (Devayānī); *dadarśa*—saw; *ha*—indeed.

TRANSLATION

After throwing Devayānī into the well, Śarmiṣṭhā went home. Meanwhile, King Yayāti, while engaged in a hunting excursion, went to the well to drink water and by chance saw Devayānī.

TEXT 19

दत्त्वा स्वमुत्तरं वासस्तस्यै राजा विवाससे ।
गृहीत्वा पाणिना पाणिमुज्जहार दयापरः ॥१९॥

dattvā svam uttaraṁ vāsas
tasyai rājā vivāsase
gṛhītvā pāṇinā pāṇim
ujjahāra dayā-paraḥ

dattvā—giving; *svam*—his own; *uttaram*—upper; *vāsaḥ*—cloth; *tasyai*—unto her (Devayānī); *rājā*—the King; *vivāsase*—because she was naked; *gṛhītvā*—catching; *pāṇinā*—with his hand; *pāṇim*—her hand; *ujjahāra*—delivered; *dayā-paraḥ*—being very kind.

TRANSLATION

Seeing Devayānī naked in the well, King Yayāti immediately gave her his upper cloth. Being very kind to her, he caught her hand with his own and lifted her out.

TEXTS 20–21

तं वीरमाहौशनसी प्रेमनिर्भरया गिरा ।
राजंस्त्वया गृहीतो मे पाणिः परपुरञ्जय ॥२०॥
हस्तग्राहोऽपरो मा भूद् गृहीतायास्त्वया हि मे ।
एष ईशकृतो वीर सम्बन्धो नौ न पौरुषः ॥२१॥

taṁ vīram āhauśanasī
prema-nirbharayā girā
rājaṁs tvayā gṛhīto me
pāṇiḥ para-purañjaya

hasta-grāho 'paro mā bhūd
gṛhītāyās tvayā hi me
eṣa īśa-kṛto vīra
sambandho nau na pauruṣaḥ

tam—unto him; *vīram*—Yayāti; *āha*—said; *auśanasī*—the daughter of Uśanā Kavi, Śukrācārya; *prema-nirbharayā*—saturated with love and kindness; *girā*—by such words; *rājan*—O King; *tvayā*—by you; *gṛhītaḥ*—accepted; *me*—my; *pāṇiḥ*—hand; *para-purañjaya*—the conqueror of the kingdoms of others; *hasta-grāhaḥ*—he who accepted my hand; *aparaḥ*—another; *mā*—may not; *bhūt*—become; *gṛhītāyāḥ*—accepted; *tvayā*—by you; *hi*—indeed; *me*—of me; *eṣaḥ*—this; *īśa-kṛtaḥ*—arranged by providence; *vīra*—O great hero; *sambandhaḥ*—relationship; *nau*—our; *na*—not; *pauruṣaḥ*—anything man-made.

TRANSLATION

With words saturated with love and affection, Devayānī said to King Yayāti: O great hero, O King, conqueror of the cities of your enemies, by accepting my hand you have accepted me as your married wife. Let me not be touched by others, for our relationship as husband and wife has been made possible by providence, not by any human being.

PURPORT

While taking Devayānī out of the well, King Yayāti must certainly have appreciated her youthful beauty, and therefore he might have asked her which caste she belonged to. Thus Devayānī would have immediately replied, "We are already married because you have accepted my hand." Uniting the hands of the bride and bridegroom is a system perpetually existing in all societies. Therefore, as soon as Yayāti accepted Devayānī's hand, they could be regarded as married. Because Devayānī was enamored with the hero Yayāti, she requested him not to change his mind and let another come to marry her.

TEXT 22

यदिदं कूपमग्नाया भवतो दर्शनं मम ।
न ब्राह्मणो मे भविता हस्तग्राहो महाभुज ।
कचस्य बार्हस्पत्यस्य शापाद् यमशपं पुरा ॥२२॥

yad idaṁ kūpa-magnāyā
bhavato darśanaṁ mama
na brāhmaṇo me bhavitā
hasta-grāho mahā-bhuja
kacasya bārhaspatyasya
śāpād yam aśapaṁ purā

yat—because of; *idam*—this; *kūpa-magnāyāḥ*—fallen in the well; *bhavataḥ*—of your good self; *darśanam*—meeting; *mama*—with me; *na*—not; *brāhmaṇaḥ*—a qualified *brāhmaṇa; me*—my; *bhavitā*—will become; *hasta-grāhaḥ*—husband; *mahā-bhuja*—O great mighty-armed one; *kacasya*—of Kaca; *bārhaspatyasya*—the son of the learned *brāhmaṇa* and celestial priest Bṛhaspati; *śāpāt*—because of the curse; *yam*—whom; *aśapam*—I cursed; *purā*—in the past.

TRANSLATION

Because of falling in the well, I met you. Indeed, this has been arranged by providence. After I cursed Kaca, the son of the learned scholar Bṛhaspati, he cursed me by saying that I would not have a brāhmaṇa for a husband. Therefore, O mighty-armed one, there is no possibility of my becoming the wife of a brāhmaṇa.

PURPORT

Kaca, the son of the learned celestial priest Bṛhaspati, had been a student of Śukrācārya, from whom he had learned the art of reviving a man who has died untimely. This art, called *mṛta-sañjīvanī,* was especially used during wartime. When there was a war, soldiers would certainly die untimely, but if a soldier's body was intact, he could be brought to life again by this art of *mṛta-sañjīvanī.* This art was known to Śukrācārya and many others, and Kaca, the son of Bṛhaspati, became Śukrācārya's student to learn it. Devayānī desired to have Kaca as her husband, but Kaca, out of regard for Śukrācārya, looked upon the *guru's* daughter as a respectable superior and therefore refused to marry her. Devayānī angrily cursed Kaca by saying that although he had learned the art of *mṛta-sañjīvanī* from her father, it would be useless. When cursed in this way, Kaca retaliated by cursing Devayānī never to have a husband who was a *brāhmaṇa.* Because Devayānī liked Yayāti, who was a *kṣatriya,* she requested him to accept her as his bona fide wife. Although this would be *pratiloma-vivāha,* a marriage between the daughter of a high family and the son of a lower family, she explained that this arrangement was made by providence.

TEXT 23

ययातिरनभिप्रेतं दैवोपहृतमात्मनः ।
मनस्तु तद्गतं बुद्ध्वा प्रतिजग्राह तद्वचः ॥२३॥

yayātir anabhipretaṁ
daivopahṛtam ātmanaḥ
manas tu tad-gataṁ buddhvā
pratijagrāha tad-vacaḥ

yayātiḥ—King Yayāti; *anabhipretam*—not liked; *daiva-upahṛtam*—brought about by providential arrangements; *ātmanaḥ*—his personal interest; *manaḥ*—mind; *tu*—however; *tat-gatam*—being attracted to her; *buddhvā*—by such intelligence; *pratijagrāha*—accepted; *tat-vacaḥ*—the words of Devayānī.

TRANSLATION

Śukadeva Gosvāmī continued: Because such a marriage is not sanctioned by regular scriptures, King Yayāti did not like it, but because it was arranged by providence and because he was attracted by Devayānī's beauty, he accepted her request.

PURPORT

According to the Vedic system, the parents would consider the horoscopes of the boy and girl who were to be married. If according to astrological calculations the boy and girl were compatible in every respect, the match was called *yoṭaka* and the marriage would be accepted. Even fifty years ago, this system was current in Hindu society. Regardless of the affluence of the boy or the personal beauty of the girl, without this astrological compatibility the marriage would not take place. A person is born in one of three categories, known as *deva-gaṇa, manuṣya-gaṇa* and *rakṣasa-gaṇa.* In different parts of the universe there are demigods and demons, and in human society also some people resemble demigods whereas others resemble demons. If according to astrological calculations there was conflict between a godly and a demoniac nature, the marriage would not take place. Similarly, there were calculations of *pratiloma* and *anuloma.* The central idea is that if the boy and girl were on an equal level the marriage would be happy, whereas inequality would lead to unhappiness. Because care is no longer taken in marriage, we now find many divorces. Indeed, divorce has now become a common affair, although formerly one's marriage would continue lifelong, and the affection between husband and wife was so great that the wife would voluntarily die when her husband died or would remain a faithful widow throughout her entire life. Now, of course, this is no longer possible, for human society has fallen to the level of animal society. Marriage now takes place simply by agreement. *Dāmpatye 'bhirucir hetuḥ* (*Bhag.* 12.2.3). The word *abhiruci* means "agreement." If the boy and girl simply agree to marry, the marriage takes place. But when the Vedic system is not rigidly observed, marriage frequently ends in divorce.

TEXT 24

गते राजनि सा धीरे तत्र स्म रुदती पितुः ।
न्यवेदयत् ततः सर्वमुक्तं शर्मिष्ठया कृतम् ।।२४।।

gate rājani sā dhīre
tatra sma rudatī pituḥ
nyavedayat tataḥ sarvam
uktaṁ śarmiṣṭhayā kṛtam

gate rājani—after the departure of the King; *sā*—she (Devayānī); *dhīre*—learned; *tatra sma*—returning to her home; *rudatī*—crying; *pituḥ*—before her father; *nyavedayat*—submitted; *tataḥ*—thereafter; *sarvam*—all; *uktam*—mentioned; *śarmiṣṭhayā*—by Śarmiṣṭhā; *kṛtam*—done.

TRANSLATION

Thereafter, when the learned King returned to his palace, Devayānī returned home crying and told her father, Śukrācārya, about all that had happened because of Śarmiṣṭhā. She told how she had been thrown into the well but was saved by the King.

TEXT 25

दुर्मना भगवान् काव्यः पौरोहित्यं विगर्हयन् ।
स्तुवन् वृत्तिं च कापोतीं दुहित्रा स ययौ पुरात् ॥२५॥

durmanā bhagavān kāvyaḥ
paurohityaṁ vigarhayan
stuvan vṛttiṁ ca kāpotīṁ
duhitrā sa yayau purāt

durmanāḥ—being very unhappy; *bhagavān*—the most powerful; *kāvyaḥ*—Śukrācārya; *paurohityam*—the business of priesthood; *vigarhayan*—condemning; *stuvan*—praising; *vṛttim*—the profession; *ca*—and; *kāpotīm*—of collecting grains from the field; *duhitrā*—with his daughter; *saḥ*—he (Śukrācārya); *yayau*—went; *purāt*—from his own residence.

TRANSLATION

As Śukrācārya listened to what had happened to Devayānī, his mind was very much aggrieved. Condemning the profession of priesthood and praising the profession of uñcha-vṛtti [collecting grains from the fields], he left home with his daughter.

PURPORT

When a *brāhmaṇa* adopts the profession of a *kapota,* or pigeon, he lives by collecting grains from the field. This is called *uñcha-vṛtti.* A *brāhmaṇa* who takes to this *uñcha-vṛtti* profession is called first class because he depends completely on the mercy of the Supreme Personality of Godhead and does not beg from anyone. Although the profession of begging is allowed for a *brāhmaṇa* or *sannyāsī*, one does better if he can avoid such a profession and completely depend on the mercy of the Supreme Personality of Godhead for maintenance. Śukrācārya was certainly very sorry that because of his daughter's complaint he had to go to his disciple to beg some mercy, which he was obliged to do because he had accepted the profession of priesthood. In his heart, Śukrācārya did not like his profession, but since he had accepted it, he was obliged to go unwillingly to his disciple to settle the grievance submitted by his daughter.

TEXT 26

वृषपर्वा तमाज्ञाय प्रत्यनीकविवक्षितम् ।
गुरुं प्रसादयन् मूर्ध्ना पादयोः पतितः पथि ॥२६॥

vṛṣaparvā tam ājñāya
pratyanīka-vivakṣitam
guruṁ prasādayan mūrdhnā
pādayoḥ patitaḥ pathi

vṛṣaparvā—the King of the demons; *tam ājñāya*—understanding the motive of Śukrācārya; *pratyanīka*—some curse; *vivakṣitam*—desiring to speak; *gurum*—his spiritual master, Śukrācārya; *prasādayat*—he satisfied immediately; *mūrdhnā*—with his head; *pādayoḥ*—at the feet; *patitaḥ*—fell down; *pathi*—on the road.

TRANSLATION

King Vṛṣaparvā understood that Śukrācārya was coming to chastise or curse him. Consequently, before Śukrācārya came to his house, Vṛṣaparvā went out and fell down in the street at the feet of his guru and satisfied him, checking his wrath.

TEXT 27

क्षणार्धमन्युर्भगवान् शिष्यं व्याचष्ट भार्गवः ।
कामोऽस्याः क्रियतां राजन् नैनां त्यक्तुमिहोत्सहे ॥२७॥

kṣaṇārdha-manyur bhagavān
śiṣyaṁ vyācaṣṭa bhārgavaḥ
kāmo 'syāḥ kriyatāṁ rājan
naināṁ tyaktum ihotsahe

kṣaṇa-ardha—lasting only a few moments; *manyuḥ*—whose anger; *bhagavān*—the most powerful; *śiṣyam*—unto his disciple, Vṛṣaparvā; *vyācaṣṭa*—said; *bhārgavaḥ*—Śukrācārya, the descendant of Bhṛgu; *kāmaḥ*—the desire; *asyāḥ*—of this Devayānī; *kriyatām*—please fulfill; *rājan*—O King; *na*—not; *enām*—this girl; *tyaktum*—to give up; *iha*—in this world; *utsahe*—I am able.

TRANSLATION

The powerful Śukrācārya was angry for a few moments, but upon being satisfied he said to Vṛṣaparvā: My dear King, kindly fulfill the desire of Devayānī, for she is my daughter and in this world I cannot give her up or neglect her.

PURPORT

Sometimes a great personality like Śukrācārya cannot neglect sons and daughters, for sons and daughters are by nature dependent on their father and the father has affection for them. Although Śukrācārya knew that the quarrel between Devayānī and Śarmiṣṭhā was childish, as Devayānī's father he had to side with his daughter. He did not like to do this, but he was obliged to because of affection. He plainly admitted that although he should not have asked the King for mercy for his daughter, because of affection he could not avoid doing so.

TEXT 28

तथेत्यवस्थिते प्राह देवयानी मनोगतम् ।
पित्रा दत्ता यतो यास्ये सानुगा यातु मामनु ॥२८॥

tathety avasthite prāha
devayānī manogatam
pitrā dattā yato yāsye
sānugā yātu mām anu

tathā iti—when King Vṛṣaparvā agreed to Śukrācārya's proposal; *avasthite*—the situation being settled in this way; *prāha*—said; *devayānī*—the daughter of Śukrācārya; *manogatam*—her desire; *pitrā*—by the father; *dattā*—given; *yataḥ*—to whomever; *yāsye*—I shall go; *sa-anugā*—with her friends; *yātu*—shall go; *mām anu*—as my follower or servant.

TRANSLATION

After hearing Śukrācārya's request, Vṛṣaparvā agreed to fulfill Devayānī's desire, and he awaited her words. Devayānī then expressed her desire as follows: "Whenever I marry by the order of my father, my friend Śarmiṣṭhā must go with me as my maidservant, along with her friends."

TEXT 29

पित्रादत्तादेवयान्यै शर्मिष्ठासानुगातदा ।
स्वानां तत् सङ्कटं वीक्ष्य तदर्थस्य च गौरवम् ।
देवयानीं पर्यचरत् स्त्रीसहस्रेण दासवत् ॥२९॥

pitrā dattā devayānyai
śarmiṣṭhā sānugā tadā
svānāṁ tat saṅkaṭaṁ vīkṣya
tad-arthasya ca gauravam
devayānīṁ paryacarat
strī-sahasreṇa dāsavat

pitrā—by the father; *dattā*—given; *devayānyai*—unto Devayānī, the daughter of Śukrācārya; *śarmiṣṭhā*—the daughter of Vṛṣaparvā; *sa-anugā*—with her friends; *tadā*—at that time; *svānām*—of his own; *tat*—that; *saṅkaṭam*—dangerous position; *vīkṣya*—observing; *tat*—from him; *arthasya*—of the benefit; *ca*—also; *gauravam*—the greatness; *devayānīm*—unto Devayānī; *paryacarat*—served; *strī-sahasreṇa*—with thousands of other women; *dāsa-vat*—acting as a slave.

TRANSLATION

Vṛṣaparvā wisely thought that Śukrācārya's displeasure would bring danger and that his pleasure would bring material gain.

Therefore he carried out Śukrācārya's order and served him like a slave. He gave his daughter Śarmiṣṭhā to Devayānī, and Śarmiṣṭhā served Devayānī like a slave, along with thousands of other women.

PURPORT

In the beginning of these affairs concerning Śarmiṣṭhā and Devayānī, we saw that Śarmiṣṭhā had many friends. Now these friends became maidservants of Devayānī. When a girl married a *kṣatriya* king, it was customary for all her girl friends to go with her to her husband's house. For instance, when Vasudeva married Devakī, the mother of Kṛṣṇa, he married all six of her sisters, and she also had many friends who accompanied her. A king would maintain not only his wife but also the many friends and maidservants of his wife. Some of these maidservants would become pregnant and give birth to children. Such children were accepted as *dāsī-putra*, the sons of the maidservants, and the king would maintain them. The female population is always greater than the male, but since a woman needs to be protected by a man, the king would maintain many girls, who acted either as friends or as maidservants of the queen. In the history of Kṛṣṇa's household life we find that Kṛṣṇa married 16,108 wives. These were not maidservants but direct queens, and Kṛṣṇa expanded Himself into 16,108 forms to maintain different establishments for each and every wife. This is not possible for ordinary men. Therefore although the kings had to maintain many, many servants and wives, not all of them had different establishments.

TEXT 30

नाहुषाय सुतां दत्त्वा सह शर्मिष्ठयोशना ।
तमाह राजञ्छर्मिष्ठामाधास्तल्पे न कर्हिचित् ॥३०॥

nāhuṣāya sutāṁ dattvā
saha śarmiṣṭhayośanā
tam āha rājañ charmiṣṭhām
ādhās talpe na karhicit

nāhuṣāya—unto King Yayāti, the descendant of Nahuṣa; *sutām*—his daughter; *dattvā*—giving in marriage; *saha*—with; *śarmiṣṭhayā*—

Śarmiṣṭhā, the daughter of Vṛṣaparvā and servant of Devayānī; *uśanā*—Śukrācārya; *tam*—unto him (King Yayāti); *āha*—said; *rājan*—my dear King; *śarmiṣṭhām*—Śarmiṣṭhā, the daughter of Vṛṣaparvā; *ādhāḥ*—allow; *talpe*—on your bed; *na*—not; *karhicit*—at any time.

TRANSLATION

When Śukrācārya gave Devayānī in marriage to Yayāti, he had Śarmiṣṭhā go with her, but he warned the King, "My dear King, never allow this girl Śarmiṣṭhā to lie with you in your bed."

TEXT 31

विलोक्यौशनसीं राजञ्छर्मिष्ठा सुप्रजां क्वचित् ।
तमेव वव्रे रहसि सख्याः पतिमृतौ सती ॥३१॥

vilokyauśanasīṁ rājañ
charmiṣṭhā suprajāṁ kvacit
tam eva vavre rahasi
sakhyāḥ patim ṛtau satī

vilokya—by seeing; *auśanasīm*—Devayānī, the daughter of Śukrācārya; *rājan*—O King Parīkṣit; *śarmiṣṭhā*—the daughter of Vṛṣaparvā; *su-prajām*—possessing nice children; *kvacit*—at some time; *tam*—him (King Yayāti); *eva*—indeed; *vavre*—requested; *rahasi*—in a secluded place; *sakhyāḥ*—of her friend; *patim*—the husband; *ṛtau*—at the appropriate time; *satī*—being in that position.

TRANSLATION

O King Parīkṣit, upon seeing Devayānī with a nice son, Śarmiṣṭhā once approached King Yayāti at the appropriate time for conception. In a secluded place, she requested the King, the husband of her friend Devayānī, to enable her to have a son also.

TEXT 32

राजपुत्र्यार्थितोऽपत्ये धर्मं चावेक्ष्य धर्मवित् ।
स्मरञ्छुक्रवचः काले दिष्टमेवाभ्यपद्यत ॥३२॥

rāja-putryārthito 'patye
dharmaṁ cāvekṣya dharmavit
smarañ chukra-vacaḥ kāle
diṣṭam evābhyapadyata

rāja-putryā—by Śarmiṣṭhā, who was the daughter of a king; *arthitaḥ*—being requested; *apatye*—for a son; *dharmam*—religious principles; *ca*—as well as; *avekṣya*—considering; *dharma-vit*—aware of all religious principles; *smaran*—remembering; *śukra-vacaḥ*—the warning of Śukrācārya; *kāle*—at the time; *diṣṭam*—circumstantially; *eva*—indeed; *abhyapadyata*—accepted (to fulfill the desire of Śarmiṣṭhā).

TRANSLATION

When Princess Śarmiṣṭhā begged King Yayāti for a son, the King was certainly aware of the principles of religion, and therefore he agreed to fulfill her desire. Although he remembered the warning of Śukrācārya, he thought of this union as the desire of the Supreme, and thus he had sex with Śarmiṣṭhā.

PURPORT

King Yayāti was completely aware of the duty of a *kṣatriya.* When a *kṣatriya* is approached by a woman, he cannot deny her. This is a religious principle. Consequently, when Dharmarāja, Yudhiṣṭhira, saw Arjuna unhappy after Arjuna returned from Dvārakā, he asked whether Arjuna had refused a woman who had begged for a son. Although Mahārāja Yayāti remembered Śukrācārya's warning, he could not refuse Śarmiṣṭhā. He thought it wise to give her a son, and thus he had sexual intercourse with her after her menstrual period. This kind of lust is not against religious principles. As stated in *Bhagavad-gītā* (7.11), *dharmāviruddho bhūteṣu kāmo 'smi:* sex life not contrary to the principles of religion is sanctioned by Kṛṣṇa. Because Śarmiṣṭhā, the daughter of a king, had begged Yayāti for a son, their combination was not lust but an act of religion.

TEXT 33

यदुं च तुर्वसुं चैव देवयानी व्यजायत ।
द्रुह्युं चानुं च पूरुं च शर्मिष्ठा वार्षपर्वणी ॥३३॥

yadurn ca turvasurn caiva
devayānī vyajāyata
druhyurn cānurn ca pūrurn ca
śarmiṣṭhā vārṣaparvaṇī

yadum—Yadu; *ca*—and; *turvasum*—Turvasu; *ca eva*—as well as; *devayānī*—the daughter of Śukrācārya; *vyajāyata*—gave birth to; *druhyum*—Druhyu; *ca*—and; *anum*—Anu; *ca*—also; *pūrum*—Pūru; *ca*—also; *śarmiṣṭhā*—Śarmiṣṭhā; *vārṣaparvaṇī*—the daughter of Vṛṣaparvā.

TRANSLATION

Devayānī gave birth to Yadu and Turvasu, and Śarmiṣṭhā gave birth to Druhyu, Anu and Pūru.

TEXT 34

गर्भसम्भवमासुर्या भर्तुर्विज्ञाय मानिनी ।
देवयानी पितुर्गेहं ययौ क्रोधविमूर्छिता ॥३४॥

garbha-sambhavam āsuryā
bhartur vijñāya māninī
devayānī pitur geharn
yayau krodha-vimūrchitā

garbha-sambhavam—pregnancy; *āsuryāḥ*—of Śarmiṣṭhā; *bhartuḥ*—made possible by her husband; *vijñāya*—knowing (from the *brāhmaṇa* astrologers); *māninī*—being very proud; *devayānī*—the daughter of Śukrācārya; *pituḥ*—of her father; *geham*—to the house; *yayau*—departed; *krodha-vimūrchitā*—frenzied because of anger.

TRANSLATION

When the proud Devayānī understood from outside sources that Śarmiṣṭhā was pregnant by her husband, she was frenzied with anger. Thus she departed for her father's house.

TEXT 35

प्रियामनुगतः कामी वचोभिरुपमन्त्रयन् ।
न प्रसादयितुं शेके पादसंवाहनादिभिः ॥३५॥

priyām anugataḥ kāmī
vacobhir upamantrayan
na prasādayituṁ śeke
pāda-saṁvāhanādibhiḥ

priyām—his beloved wife; *anugataḥ*—following; *kāmī*—very, very lusty; *vacobhiḥ*—by great words; *upamantrayan*—appeasing; *na*—not; *prasādayitum*—to appease; *śeke*—was able; *pāda-saṁvāhana-ādibhiḥ*—even by massaging her feet.

TRANSLATION

King Yayāti, who was very lusty, followed his wife, caught her and tried to appease her by speaking pleasing words and massaging her feet, but he could not satisfy her by any means.

TEXT 36

शुक्रस्तमाह कुपितः स्त्रीकामानृतपूरुष ।
त्वां जरा विशतां मन्द विरूपकरणी नृणाम् ॥३६॥

śukras tam āha kupitaḥ
strī-kāmānṛta-pūruṣa
tvāṁ jarā viśatāṁ manda
virūpa-karaṇī nṛṇām

śukraḥ—Śukrācārya; *tam*—unto him (King Yayāti); *āha*—said; *kupitaḥ*—being very angry at him; *strī-kāma*—O you who have lusty desires for women; *anṛta-pūruṣa*—O untruthful person; *tvām*—unto you; *jarā*—old age, invalidity; *viśatām*—may enter; *manda*—you fool; *virūpa-karaṇī*—which disfigures; *nṛṇām*—the bodies of human beings.

TRANSLATION

Śukrācārya was extremely angry. "You untruthful fool, lusting after women! You have done a great wrong," he said. "I therefore curse you to be attacked and disfigured by old age and invalidity."

TEXT 37

श्रीययातिरुवाच
अतृप्तोऽस्म्यद्य कामानां ब्रह्मन् दुहितरि स्म ते ।
व्यत्यस्यतां यथाकामं वयसा योऽभिधास्यति ॥३७॥

śrī-yayātir uvāca
atṛpto 'smy adya kāmānāṁ
brahman duhitari sma te
vyatyasyatāṁ yathā-kāmaṁ
vayasā yo 'bhidhāsyati

śrī-yayātiḥ uvāca—King Yayāti said; *atṛptaḥ*—unsatisfied; *asmi*—I am; *adya*—till now; *kāmānām*—to satisfy my lusty desires; *brahman*—O learned *brāhmaṇa; duhitari*—in connection with the daughter; *sma*—in the past; *te*—your; *vyatyasyatām*—just exchange; *yathā-kāmam*—as long as you are lusty; *vayasā*—with youth; *yaḥ abhidhāsyati*—of one who agrees to exchange your old age for his youth.

TRANSLATION

King Yayāti said, "O learned, worshipable brāhmaṇa, I have not yet satisfied my lusty desires with your daughter." Śukrācārya then replied, "You may exchange your old age with someone who will agree to transfer his youth to you."

PURPORT

When King Yayāti said that he had not yet satisfied his lusty desires with Śukrācārya's daughter, Śukrācārya saw that it was against the interests of his own daughter for Yayāti to continue in old age and invalidity, for certainly his lusty daughter would not be satisfied. Therefore Śukrācārya blessed his son-in-law by saying that he could exchange his old age for someone else's youth. He indicated that if Yayāti's son would exchange his youth for Yayāti's old age, Yayāti could continue to enjoy sex with Devayānī.

TEXT 38

इति लब्धव्यवस्थानः पुत्रं ज्येष्ठमवोचत ।
यदो तात प्रतीच्छेमां जरां देहि निजं वयः ॥३८॥

iti labdha-vyavasthānaḥ
putraṁ jyeṣṭham avocata
yado tāta pratīcchemāṁ
jarāṁ dehi nijaṁ vayaḥ

iti—thus; *labdha-vyavasthānaḥ*—getting the opportunity to exchange his old age; *putram*—unto his son; *jyeṣṭham*—the eldest; *avocata*—he requested; *yado*—O Yadu; *tāta*—you are my beloved son; *pratīccha*—kindly exchange; *imām*—this; *jarām*—invalidity; *dehi*—and give; *nijam*—your own; *vayaḥ*—youth.

TRANSLATION

When Yayāti received this benediction from Śukrācarya, he requested his eldest son: My dear son Yadu, please give me your youth in exchange for my old age and invalidity.

TEXT 39

मातामहकृतां वत्स न तृप्तो विषयेष्वहम् ।
वयसा भवदीयेन रंस्ये कतिपयाः समाः ॥३९॥

mātāmaha-kṛtāṁ vatsa
na tṛpto viṣayeṣv aham
vayasā bhavadīyena
raṁsye katipayāḥ samāḥ

mātāmaha-kṛtām—given by your maternal grandfather, Śukrācārya; *vatsa*—my dear son; *na*—not; *tṛptaḥ*—satisfied; *viṣayeṣu*—in sex life, sense gratification; *aham*—I (am); *vayasā*—by age; *bhavadīyena*—of your good self; *raṁsye*—I shall enjoy sex life; *katipayāḥ*—for a few; *samāḥ*—years.

TRANSLATION

My dear son, I am not yet satisfied in my sexual desires. But if you are kind to me, you can take the old age given by your maternal grandfather, and I may take your youth so that I may enjoy life for a few years more.

PURPORT

This is the nature of lusty desires. In *Bhagavad-gītā* (7.20) it is said, *kāmais tais tair hṛta-jñānāḥ:* when one is too attached to sense gratification, he actually loses his sense. The word *hṛta-jñānāḥ* refers to one who has lost his sense. Here is an example: the father shamelessly asked his son to exchange youth for old age. Of course, the entire world is under such illusion. Therefore it is said that everyone is *pramattaḥ,* or exclusively mad. *Nūnaṁ pramattaḥ kurute vikarma:* when one becomes almost like a madman, he indulges in sex and sense gratification. Sex and sense gratification can be controlled, however, and one achieves perfection when he has no desires for sex. This is possible only when one is fully Kṛṣṇa conscious.

yadavadhi mama cetaḥ kṛṣṇa-pādāravinde
nava-nava-rasa-dhāmany udyataṁ rantum āsīt
tadavadhi bata nārī-saṅgame smaryamāne
bhavati mukha-vikāraḥ suṣṭhu-niṣṭhīvanaṁ ca

"Since I have been engaged in the transcendental loving service of Kṛṣṇa, realizing ever-new pleasure in Him, whenever I think of sex pleasure, I spit at the thought, and my lips curl with distaste." Sexual desire can be stopped only when one is fully Kṛṣṇa conscious, and not otherwise. As long as one has desires for sex, one must change his body and transmigrate from one body to another to enjoy sex in different species or forms. But although the forms may differ, the business of sex is the same. Therefore it is said, *punaḥ punaś carvita-carvaṇānām.* Those who are very much attached to sex transmigrate from one body to another, with the same business of "chewing the chewed," tasting sex enjoyment as a dog, sex enjoyment as a hog, sex enjoyment as a demigod, and so on.

TEXT 40

श्रीयदुरुवाच

नोत्सहे जरसा स्थातुमन्तरा प्राप्तया तव ।
अविदित्वा सुखं ग्राम्यं वैतृष्ण्यं नैति पूरुषः ॥४०॥

śrī-yadur uvāca
notsahe jarasā sthātum
antarā prāptayā tava
aviditvā sukhaṁ grāmyaṁ
vaitṛṣṇyaṁ naiti pūruṣaḥ

śrī-yaduḥ uvāca—Yadu, the eldest son to Yayāti, replied; *na utsahe*—I am not enthusiastic; *jarasā*—with your old age and invalidity; *sthātum*—to remain; *antarā*—while in youth; *prāptayā*—accepted; *tava*—your; *aviditvā*—without experiencing; *sukham*—happiness; *grāmyam*—material or bodily; *vaitṛṣṇyam*—indifference to material enjoyment; *na*—does not; *eti*—attain; *pūruṣaḥ*—a person.

TRANSLATION

Yadu replied: My dear father, you have already achieved old age, although you also were a young man. But I do not welcome your old age and invalidity, for unless one enjoys material happiness, one cannot attain renunciation.

PURPORT

Renunciation of material enjoyment is the ultimate goal of human life. Therefore the *varṇāśrama* institution is most scientific. It aims at giving one the facility to return home, back to Godhead, which one cannot do without completely renouncing all connections with the material world. Śrī Caitanya Mahāprabhu said, *niṣkiñcanasya bhagavad-bhajanonmukhasya:* one who wants to go back home, back to Godhead, must be *niṣkiñcana,* free from all affinity for material enjoyment. *Brahmaṇy upaśamāśrayam:* unless one is fully renounced, one cannot engage in devotional service or stay in Brahman. Devotional service is rendered on the Brahman platform. Therefore, unless one attains the Brahman platform, or spiritual platform, one cannot engage in devotional service; or, in other words, a person engaged in devotional service is already on the Brahman platform.

māṁ ca yo 'vyabhicāreṇa
bhakti-yogena sevate

sa guṇān samatītyaitān
brahma-bhūyāya kalpate

"One who engages in full devotional service, who does not fall down in any circumstance, at once transcends the modes of material nature and thus comes to the level of Brahman." (Bg. 14.26) If one attains devotional service, therefore, he is certainly liberated. Generally, unless one enjoys material happiness, one cannot attain renunciation. *Varṇāśrama* therefore gives the opportunity for gradual elevation. Yadu, the son of Mahārāja Yayāti, explained that he was unable to give up his youth, for he wanted to use it to attain the renounced order in the future.

Mahārāja Yadu was different from his brothers. As stated in the next verse, *turvasuś coditaḥ pitrā druhyuś cānuś ca bhārata/ pratyācakhyur adharmajñāḥ.* Mahārāja Yadu's brothers refused to accept their father's proposal because they were not completely aware of *dharma.* To accept orders that follow religious principles, especially the orders of one's father, is very important. Therefore when the brothers of Mahārāja Yadu refused their father's order, this was certainly irreligious. Mahārāja Yadu's refusal, however, was religious. As stated in the Tenth Canto, *yadoś ca dharma-śīlasya:* Mahārāja Yadu was completely aware of the principles of religion. The ultimate principle of religion is to engage oneself in devotional service to the Lord. Mahārāja Yadu was very eager to engage himself in the Lord's service, but there was an impediment: during youth the material desire to enjoy the material senses is certainly present, and unless one fully satisfies these lusty desires in youth, there is a chance of one's being disturbed in rendering service to the Lord. We have actually seen that many *sannyāsīs* who accept *sannyāsa* prematurely, not having satisfied their material desires, fall down because they are disturbed. Therefore the general process is to go through *gṛhastha* life and *vānaprastha* life and finally come to *sannyāsa* and devote oneself completely to the service of the Lord. Mahārāja Yadu was ready to accept his father's order and exchange youth for old age because he was confident that the youth taken by his father would be returned. But because this exchange would delay his complete engagement in devotional service, he did not want to accept his father's old age, for he was eager to achieve freedom from disturbances. Moreover, among the descendants of Yadu would be Lord Kṛṣṇa. Therefore, because Yadu was eager to see the Lord's appearance in his dynasty as soon as possible, Yadu refused to accept his father's proposal. This was not irreligious, however, because Yadu's purpose was to serve the Lord. Because Yadu was a faithful servant of the Lord, Lord Kṛṣṇa appeared in his dynasty. As confirmed in the prayers of Kuntī, *yadoḥ priyasyānvavāye*. Yadu was very dear to Kṛṣṇa, who was therefore eager to descend in Yadu's dynasty. In conclusion, Mahārāja Yadu should not be considered *adharma-jña*, ignorant of religious principles, as the next verse designates his brothers. He was like the four Sanakas (*catuḥ-sana*), who refused the order of their father, Brahmā, for the sake of a better cause. Because the four Kumāras wanted to engage themselves completely in the service of the Lord as *brahmacārīs*, their refusal to obey their father's order was not irreligious.

TEXT 41

तुर्वसुश्चोदितः पित्रा द्रुह्युश्चानुश्च भारत ।
प्रत्याचख्युरधर्मज्ञा ह्यनित्ये नित्यबुद्धयः ॥४१॥

turvasuś coditaḥ pitrā
druhyuś cānuś ca bhārata
pratyācakhyur adharmajñā
hy anitye nitya-buddhayaḥ

turvasuḥ—Turvasu, another son; *coditaḥ*—requested; *pitrā*—by the father (to exchange old age and invalidity for his youth); *druhyuḥ*—Druhyu, another son; *ca*—and; *anuḥ*—Anu, another son; *ca*—also; *bhārata*—O King Parīkṣit; *pratyācakhyuḥ*—refused to accept; *adharma-jñāḥ*—because they did not know religious principles; *hi*—indeed; *a-nitye*—temporary youth; *nitya-buddhayaḥ*—thinking to be permanent.

TRANSLATION

O Mahārāja Parīkṣit, Yayāti similarly requested his sons Turvasu, Druhyu and Anu to exchange their youth for his old age, but because they were unaware of religious principles, they thought that their flickering youth was eternal, and therefore they refused to carry out their father's order.

TEXT 42

अपृच्छत् तनयं पूरुं वयसोनं गुणाधिकम् ।
न त्वमग्रजवद् वत्स मां प्रत्याख्यातुमर्हसि ॥४२॥

apṛcchat tanayaṁ pūruṁ
vayasonaṁ guṇādhikam
na tvam agrajavad vatsa
māṁ pratyākhyātum arhasi

apṛcchat—requested; *tanayam*—the son; *pūrum*—Pūru; *vayasā*—by age; *ūnam*—although younger; *guṇa-adhikam*—better than the others by quality; *na*—not; *tvam*—you; *agraja-vat*—like your older brothers; *vatsa*—my dear son; *mām*—me; *pratyākhyātum*—to refuse; *arhasi*—ought.

TRANSLATION

King Yayāti then requested Pūru, who was younger than these three brothers but more qualified, "My dear son, do not be disobedient like your elder brothers, for that is not your duty."

TEXT 43

श्रीपूरुरुवाच

को नु लोके मनुष्येन्द्र पितुरात्मकृतः पुमान् ।
प्रतिकर्तुं क्षमो यस्य प्रसादाद् विन्दते परम् ॥४३॥

śrī-pūrur uvāca
ko nu loke manuṣyendra
pitur ātma-kṛtaḥ pumān
pratikartuṁ kṣamo yasya
prasādād vindate param

śrī-pūruḥ uvāca—Pūru said; *kaḥ*—what; *nu*—indeed; *loke*—in this world; *manuṣya-indra*—O Your Majesty, best of human beings; *pituḥ*—the father; *ātma-kṛtaḥ*—who has given this body; *pumān*—a person; *pratikartum*—to repay; *kṣamaḥ*—is able; *yasya*—of whom; *prasādāt*—by the mercy; *vindate*—one enjoys; *param*—superior life.

TRANSLATION

Pūru replied: O Your Majesty, who in this world can repay his debt to his father? By the mercy of one's father, one gets the human form of life, which can enable one to become an associate of the Supreme Lord.

PURPORT

The father gives the seed of the body, and this seed gradually grows and develops until one ultimately attains the developed human body, with consciousness higher than that of the animals. In the human body one can be elevated to the higher planets, and, furthermore, if one cultivates Kṛṣṇa consciousness, one can return home, back to Godhead. This important human body is obtained by the grace of the father, and therefore everyone is indebted to his father. Of course, in other lives one also gets a father and mother; even cats and dogs have fathers and mothers. But in the human form of life the father and mother can award their son the greatest benediction by teaching him to become a devotee. When one becomes a devotee, he achieves the greatest benediction because he completely averts the repetition of birth and death. Therefore the father who trains his child in Kṛṣṇa consciousness is the most benevolent father in this world. It is said:

janame janame sabe pitāmātā pāya
kṛṣṇa guru nahi mile bhaja hari ei

Everyone gets a father and mother, but if one gets the benediction of Kṛṣṇa and *guru,* he can conquer material nature and return home, back to Godhead.

TEXT 44

उत्तमश्चिन्तितं कुर्यात् प्रोक्तकारी तु मध्यमः ।
अधमोऽश्रद्धया कुर्यादकर्तोच्चरितं पितुः ॥४४॥

uttamaś cintitaṁ kuryāt
prokta-kārī tu madhyamaḥ

adhamo 'śraddhayā kuryād
akartoccaritaṁ pituḥ

uttamaḥ—the best; *cintitam*—considering the father's idea; *kuryāt*—acts accordingly; *prokta-kārī*—one who acts on the order of the father; *tu*—indeed; *madhyamaḥ*—mediocre; *adhamaḥ*—lower class; *aśraddhayā*—without any faith; *kuryāt*—acts; *akartā*—unwilling to do; *uccaritam*—like stool; *pituḥ*—of the father.

TRANSLATION

A son who acts by anticipating what his father wants him to do is first class, one who acts upon receiving his father's order is second class, and one who executes his father's order irreverently is third class. But a son who refuses his father's order is like his father's stool.

PURPORT

Pūru, Yayāti's last son, immediately accepted his father's proposal, for although he was the youngest, he was very qualified. Pūru thought, "I should have accepted my father's proposal before he asked, but I did not. Therefore I am not a first-class son. I am second class. But I do not wish to become the lowest type of son, who is compared to his father's stool." One Indian poet has spoken of *putra* and *mūtra. Putra* means "son," and *mūtra* means "urine." Both a son and urine come from the same genitals. If a son is an obedient devotee of the Lord he is called *putra*, or a real son; otherwise, if he is not learned and is not a devotee, a son is nothing better than urine.

TEXT 45

इति प्रमुदितः पूरुः प्रत्यगृह्णाज्जरां पितुः ।
सोऽपि तद्वयसा कामान् यथावज्जुजुषे नृप ॥४५॥

iti pramuditaḥ pūruḥ
pratyagṛhṇāj jarāṁ pituḥ
so 'pi tad-vayasā kāmān
yathāvaj jujuṣe nṛpa

iti—in this way; *pramuditaḥ*—very pleased; *pūruḥ*—Pūru; *pratyagṛhṇāt*—accepted; *jarām*—the old age and invalidity; *pituḥ*—of his father; *saḥ*—that father (Yayāti); *api*—also; *tat-vayasā*—by the youth of his son; *kāmān*—all desires; *yathā-vat*—as required; *jujuṣe*—satisfied; *nṛpa*—O Mahārāja Parīkṣit.

TRANSLATION

Śukadeva Gosvāmī said: In this way, O Mahārāja Parīkṣit, the son named Pūru was very pleased to accept the old age of his father, Yayāti, who took the youth of his son and enjoyed this material world as he required.

TEXT 46

सप्तद्वीपपतिः सम्यक् पितृवत् पालयन् प्रजाः ।
यथोपजोषं विषयाञ्जुजुषेऽव्याहतेन्द्रियः ॥४६॥

sapta-dvīpa-patiḥ samyak
pitṛvat pālayan prajāḥ
yathopajoṣaṁ viṣayāñ
jujuṣe 'vyāhatendriyaḥ

sapta-dvīpa-patiḥ—the master of the entire world, consisting of seven islands; *samyak*—completely; *pitṛ-vat*—exactly like a father; *pālayan*—ruling; *prajāḥ*—the subjects; *yathā-upajoṣam*—as much as he wanted; *viṣayān*—material happiness; *jujuṣe*—enjoyed; *avyāhata*—without being disturbed; *indriyaḥ*—his senses.

TRANSLATION

Thereafter, King Yayāti became the ruler of the entire world, consisting of seven islands, and ruled the citizens exactly like a father. Because he had taken the youth of his son, his senses were unimpaired, and he enjoyed as much material happiness as he desired.

TEXT 47

देवयान्यप्यनुदिनं मनोवाग्देहवस्तुभिः ।
प्रेयसः परमां प्रीतिमुवाह प्रेयसी रहः ॥४७॥

devayāny apy anudinaṁ
mano-vāg-deha-vastubhiḥ
preyasaḥ paramāṁ prītim
uvāha preyasī rahaḥ

devayānī—Mahārāja Yayāti's wife, the daughter of Śukrācārya; *api*—also; *anudinam*—twenty-four hours, day after day; *manaḥ-vāk*—by her mind and words; *deha*—body; *vastubhiḥ*—with all requisite things; *preyasaḥ*—of her beloved husband; *paramām*—transcendental; *prītim*—bliss; *uvāha*—executed; *preyasī*—very dear to her husband; *rahaḥ*—in seclusion, without any disturbance.

TRANSLATION

In secluded places, engaging her mind, words, body and various paraphernalia, Devayānī, the dear wife of Mahārāja Yayāti, always brought her husband the greatest possible transcendental bliss.

TEXT 48

अयजद् यज्ञपुरुषं क्रतुभिर्भूरिदक्षिणैः ।
सर्वदेवमयं देवं सर्ववेदमयं हरिम् ॥४८॥

ayajad yajña-puruṣaṁ
kratubhir bhūri-dakṣiṇaiḥ
sarva-devamayaṁ devaṁ
sarva-vedamayaṁ harim

ayajat—worshiped; *yajña-puruṣam*—the *yajña-puruṣa,* the Lord; *kratubhiḥ*—by performing various sacrifices; *bhūri-dakṣiṇaiḥ*—giving abundant gifts to the *brāhmaṇas; sarva-deva-mayam*—the reservoir of all the demigods; *devam*—the Supreme Lord; *sarva-veda-mayam*—the ultimate object of all Vedic knowledge; *harim*—the Lord, the Supreme Personality of Godhead.

TRANSLATION

King Yayāti performed various sacrifices, in which he offered abundant gifts to the brāhmaṇas to satisfy the Supreme Lord, Hari, who is the reservoir of all the demigods and the object of all Vedic knowledge.

TEXT 49

यस्मिन्निदं विरचितं व्योम्नीव जलदावलिः ।
नानेव भाति नाभाति स्वप्नमायामनोरथः ॥४९॥

yasminn idaṁ viracitaṁ
vyomnīva jaladāvaliḥ
nāneva bhāti nābhāti
svapna-māyā-manorathaḥ

yasmin—in whom; *idam*—this entire cosmic manifestation; *viracitam*—created; *vyomni*—in the sky; *iva*—just like; *jalada-āvaliḥ*—clouds; *nānā iva*—as if in different varieties; *bhāti*—is manifested; *na ābhāti*—is unmanifested; *svapna-māyā*—illusion, like a dream; *manaḥ-rathaḥ*—created to be traversed by the chariot of the mind.

TRANSLATION

The Supreme Lord, Vāsudeva, who created the cosmic manifestation, exhibits Himself as all-pervading, like the sky that holds clouds. And when the creation is annihilated, everything enters into the Supreme Lord, Viṣṇu, and varieties are no longer manifested.

PURPORT

As stated by the Lord Himself in *Bhagavad-gītā* (7.19):

bahūnāṁ janmanāṁ ante
jñānavān māṁ prapadyate

vāsudevaḥ sarvam iti
sa mahātmā sudurlabhaḥ

"After many births and deaths, he who is actually in knowledge surrenders unto Me, knowing Me to be the cause of all causes and all that is. Such a great soul is very rare." The Supreme Personality of Godhead, Vāsudeva, is one with the Supreme Brahman, the Supreme Absolute Truth. Everything is in Him in the beginning, and at the end all manifestations enter into Him. He is situated in everyone's heart (*sarvasya cāhaṁ hṛdi sanniviṣṭaḥ*). And from Him everything has emanated (*janmādy asya yataḥ*). All material manifestations, however, are temporary. The word *svapna* means "dreams," *māyā* means "illusion," and *manoratha* means "mental creations." Dreams, illusions and mental creations are temporary. Similarly, all material creation is temporary, but Vāsudeva, the Supreme Personality of Godhead, is the eternal Absolute Truth.

TEXT 50

तमेव हृदि विन्यस्य वासुदेवं गुहाशयम् ।
नारायणमणीयांसं निराशीरयजत् प्रभुम् ॥५०॥

tam eva hṛdi vinyasya
vāsudevaṁ guhāśayam
nārāyaṇam aṇīyāṁsaṁ
nirāśīr ayajat prabhum

tam eva—Him only; *hṛdi*—within the heart; *vinyasya*—placing; *vāsudevam*—Lord Vāsudeva; *guha-āśayam*—who exists in everyone's heart; *nārāyaṇam*—who is Nārāyaṇa, or an expansion of Nārāyaṇa; *aṇīyāṁsam*—invisible to material eyes, although existing everywhere; *nirāśīḥ*—Yayāti, without any material desires; *ayajat*—worshiped; *prabhum*—the Supreme Lord.

TRANSLATION

Without material desires, Mahārāja Yayāti worshiped the Supreme Lord, who is situated in everyone's heart as Nārāyaṇa and is invisible to material eyes, although existing everywhere.

PURPORT

King Yayāti, although externally seeming very fond of material enjoyment, was internally thinking of becoming an eternal servant of the Lord.

TEXT 51

एवं वर्षसहस्राणि मनःषष्ठैर्मनःसुखम् ।
विदधानोऽपि नातृप्यत् सार्वभौमः कदिन्द्रियैः ॥५१॥

evaṁ varṣa-sahasrāṇi
manaḥ-ṣaṣṭhair manaḥ-sukham
vidadhāno 'pi nātṛpyat
sārva-bhaumaḥ kad-indriyaiḥ

evam—in this way; *varṣa-sahasrāṇi*—for one thousand years; *manaḥ-ṣaṣṭhaiḥ*—by the mind and five knowledge-acquiring senses; *manaḥ-sukham*—temporary happiness created by the mind; *vidadhānaḥ*—executing; *api*—although; *na atṛpyat*—could not be satisfied; *sārva-bhaumaḥ*—although he was the king of the entire world; *kat-indriyaiḥ*—because of possessing impure senses.

TRANSLATION

Although Mahārāja Yayāti was the king of the entire world and he engaged his mind and five senses in enjoying material possessions for one thousand years, he was unable to be satisfied.

PURPORT

The *kad-indriya*, or unpurified senses, can be purified if one engages the senses and the mind in Kṛṣṇa consciousness. *Sarvopādhi-vinirmuktaṁ tat-paratvena nirmalam.* One must be freed from all designations. When one identifies himself with the material world, his senses are impure. But when one achieves spiritual realization and identifies himself as a servant of the Lord, his senses are purified immediately. Engagement of the purified senses in the service of the Lord is called *bhakti. Hṛṣīkeṇa hṛṣīkeśa-sevanaṁ bhaktir ucyate.* One may enjoy the senses for many thousands of years, but unless one purifies the senses, one cannot be happy.

Thus end the Bhaktivedanta purports of the Ninth Canto, Eighteenth Chapter, of the Śrīmad-Bhāgavatam, *entitled "King Yayāti Regains His Youth."*

CHAPTER NINETEEN

King Yayāti Achieves Liberation

This Nineteenth Chapter describes how Mahārāja Yayāti achieved liberation after he recounted the figurative story of the he-goat and she-goat.

After many, many years of sexual relationships and enjoyment in the material world, King Yayāti finally became disgusted with such materialistic happiness. When satiated with material enjoyment, he devised a story of a he-goat and she-goat, corresponding to his own life, and narrated the story before his beloved Devayānī. The story is as follows. Once upon a time, while a goat was searching in a forest for different types of vegetables to eat, by chance he came to a well, in which he saw a she-goat. He became attracted to this she-goat and somehow or other delivered her from the well, and thus they were united. One day thereafter, when the she-goat saw the he-goat enjoying sex with another she-goat, she became angry, abandoned the he-goat, and returned to her *brāhmaṇa* owner, to whom she described her husband's behavior. The *brāhmaṇa* became very angry and cursed the he-goat to lose his sexual power. Thereupon, the he-goat begged the *brāhmaṇa's* pardon and was given back the power for sex. Then the he-goat enjoyed sex with the she-goat for many years, but still he was not satisfied. If one is lusty and greedy, even the total stock of gold in this world cannot satisfy one's lusty desires. These desires are like a fire. One may pour clarified butter on a blazing fire, but one cannot expect the fire to be extinguished. To extinguish such a fire, one must adopt a different process. The *śāstra* therefore advises that by intelligence one renounce the life of enjoyment. Without great endeavor, those with a poor fund of knowledge cannot give up sense enjoyment, especially in relation to sex, because a beautiful woman bewilders even the most learned man. King Yayāti, however, renounced worldly life and divided his property among his sons. He personally adopted the life of a mendicant, or *sannyāsī*, giving up all attraction to material enjoyment, and engaged himself fully in devotional service to the Lord. Thus he attained perfection. Later, when his beloved wife, Devayānī, was freed from her mistaken way of life, she also engaged herself in the devotional service of the Lord.

TEXT 1

श्रीशुक उवाच

स इत्थमाचरन् कामान् स्त्रैणोऽपह्नवमात्मनः ।
बुद्ध्वा प्रियायै निर्विण्णो गाथामेतामगायत ॥ १ ॥

śrī-śuka uvāca
sa ittham ācaran kāmān
straiṇo 'pahnavam ātmanaḥ
buddhvā priyāyai nirviṇṇo
gāthām etām agāyata

śrī-śukaḥ uvāca—Śrī Śukadeva Gosvāmī said; *saḥ*—Mahārāja Yayāti; *ittham*—in this way; *ācaran*—behaving; *kāmān*—in regard to lusty desires; *straiṇaḥ*—very much attached to woman; *apahnavam*—counteraction; *ātmanaḥ*—of his own welfare; *buddhvā*—understanding with intelligence; *priyāyai*—unto his beloved wife, Devayānī; *nirviṇṇaḥ*—disgusted; *gāthām*—story; *etām*—this (as follows); *agāyata*—narrated.

TRANSLATION

Śukadeva Gosvāmī said: O Mahārāja Parīkṣit, Yayāti was very much attached to woman. In due course of time, however, when disgusted with sexual enjoyment and its bad effects, he renounced this way of life and narrated the following story to his beloved wife.

TEXT 2

शृणु भार्गव्यमूं गाथां मद्विधाचरितां भुवि ।
धीरा यस्यानुशोचन्ति वने ग्रामनिवासिनः ॥ २ ॥

śṛṇu bhārgavy amūṁ gāthāṁ
mad-vidhācaritāṁ bhuvi
dhīrā yasyānuśocanti
vane grāma-nivāsinaḥ

śṛṇu—please hear; *bhārgavi*—O daughter of Śukrācārya; *amūm*—this; *gāthām*—history; *mat-vidhā*—exactly resembling my behavior; *ācaritām*—behavior; *bhuvi*—within this world; *dhīrāḥ*—those who are sober and intelligent; *yasya*—of whom; *anuśocanti*—lament very much; *vane*—in the forest; *grāma-nivāsinaḥ*—very much attached to materialistic enjoyment.

TRANSLATION

My dearly beloved wife, daughter of Śukrācārya, in this world there was someone exactly like me. Please listen as I narrate the history of his life. By hearing about the life of such a householder, those who have retired from householder life always lament.

PURPORT

Persons who live in the village or town are called *grāma-nivāsī,* and those who live in the forest are called *vana-vāsī* or *vānaprastha.* The *vānaprasthas,* who have retired from family life, generally lament about their past family life because it engaged them in trying to fulfill lusty desires. Prahlāda Mahārāja said that one should retire from family life as soon as possible, and he described family life as the darkest well (*hitvātma-pātaṁ gṛham andha-kūpam*). If one continuously or permanently concentrates on living with his family, he should be understood to be killing himself. In the Vedic civilization, therefore, it is recommended that one retire from family life at the end of his fiftieth year and go to *vana,* the forest. When he becomes expert or accustomed to forest life, or retired life as a *vānaprastha,* he should accept *sannyāsa. Vanaṁ gato yad dharim āśrayeta. Sannyāsa* means accepting unalloyed engagement in the service of the Lord. Vedic civilization therefore recommends four different stages of life—*brahmacarya, gṛhastha, vānaprastha* and *sannyāsa.* One should be very much ashamed of remaining a householder and not promoting oneself to the two higher stages, namely *vānaprastha* and *sannyāsa.*

TEXT 3

बस्त एको वने कश्चिद् विचिन्वन् प्रियमात्मनः ।
ददर्श कूपे पतितां स्वकर्मवशगामजाम् ॥ ३ ॥

basta eko vane kaścid
vicinvan priyam ātmanaḥ
dadarśa kūpe patitāṁ
sva-karma-vaśagām ajām

bastaḥ—goat; *ekaḥ*—one; *vane*—in a forest; *kaścit*—some; *vicinvan*—searching for food; *priyam*—very dear; *ātmanaḥ*—for himself; *dadarśa*—saw by chance; *kūpe*—within a well; *patitām*—fallen; *sva-karma-vaśa-gām*—under the influence of the results of fruitive activities; *ajām*—a she-goat.

TRANSLATION

While wandering in the forest, eating to satisfy his senses, a he-goat by chance approached a well, in which he saw a she-goat standing helplessly, having fallen into it by the influence of the results of fruitive activities.

PURPORT

Here Mahārāja Yayāti compares himself to a he-goat and Devayānī to a she-goat and describes the nature of man and woman. Like a he-goat, a man searches for sense gratification, wandering here and there, and a woman without the shelter of a man or husband is like a she-goat that has fallen into a well. Without being cared for by a man, a woman cannot be happy. Indeed, she is just like a she-goat that has fallen into a well and is struggling for existence. Therefore a woman must take shelter of her father, as Devayānī did when under the care of Śukrācārya, and then the father must give the daughter in charity to a suitable man, or a suitable man should help the woman by placing her under the care of a husband. This is shown vividly by the life of Devayānī. When King Yayāti delivered Devayānī from the well, she felt great relief and requested Yayāti to accept her as his wife. But when Mahārāja Yayāti accepted Devayānī, he became too attached and had sex life not only with her but with others, like Śarmiṣṭhā. Yet still he was dissatisfied. Therefore one should retire by force from such family life as Yayāti's. When one is fully convinced of the degrading nature of worldly family life, one should completely renounce this way of life, take *sannyāsa*, and engage himself fully in the service of the Lord. Then one's life will be successful.

TEXT 4

तस्या उद्धरणोपायं बस्तः कामी विचिन्तयन् ।
व्यधत्त तीर्थमुद्धृत्य विषाणाग्रेण रोधसी ॥ ४ ॥

tasyā uddharaṇopāyaṁ
bastaḥ kāmī vicintayan
vyadhatta tīrtham uddhṛtya
viṣāṇāgreṇa rodhasī

tasyāḥ—of the she-goat; *uddharaṇa-upāyam*—the means of deliverance (from the well); *bastaḥ*—the he-goat; *kāmī*—having lusty desires; *vicintayan*—planning; *vyadhatta*—executed; *tīrtham*—a way to come out; *uddhṛtya*—digging the earth; *viṣāṇa-agreṇa*—by the point of the horns; *rodhasī*—at the edge of the well.

TRANSLATION

After planning how to get the she-goat out of the well, the lusty he-goat dug up the earth on the well's edge with the point of his horns in such a way that she was able to come out very easily.

PURPORT

Attraction for woman is the impetus for economic development, housing and many other things meant for living comfortably in this material world. Digging up the earth to make a way out for the she-goat was a laborious task, but before accepting the she-goat, the he-goat underwent this labor. *Aho gṛha-kṣetra-sutāpta-vittair janasya moho 'yam ahaṁ mameti.* The union between male and female provides the impetus for gaining a nice apartment, a good income, children and friends. Thus one becomes entangled in this material world.

TEXTS 5–6

सोत्तीर्य कूपात् सुश्रोणी तमेव चकमे किल ।
तया वृतं समुद्वीक्ष्य बह्व्योऽजाः कान्तकामिनीः ॥५॥

पीवानं श्मश्रुलं प्रेष्ठं मीढ्वांसं याभकोविदम् ।
स एकोऽजवृषस्तासां बह्वीनां रतिवर्धनः ।
रेमे कामग्रहग्रस्त आत्मानं नावबुध्यत ॥ ६ ॥

sottīrya kupāt suśroṇī
tam eva cakame kila
tayā vṛtaṁ samudvīkṣya
bahvyo 'jāḥ kānta-kāminīḥ

pīvānaṁ śmaśrulaṁ preṣṭhaṁ
mīḍhvāṁsaṁ yābha-kovidam
sa eko 'javṛṣas tāsāṁ
bahvīnāṁ rati-vardhanaḥ
reme kāma-graha-grasta
ātmānaṁ nāvabudhyata

sā—the she-goat; *uttīrya*—getting out; *kupāt*—from the well; *su-śroṇī*—possessing very nice hips; *tam*—unto the he-goat; *eva*—indeed; *cakame*—desired to get as her husband; *kila*—indeed; *tayā*—by her; *vṛtam*—accepted; *samudvīkṣya*—seeing; *bahvyaḥ*—many others; *ajāḥ*—she-goats; *kānta-kāminīḥ*—desiring to get the he-goat as their husband; *pīvānam*—very stout and strong; *śmaśrulam*—having a very nice mustache and beard; *preṣṭham*—first-class; *mīḍhvāṁsam*—expert in discharging semen; *yābha-kovidam*—expert in the art of sexual intercourse; *saḥ*—that he-goat; *ekaḥ*—alone; *aja-vṛṣaḥ*—the hero of the goats; *tāsām*—of all the she-goats; *bahvīnām*—a great number; *rati-vardhanaḥ*—could increase the lusty desire; *reme*—he enjoyed; *kāma-graha-grastaḥ*—being haunted by the ghost of lusty desire; *ātmānam*—his own self; *na*—not; *avabudhyata*—could understand.

TRANSLATION

When the she-goat, who had very nice hips, got out of the well and saw the very handsome he-goat, she desired to accept him as her husband. When she did so, many other she-goats also desired him as their husband because he had a very beautiful bodily structure and a nice mustache and beard and was expert in discharging

semen and in the art of sexual intercourse. Therefore, just as a person haunted by a ghost exhibits madness, the best of the he-goats, attracted by the many she-goats, engaged in erotic activities and naturally forgot his real business of self-realization.

PURPORT

Materialists are certainly very much attracted by sexual intercourse. *Yan maithunādi-gṛhamedhi-sukhaṁ hi tuccham.* Although one becomes a *gṛhastha*, or householder, to enjoy sex life to his heart's content, one is never satisfied. Such a lusty materialist is like a goat, for it is said that if goats meant for slaughter get the opportunity, they enjoy sex before being killed. Human beings, however, are meant for self-realization.

tapo divyaṁ putrakā yena sattvaṁ
śuddhyed yasmād brahma-saukhyaṁ tv anantam

Human life is meant for realization of the self, the spiritual soul within the body (*dehino 'smin yathā dehe*). A materialistic rascal does not know that he is not the body but a spiritual soul within the body. However, one should understand his real position and cultivate knowledge by which to get free from bodily entanglement. Like an unfortunate person who acts madly, haunted by ghosts, a materialist haunted by the ghost of lust forgets his real business so that he can enjoy so-called happiness in the bodily concept of life.

TEXT 7

तमेव प्रेष्ठतमया रममाणमजान्यया ।
विलोक्य कूपसंविग्ना नामृष्यद् बस्तकर्म तत् ॥ ७ ॥

tam eva preṣṭhatamayā
ramamāṇam ajānyayā
vilokya kūpa-saṁvignā
nāmṛṣyad basta-karma tat

tam—the he-goat; *eva*—indeed; *preṣṭhatamayā*—beloved; *ramamāṇam*—engaged in sexual activities; *ajā*—the she-goat; *anyayā*—with another she-goat; *vilokya*—by seeing; *kūpa-saṁvignā*—the she-goat who had fallen into the well; *na*—not; *amṛṣyat*—tolerated; *basta-karma*—the business of the goat; *tat*—that (sex is accepted here as the business of the goat).

TRANSLATION

When the she-goat who had fallen into the well saw her beloved goat engaged in sexual affairs with another she-goat, she could not tolerate the goat's activities.

TEXT 8

तं दुर्हृदं सुहृद्रूपं कामिनं क्षणसौहृदम् ।
इन्द्रियाराममुत्सृज्य स्वामिनं दुःखिता ययौ ॥ ८ ॥

taṁ durhṛdaṁ suhṛd-rūpaṁ
kāminaṁ kṣaṇa-sauhṛdam
indriyārāmam utsṛjya
svāminaṁ duḥkhitā yayau

tam—him (the he-goat); *durhṛdam*—cruel hearted; *suhṛt-rūpam*—pretending to be a friend; *kāminam*—very lusty; *kṣaṇa-sauhṛdam*—having friendship for the time being; *indriya-ārāmam*—interested only in sense gratification or sensuality; *utsṛjya*—giving up; *svāminam*—to her present husband, or to the former maintainer; *duḥkhitā*—being very much aggrieved; *yayau*—she left.

TRANSLATION

Aggrieved by her husband's behavior with another, the she-goat thought that the he-goat was not actually her friend but was hard-hearted and was her friend only for the time being. Therefore, because her husband was lusty, she left him and returned to her former maintainer.

PURPORT

The word *svāminam* is significant. *Svāmī* means "caretaker" or "master." Devayānī was cared for by Śukrācārya before her marriage, and after her marriage she was cared for by Yayāti, but here the word *svāminam* indicates that Devayānī left the protection of her husband, Yayāti, and returned to her former protector, Śukrācārya. Vedic civilization recommends that a woman stay under the protection of a man. During childhood she should be cared for by her father, in youth by her husband, and in old age by a grown son. In any stage of life, a woman should not have independence.

TEXT 9

सोऽपि चानुगतः स्त्रैणः कृपणस्तां प्रसादितुम् ।
कुर्वन्निडविडाकारं नाशक्नोत् पथि संधितुम् ॥ ९ ॥

so 'pi cānugataḥ straiṇaḥ
kṛpaṇas tāṁ prasāditum
kurvann iḍaviḍā-kāraṁ
nāśaknot pathi sandhitum

saḥ—that he-goat; *api*—also; *ca*—also; *anugataḥ*—following the she-goat; *straiṇaḥ*—henpecked; *kṛpaṇaḥ*—very poor; *tām*—her; *prasāditum*—to satisfy; *kurvan*—making; *iḍaviḍā-kāram*—an utterance in the language of the goats; *na*—not; *aśaknot*—was able; *pathi*—on the road; *sandhitum*—to satisfy.

TRANSLATION

Being very sorry, the he-goat, who was subservient to his wife, followed the she-goat on the road and tried his best to flatter her, but he could not pacify her.

TEXT 10

तस्यतत्र द्विजः कश्चिदजास्वाम्यच्छिनद् रुषा ।
लम्बन्तं वृषणं भूयः सन्दधेऽर्थाय योगवित् ॥१०॥

tasya tatra dvijaḥ kaścid
ajā-svāmy acchinad ruṣā

lambantaṁ vṛṣaṇaṁ bhūyaḥ
sandadhe 'rthāya yogavit

tasya—of the he-goat; *tatra*—thereupon; *dvijaḥ*—*brāhmaṇa; kaścit*—some; *ajā-svāmī*—the maintainer of another she-goat; *acchinat*—castrated, made effeminate; *ruṣā*—out of anger; *lambantam*—long; *vṛṣaṇam*—testicles; *bhūyaḥ*—again; *sandadhe*—joined; *arthāya*—for self-interest; *yoga-vit*—expert in the power of mystic *yoga.*

TRANSLATION

The she-goat went to the residence of a brāhmaṇa who was the maintainer of another she-goat, and that brāhmaṇa angrily cut off the he-goat's dangling testicles. But at the he-goat's request, the brāhmaṇa later rejoined them by the power of mystic yoga.

PURPORT

Here Śukrācārya is figuratively described as the husband of another she-goat. This indicates that the relationship between husband and wife in any society, whether higher or lower than human society, is nothing but the same relationship between he-goat and she-goat, for the material relationship between man and woman is one of sex. *Yan maithunādi-gṛhamedhi-sukhaṁ hi tuccham.* Śukrācārya was an *ācārya*, or expert, in family affairs, which involve the transfer of semen from he-goat to she-goat. The words *kaścid ajā-svāmī* expressly indicate herein that Śukrācārya was no better than Yayāti, for both of them were interested in family affairs generated by *śukra*, or semen. Śukrācārya first cursed Yayāti to become old so that he could no longer indulge in sex, but when Śukrācārya saw that Yayāti's emasculation would make his own daughter a victim of punishment, he used his mystic power to restore Yayāti's masculinity. Because he used his power of mystic *yoga* for family affairs and not to realize the Supreme Personality of Godhead, this exercise in the magic of *yoga* was no better than the affairs of he-goats and she-goats. Yogic power should properly be used to realize the Supreme Personality of Godhead. As the Lord Himself recommends in *Bhagavad-gītā* (6.47):

yoginām api sarveṣāṁ
mad-gatenāntarātmanā
śraddhāvān bhajate yo māṁ
sa me yuktatamo mataḥ

"Of all *yogīs,* he who always abides in Me with great faith, worshiping Me in transcendental loving service, is most intimately united with Me in *yoga* and is the highest of all."

TEXT 11

सम्बद्धवृषणः सोऽपि ह्यजया कूपलब्धया ।
कालं बहुतिथं भद्रे कामैर्नाद्यापि तुष्यति ॥११॥

sambaddha-vṛṣaṇaḥ so 'pi
hy ajayā kūpa-labdhayā
kālaṁ bahu-tithaṁ bhadre
kāmair nādyāpi tuṣyati

sambaddha-vṛṣaṇaḥ—rejoined with his testicles; *saḥ*—he; *api*—also; *hi*—indeed; *ajayā*—with the she-goat; *kūpa-labdhayā*—whom he got from the well; *kālam*—for a time; *bahu-titham*—of a long, long duration; *bhadre*—O my dear wife; *kāmaiḥ*—with such lusty desires; *na*—not; *adya api*—even until now; *tuṣyati*—is satisfied.

TRANSLATION

My dear wife, when the he-goat had his testicles restored, he enjoyed the she-goat he had gotten from the well, but although he continued to enjoy for many, many years, even now he has not been fully satisfied.

PURPORT

When one is bound by affection for one's wife, one is attached to sexual desires that are very difficult to overcome. Therefore, according to Vedic civilization, one must voluntarily leave his so-called home and go to the forest. *Pañcāśordhvaṁ vanaṁ vrajet.* Human life is meant for such *tapasya,* or austerity. By the austerity of voluntarily stopping sex life at home and going to the forest to engage in spiritual activities in the association of devotees, one achieves the actual purpose of human life.

TEXT 12

तथाहं कृपणः सुभ्रु भवत्याः प्रेमयन्त्रितः ।
आत्मानं नाभिजानामि मोहितस्तव मायया ॥१२॥

tathāhaṁ kṛpaṇaḥ subhru
bhavatyāḥ prema-yantritaḥ
ātmānaṁ nābhijānāmi
mohitas tava māyayā

tathā—exactly like the he-goat; *aham*—I; *kṛpaṇaḥ*—a miser with no sense of the importance of life; *su-bhru*—O my wife, with beautiful eyebrows; *bhavatyāḥ*—in your company; *prema-yantritaḥ*—as if tied in love, although it is actually lust; *ātmānam*—self-realization (what I am and what my duty is); *na abhijānāmi*—I could not realize even until now; *mohitaḥ*—being bewildered; *tava*—your; *māyayā*—by the materially attractive feature.

TRANSLATION

O my dear wife with beautiful eyebrows, I am exactly like that he-goat, for I am so poor in intelligence that I am captivated by your beauty and have forgotten the real task of self-realization.

PURPORT

If one remains a victim of the so-called beauty of his wife, his family life is nothing but a dark well. *Hitvātma-pātaṁ gṛham andha-kūpam.* Existence in such a dark well is certainly suicidal. If one wants relief from the miserable condition of material life, one must voluntarily give up his lusty relationship with his wife; otherwise there is no question of self-realization. Unless one is extremely advanced in spiritual consciousness, household life is nothing but a dark well in which one commits suicide. Prahlāda Mahārāja therefore recommended that in due time, at least after one's fiftieth year, one must give up household life and go to the forest. *Vanaṁ gato yad dharim āśrayeta.* There one should seek shelter at the lotus feet of Hari.

TEXT 13

यत् पृथिव्यां व्रीहियवं हिरण्यं पशवः स्त्रियः ।
न दुह्यन्ति मनःप्रीतिं पुंसः कामहतस्य ते ॥१३॥

yat pṛthivyāṁ vrīhi-yavaṁ
hiraṇyaṁ paśavaḥ striyaḥ
na duhyanti manaḥ-prītiṁ
puṁsaḥ kāma-hatasya te

yat—what; *pṛthivyām*—within this world; *vrīhi*—food grains, rice; *yavam*—barley; *hiraṇyam*—gold; *paśavaḥ*—animals; *striyaḥ*—wives or other women; *na duhyanti*—do not give; *manaḥ-prītim*—satisfaction of the mind; *puṁsaḥ*—to a person; *kāma-hatasya*—because of being victimized by lusty desires; *te*—they.

TRANSLATION

A person who is lusty cannot satisfy his mind even if he has enough of everything in this world, including rice, barley and other food grains, gold, animals and women. Nothing can satisfy him.

PURPORT

Improvement of one's economic condition is the aim and object of a materialist, but there is no end to this material advancement, for if one cannot control his lusty desires, he will never be pleased, even if he gets all the material wealth of the world. In this age we see much material improvement, but still people are struggling to get more and more material opulence. *Manaḥ ṣaṣṭhānīndriyāṇi prakṛti-sthāni karṣati.* Although every living entity is a part of the Supreme Being, because of lusty desires one continuously struggles for so-called betterment of one's economic condition. To have a satisfied mind, one must give up his heart disease of lusty desires. This can be done only when one is Kṛṣṇa conscious.

bhaktiṁ parāṁ bhagavati pratilabhya kāmaṁ
hṛd-rogam āśv apahinoty acireṇa dhīraḥ
(*Bhāg.* 10.33.39)

If one becomes Kṛṣṇa conscious, then he can give up this heart disease; otherwise this disease of lusty desires will continue, and one cannot have peace in his mind.

TEXT 14

न जातु कामः कामानामुपभोगेन शाम्यति ।
हविषा कृष्णवर्त्मेव भूय एवाभिवर्धते ॥१४॥

na jātu kāmaḥ kāmānām
upabhogena śāṁyati
haviṣā kṛṣṇa-vartmeva
bhūya evābhivardhate

na—not; *jātu*—at any time; *kāmaḥ*—lusty desires; *kāmānām*—of persons who are very lusty; *upabhogena*—by enjoyment of lusty desires; *śāṁyati*—can be pacified; *haviṣā*—by supplying butter; *kṛṣṇa-vartmā*—fire; *iva*—like; *bhūyaḥ*—again and again; *eva*—indeed; *abhivardhate*—increases more and more.

TRANSLATION

As supplying butter to a fire does not diminish the fire but instead increases it more and more, the endeavor to stop lusty desires by continual enjoyment can never be successful. [In fact, one must voluntarily cease from material desires.]

PURPORT

One may have enough money and enough resources to satisfy the senses but still not be satisfied, for the endeavor to stop lusty desires by enjoying can never be successful. The example given here is very appropriate. One cannot stop a blazing fire by trying to extinguish it with butter.

TEXT 15

यदा न कुरुते भावं सर्वभूतेष्वमङ्गलम् ।
समदृष्टेस्तदा पुंसः सर्वाः सुखमया दिशः ॥१५॥

yadā na kurute bhāvaṁ
sarva-bhūteṣv amaṅgalam
sama-dṛṣṭes tadā puṁsaḥ
sarvāḥ sukhamayā diśaḥ

yadā—when; *na*—not; *kurute*—does; *bhāvam*—a different attitude of attachment or envy; *sarva-bhūteṣu*—to all living entities; *amaṅgalam*—inauspicious; *sama-dṛṣṭeḥ*—because of being equipoised; *tadā*—at that time; *puṁsaḥ*—of the person; *sarvāḥ*—all; *sukhamayāḥ*—in a happy condition; *diśaḥ*—directions.

TRANSLATION

When a man is nonenvious and does not desire ill fortune for anyone, he is equipoised. For such a person, all directions appear happy.

PURPORT

Prabodhānanda Sarasvatī said, *viśvaṁ pūrṇa-sukhāyate:* when one becomes Kṛṣṇa conscious by the mercy of Lord Caitanya, for him the entire world appears happy, and he has nothing for which to hanker. On the *brahma-bhūta* stage, or the platform of spiritual realization, there is no lamentation and no material hankering (*na śocati na kāṅkṣati*). As long as one lives in the material world, actions and reactions will continue, but when one is unaffected by such material actions and reactions, he is to be considered free from the danger of being victimized by material desires. The symptoms of those who are satiated with lusty desires are described in this verse. As explained by Śrīla Viśvanātha Cakravartī Ṭhākura, when one is not envious even of his enemy, does not expect honor from anyone, but instead desires all well-being even for his enemy, he is understood to be a *paramahaṁsa*, one who has fully subdued the lusty desires for sense gratification.

TEXT 16

या दुस्त्यजा दुर्मतिभिर्जीर्यतो या न जीर्यते ।
तां तृष्णां दुःखनिवहां शर्मकामो द्रुतं त्यजेत् ॥१६॥

yā dustyajā durmatibhir
jīryato yā na jīryate
tāṁ tṛṣṇāṁ duḥkha-nivahāṁ
śarma-kāmo drutaṁ tyajet

yā—that which; *dustyajā*—extremely difficult to give up; *durmatibhiḥ*—by persons too attached to material enjoyment; *jīryataḥ*—even by one who is an invalid because of old age; *yā*—that which; *na*—not; *jīryate*—is vanquished; *tām*—such; *tṛṣṇām*—desire; *duḥkha-nivahām*—which is the cause of all tribulations; *śarma-kāmaḥ*—a person desiring his own happiness; *drutam*—very soon; *tyajet*—should give up.

TRANSLATION

For those who are too attached to material enjoyment, sense gratification is very difficult to give up. Even when one is an invalid because of old age, one cannot give up such desires for sense gratification. Therefore, one who actually desires happiness must give up such unsatisfied desires, which are the cause of all tribulations.

PURPORT

We have actually seen, especially in the Western countries, that men who have reached more than eighty years of age still go to nightclubs and pay heavy fees to drink wine and associate with women. Although such men are too old to enjoy anything, their desires have not ceased. Time deteriorates even the body itself, which is the medium for all sensual satisfaction, but even when a man becomes old and invalid, his desires are strong enough to dictate that he go here and there to satisfy the desires of his senses. Therefore, by the practice of *bhakti-yoga,* one should give up his lusty desires. As explained by Śrī Yāmunācārya:

yadavadhi mama cetaḥ kṛṣṇa-pādāravinde
nava-nava-rasa-dhāmany udyataṁ rantum āsīt
tadavadhi bata nārī-saṅgame smaryamāne
bhavati mukha-vikāraḥ suṣṭhu-niṣṭhīvanaṁ ca

When one is Kṛṣṇa conscious, he gets more and more happiness by discharging duties for Kṛṣṇa. Such a person spits on sense gratification, especially that of sexual enjoyment. An experienced, advanced devotee is no longer interested in sex life. The strong desire for sex can be subdued only by advancement in Kṛṣṇa consciousness.

TEXT 17

मात्रा स्वस्रा दुहित्रा वा नाविविक्तासनो भवेत् ।
बलवानिन्द्रियग्रामो विद्वांसमपि कर्षति ॥१७॥

mātrā svasrā duhitrā vā
nāviviktāsano bhavet
balavān indriya-grāmo
vidvāṁsam api karṣati

mātrā—with one's mother; *svasrā*—with one's sister; *duhitrā*—with one's own daughter; *vā*—either; *na*—not; *avivikta-āsanaḥ*—seated closely on one seat; *bhavet*—one should be; *balavān*—very strong; *indriya-grāmaḥ*—the group of senses; *vidvāṁsam*—the very learned and advanced person; *api*—even; *karṣati*—agitates.

TRANSLATION

One should not allow oneself to sit on the same seat even with one's own mother, sister or daughter, for the senses are so strong that even though one is very advanced in knowledge, he may be attracted by sex.

PURPORT

Learning the etiquette of how to deal with women does not free one from sexual attraction. As specifically mentioned herewith, such attraction is possible even with one's mother, sister or daughter. Generally, of course, one is not sexually attracted to his mother, sister or daughter, but if one allows himself to sit very close to such a woman, one may be attracted. This is a psychological fact. It may be said that one is liable to be attracted if he is not very advanced in civilized life; however, as specifically mentioned here, *vidvāṁsam api karṣati:* even if one is highly advanced, materially or spiritually, he may be attracted by lusty desires. The object of attraction may even be one's mother, sister or daughter. Therefore, one should be extremely careful in dealings with women. Śrī Caitanya Mahāprabhu was most strict in such dealings, especially after He accepted the *sannyāsa* order. Indeed, no woman could come near Him to offer Him respect. Again, one is warned herewith that one should be extremely careful in dealings with women. A *brahmacārī* is forbidden even to see the wife of his spiritual master if she happens to be young. The wife of the spiritual master may sometimes take some service from the disciple of her husband, as she would from a son, but if the wife of the spiritual master is young, a *brahmacārī* is forbidden to render service to her.

TEXT 18

पूर्णं वर्षसहस्रं मे विषयान् सेवतोऽसकृत् ।
तथापि चानुसवनं तृष्णा तेषूपजायते ॥१८॥

pūrṇaṁ varṣa-sahasraṁ me
viṣayān sevato 'sakṛt
tathāpi cānusavanaṁ
tṛṣṇā teṣūpajāyate

pūrṇam—completely; *varṣa-sahasram*—one thousand years; *me*—my; *viṣayān*—sense gratification; *sevataḥ*—enjoying; *asakṛt*—without cessation, continuously; *tathā api*—still; *ca*—indeed; *anusavanam*—more and more; *tṛṣṇā*—lusty desires; *teṣu*—in sense gratification; *upajāyate*—are increased.

TRANSLATION

I have spent a full one thousand years enjoying sense gratification, yet my desire to enjoy such pleasure increases daily.

PURPORT

Mahārāja Yayāti is explaining, in terms of his actual experience, how strong are sexual desires, even in old age.

TEXT 19

तस्मादेतामहं त्यक्त्वा ब्रह्मण्यध्याय मानसम् ।
निर्द्वन्द्वो निरहंकारश्चरिष्यामि मृगैः सह ॥१९॥

tasmād etām ahaṁ tyaktvā
brahmaṇy adhyāya mānasam
nirdvandvo nirahaṅkāraś
cariṣyāmi mṛgaiḥ saha

tasmāt—therefore; *etām*—such strong desires for lusty affairs; *aham*—I; *tyaktvā*—giving up; *brahmaṇi*—upon the Supreme Absolute Truth; *adhyāya*—fixing; *mānasam*—the mind; *nirdvandvaḥ*—without duality; *nirahaṅkāraḥ*—without an identity of false prestige; *cariṣyāmi*—I shall loiter or wander in the forest; *mṛgaiḥ saha*—with the forest animals.

TRANSLATION

Therefore, I shall now give up all these desires and meditate upon the Supreme Personality of Godhead. Free from the dualities of mental concoction and free from false prestige, I shall wander in the forest with the animals.

PURPORT

To go to the forest and live there with the animals, meditating upon the Supreme Personality of Godhead, is the only means by which to give up lusty desires. Unless one gives up such desires, one's mind cannot be freed from material contamination. Therefore, if one is at all interested in being freed from the bondage of repeated birth, death, old age and disease, after a certain age one must go to the forest. *Pañcāśordhvaṁ vanaṁ vrajet.* After fifty years of age, one should voluntarily give up family life and go to the forest. The best forest is Vṛndāvana, where one need not live with the animals but can associate with the Supreme Personality of Godhead, who never leaves Vṛndāvana. Cultivating Kṛṣṇa consciousness in Vṛndāvana is the best means of being liberated from material bondage, for in Vṛndāvana one can automatically meditate upon Kṛṣṇa. Vṛndāvana has many temples, and in one or more of these temples one may see the form of the Supreme Lord as Rādhā-Kṛṣṇa or Kṛṣṇa-Balarāma and meditate upon this form. As expressed here by the words *brahmaṇy adhyāya,* one should concentrate one's mind upon the Supreme Lord, Parabrahman. This Parabrahman is Kṛṣṇa, as confirmed by Arjuna in *Bhagavad-gītā* (*paraṁ brahma paraṁ dhāma pavitraṁ paramaṁ bhavān*). Kṛṣṇa and His abode, Vṛndāvana, are not different. Śrī Caitanya Mahāprabhu said, *ārādhyo bhagavān vrajeśa-tanayas tad-dhāma vṛndāvanam.* Vṛndāvana is as good as Kṛṣṇa. Therefore, if one somehow or other gets the opportunity to live in Vṛndāvana, and if one is not a pretender but simply lives in Vṛndāvana and concentrates his mind upon Kṛṣṇa, one is liberated from material bondage. One's mind is not purified, however, even in Vṛndāvana, if one is agitated by lusty desires. One should not live in Vṛndāvana and commit offenses, for a life of offenses in Vṛndāvana is no better than the lives of the monkeys and hogs there. Many monkeys and hogs live in Vṛndāvana, and they are concerned with their sexual desires. Men who have gone to Vṛndāvana but who still hanker for sex should immediately leave Vṛndāvana and stop their grievous offenses at the lotus feet of the Lord. There are many misguided men who live in Vṛndāvana to satisfy their sexual desires, but they are certainly no better than the monkeys and hogs. Those who are under the control of *māyā,* and specifically under the control of lusty desires, are called *māyā-mṛga.* Indeed, everyone in the conditional stage of material life is a *māyā-mṛga.* It is said, *māyā-mṛgaṁ dayitayepsitam anvadhāvad:* Śrī Caitanya Mahāprabhu took *sannyāsa* to show His causeless mercy to the *māyā-mṛgas,* the people of this material world, who suffer because of lusty desires. One should follow the principles of Śrī Caitanya Mahāprabhu and always think of Kṛṣṇa in full Kṛṣṇa consciousness. Then one will be eligible to live in Vṛndāvana, and his life will be successful.

TEXT 20

दृष्टं श्रुतमसद् बुद्ध्वा नानुध्यायेन्न सन्दिशेत् ।
संसृतिं चात्मनाशं च तत्र विद्वान् स आत्मदृक् ॥२०॥

dṛṣṭaṁ śrutam asad buddhvā
nānudhyāyen na sandiśet
saṁsṛtiṁ cātma-nāśaṁ ca
tatra vidvān sa ātma-dṛk

dṛṣṭam—the material enjoyment we experience in our present life; *śrutam*—material enjoyment as promised to the fruitive workers for future happiness (either in this life or in the next, in the heavenly planets and so on); *asat*—all temporary and bad; *buddhvā*—knowing; *na*—not; *anudhyāyet*—one should even think of; *na*—nor; *sandiśet*—should actually enjoy; *saṁsṛtim*—prolongation of material existence; *ca*—and; *ātma-nāśam*—forgetfulness of one's own constitutional position; *ca*—as well as; *tatra*—in such a subject matter; *vidvān*—one who is completely aware; *saḥ*—such a person; *ātma-dṛk*—a self-realized soul.

TRANSLATION

One who knows that material happiness, whether good or bad, in this life or in the next, on this planet or on the heavenly planets, is temporary and useless, and that an intelligent person should not try to enjoy or even think of such things, is the knower of the self. Such a self-realized person knows quite well that material happiness is the very cause of continued material existence and forgetfulness of one's own constitutional position.

PURPORT

The living entity is a spiritual soul, and the material body is his encagement. This is the beginning of spiritual understanding.

dehino 'smin yathā dehe
kaumāraṁ yauvanaṁ jarā

tathā dehāntara-prāptir
dhīras tatra na muhyati

"As the embodied soul continually passes, in this body, from boyhood to youth to old age, the soul similarly passes into another body at death. The self-realized soul is not bewildered by such a change." (Bg. 2.13) The real mission of human life is to get free from encagement in the material body. Therefore Kṛṣṇa descends to teach the conditioned soul about spiritual realization and how to become free from material bondage. *Yadā yadā hi dharmasya glānir bhavati bhārata.* The words *dharmasya glāniḥ* mean "pollution of one's existence." Our existence is now polluted, and it must be purified (*sattvaṁ śuddhyet*). The human life is meant for this purification, not for thinking of happiness in terms of the external body, which is the cause of material bondage. Therefore, in this verse, Mahārāja Yayāti advises that whatever material happiness we see and whatever is promised for enjoyment is all merely flickering and temporary. *Ābrahma-bhuvanāl lokāḥ punar āvartino 'rjuna.* Even if one is promoted to Brahmaloka, if one is not freed from material bondage one must return to this planet earth and continue in the miserable condition of material existence (*bhūtvā bhūtvā pralīyate*). One should always keep this understanding in mind so as not to be allured by any kind of sense enjoyment, in this life or in the next. One who is fully aware of this truth is self-realized (*sa ātma-dṛk*), but aside from him, everyone suffers in the cycle of birth and death (*mṛtyu-saṁsāra-vartmani*). This understanding is one of true intelligence, and anything contrary to this is but a cause of unhappiness. *Kṛṣṇa-bhakta——niṣkāma, ataeva 'śānta.'* Only a Kṛṣṇa conscious person, who knows the aim and object of life, is peaceful. All others, whether *karmīs, jñānīs* or *yogīs*, are restless and cannot enjoy real peace.

TEXT 21

इत्युक्त्वा नाहुषो जायां तदीयं पूरवे वयः ।
दत्त्वा स्वजरसं तस्मादाददे विगतस्पृहः ॥२१॥

ity uktvā nāhuṣo jāyāṁ
tadīyaṁ pūrave vayaḥ

dattvā sva-jarasaṁ tasmād
ādade vigata-spṛhaḥ

iti uktvā—saying this; *nāhuṣaḥ*—Mahārāja Yayāti, the son of King Nahuṣa; *jāyām*—unto his wife, Devayānī; *tadīyam*—his own; *pūrave*—unto his son Pūru; *vayaḥ*—youth; *dattvā*—delivering; *sva-jarasam*—his own invalidity and old age; *tasmāt*—from him; *ādade*—took back; *vigata-spṛhaḥ*—being freed from all material lusty desires.

TRANSLATION

Śukadeva Gosvāmī said: After speaking in this way to his wife, Devayānī, King Yayāti, who was now free from all material desires, called his youngest son, Pūru, and returned Pūru's youth in exchange for his own old age.

TEXT 22

दिशि दक्षिणपूर्वस्यां द्रुह्युं दक्षिणतो यदुम् ।
प्रतीच्यां तुर्वसुं चक्र उदीच्यामनुमीश्वरम् ॥२२॥

diśi dakṣiṇa-pūrvasyāṁ
druhyuṁ dakṣiṇato yadum
pratīcyāṁ turvasuṁ cakra
udīcyām anum īśvaram

diśi—in the direction; *dakṣiṇa-pūrvasyām*—southeast; *druhyum*—his son named Druhyu; *dakṣiṇataḥ*—in the southern side of the world; *yadum*—Yadu; *pratīcyām*—in the western side of the world; *turvasum*—his son known as Turvasu; *cakre*—he made; *udīcyām*—in the northern side of the world; *anum*—his son named Anu; *īśvaram*—the King.

TRANSLATION

King Yayāti gave the southeast to his son Druhyu, the south to his son Yadu, the west to his son Turvasu, and the north to his son Anu. In this way he divided the kingdom.

TEXT 23

भूमण्डलस्य सर्वस्य पूरुमर्हत्तमं विशाम् ।
अभिषिच्याग्रजांस्तस्य वशे स्थाप्य वनं ययौ ॥२३॥

bhū-maṇḍalasya sarvasya
pūrum arhattamaṁ viśām
abhiṣicyāgrajāṁs tasya
vaśe sthāpya vanaṁ yayau

bhū-maṇḍalasya—of the entire planet earth; *sarvasya*—of all wealth and riches; *pūrum*—his youngest son, Pūru; *arhat-tamam*—the most worshipable person, the king; *viśām*—of the citizens or the subjects of the world; *abhiṣicya*—crowning on the throne of the emperor; *agrajān*—all his elder brothers, beginning from Yadu; *tasya*—of Pūru; *vaśe*—under the control; *sthāpya*—establishing; *vanam*—in the forest; *yayau*—he went away.

TRANSLATION

Yayāti enthroned his youngest son, Pūru, as the emperor of the entire world and the proprietor of all its riches, and he placed all the other sons, who were older than Pūru, under Pūru's control.

TEXT 24

आसेवितं वर्षपूगान् षड्वर्गं विषयेषु सः ।
क्षणेन मुमुचे नीडं जातपक्ष इव द्विजः ॥२४॥

āsevitaṁ varṣa-pūgān
ṣaḍ-vargaṁ viṣayeṣu saḥ
kṣaṇena mumuce nīḍaṁ
jāta-pakṣa iva dvijaḥ

āsevitam—being always engaged in; *varṣa-pūgān*—for many, many years; *ṣaṭ-vargam*—the six senses, including the mind; *viṣayeṣu*—in sense enjoyment; *saḥ*—King Yayāti; *kṣaṇena*—within a moment;

mumuce—gave up; *nīḍam*—nest; *jāta-pakṣaḥ*—one that has grown its wings; *iva*—like; *dvijaḥ*—a bird.

TRANSLATION

Having enjoyed sense gratification for many, many years, O King Parīkṣit, Yayāti was accustomed to it, but he gave it up entirely in a moment, just as a bird flies away from the nest as soon as its wings have grown.

PURPORT

That Mahārāja Yayāti was immediately liberated from the bondage of conditioned life is certainly astonishing. But the example given herewith is appropriate. A tiny baby bird, dependent fully on its father and mother even to eat, suddenly flies away from the nest when its wings have grown. Similarly, if one fully surrenders to the Supreme Personality of Godhead, one is immediately liberated from the bondage of conditioned life, as promised by the Lord Himself (*ahaṁ tvāṁ sarva-pāpebhyo mokṣayiṣyāmi*). As stated in *Śrīmad-Bhāgavatam* (2.4.18):

kirāta-hūṇāndhra-pulinda-pulkaśā
ābhīra-śumbhā yavanāḥ khasādayaḥ
ye 'nye ca pāpā yad-apāśrayāśrayāḥ
śudhyanti tasmai prabhaviṣṇave namaḥ

"Kirāta, Hūṇa, Āndhra, Pulinda, Pulkaśa, Ābhīra, Śumbha, Yavana and the Khasa races and even others addicted to sinful acts can be purified by taking shelter of the devotees of the Lord, for He is the supreme power. I beg to offer my respectful obeisances unto Him." Lord Viṣṇu is so powerful that He can deliver anyone at once if He is pleased to do so. And Lord Viṣṇu, the Supreme Personality of Godhead, Kṛṣṇa, can be pleased immediately if we accept His order by surrendering unto Him, as Mahārāja Yayāti did. Mahārāja Yayāti was eager to serve Vāsudeva, Kṛṣṇa, and therefore as soon as he wanted to renounce material life, Lord Vāsudeva helped him. We must therefore be very sincere in surrendering ourselves unto the lotus feet of the Lord. Then we can immediately be liberated from all the bondage of conditioned life. This is clearly expressed in the next verse.

TEXT 25

स तत्र निर्मुक्तसमस्तसङ्ग
आत्मानुभूत्या विधुतत्रिलिङ्गः ।
परेऽमले ब्रह्मणि वासुदेवे
लेभे गतिं भागवतीं प्रतीतः ॥२५॥

sa tatra nirmukta-samasta-saṅga
ātmānubhūtyā vidhuta-triliṅgaḥ
pare 'male brahmaṇi vāsudeve
lebhe gatiṁ bhāgavatīṁ pratītaḥ

saḥ—Mahārāja Yayāti; *tatra*—upon doing this; *nirmukta*—was immediately liberated from; *samasta-saṅgaḥ*—all contamination; *ātma-anubhūtyā*—simply by understanding his constitutional position; *vidhuta*—was cleansed of; *tri-liṅgaḥ*—the contamination caused by the three modes of material nature (*sattva-guṇa, rajo-guṇa* and *tamo-guṇa*); *pare*—unto the Transcendence; *amale*—without material contact; *brahmaṇi*—the Supreme Lord; *vāsudeve*—Vāsudeva, Kṛṣṇa, the Absolute Truth, Bhagavān; *lebhe*—achieved; *gatim*—the destination; *bhāgavatīm*—as an associate of the Supreme Personality of Godhead; *pratītaḥ*—famous.

TRANSLATION

Because King Yayāti completely surrendered unto the Supreme Personality of Godhead, Vāsudeva, he was freed from all contamination of the material modes of nature. Because of his self-realization, he was able to fix his mind upon the Transcendence [Parabrahman, Vāsudeva], and thus he ultimately achieved the position of an associate of the Lord.

PURPORT

The word *vidhuta*, meaning "cleansed," is very significant. Everyone in this material world is contaminated (*kāraṇaṁ guṇa-saṅgo 'sya*).

Because we are in a material condition, we are contaminated either by *sattva-guṇa*, by *rajo-guṇa* or by *tamo-guṇa*. Even if one becomes a qualified *brāhmaṇa* in the mode of goodness (*sattva-guṇa*), he is still materially contaminated. One must come to the platform of *śuddha-sattva*, transcending the *sattva-guṇa*. Then one is *vidhuta-triliṅga*, cleansed of the contamination caused by the three modes of material nature. This is possible by the mercy of Kṛṣṇa. As stated in *Śrīmad-Bhāgavatam* (1.2.17):

śṛṇvatāṁ sva-kathāḥ kṛṣṇaḥ
puṇya-śravaṇa-kīrtanaḥ
hṛdy antaḥ-stho hy abhadrāṇi
vidhunoti suhṛt-satām

"Śrī Kṛṣṇa, the Personality of Godhead, who is the Paramātmā [Supersoul] in everyone's heart and the benefactor of the truthful devotee, cleanses desire for material enjoyment from the heart of the devotee who has developed the urge to hear His messages, which are in themselves virtuous when properly heard and chanted." A person trying to be perfectly Kṛṣṇa conscious by hearing the words of Kṛṣṇa from *Śrīmad-Bhāgavatam* or *Bhagavad-gītā* certainly has all the dirty things cleansed from the core of his heart. Caitanya Mahāprabhu also says, *ceto-darpaṇa-mārjanam:* the process of hearing and chanting the glories of the Supreme Lord washes away the dirty things accumulated in the core of the heart. As soon as one is freed from all the dirt of material contamination, as Mahārāja Yayāti was, one's original position as an associate of the Lord is revealed. This is called *svarūpa-siddhi*, or personal perfection.

TEXT 26

श्रुत्वा गाथां देवयानी मेने प्रस्तोभमात्मनः ।
स्त्रीपुंसोः स्नेहवैक्लव्यात् परिहासमिवेरितम् ॥२६॥

śrutvā gāthāṁ devayānī
mene prastobham ātmanaḥ
strī-puṁsoḥ sneha-vaiklavyāt
parihāsam iveritam

śrutvā—hearing; *gāthām*—the narration; *devayānī*—Queen Devayānī, the wife of Mahārāja Yayāti; *mene*—understood; *prastobham ātmanaḥ*—when instructed for her self-realization; *strī-puṁsoḥ*—between the husband and wife; *sneha-vaiklavyāt*—from an exchange of love and affection; *parihāsam*—a funny joke or story; *iva*—like; *īritam*—spoken (by Mahārāja Yayāti).

TRANSLATION

When Devayānī heard Mahārāja Yayāti's story of the he-goat and she-goat, she understood that this story, which was presented as if a funny joke for entertainment between husband and wife, was intended to awaken her to her constitutional position.

PURPORT

When one actually awakens from material life, one understands his real position as an eternal servant of Kṛṣṇa. This is called liberation. *Muktir hitvānyathā rūpaṁ svarūpeṇa vyavasthitiḥ* (*Bhāg.* 2.10.6). Under the influence of *māyā*, everyone living in this material world thinks that he is the master of everything (*ahaṅkāra-vimūḍhātmā kartāham iti manyate*). One thinks that there is no God or controller and that one is independent and can do anything. This is the material condition, and when one awakens from this ignorance, he is called liberated. Mahārāja Yayāti had delivered Devayānī from the well, and finally, as a dutiful husband, he instructed her with the story about the he-goat and she-goat and thus delivered her from the misconception of material happiness. Devayānī was quite competent to understand her liberated husband, and therefore she decided to follow him as his faithful wife.

TEXTS 27–28

सा संनिवासं सुहृदां प्रपायामिव गच्छताम् ।
विज्ञायेश्वरतन्त्राणां मायाविरचितं प्रभोः ॥२७॥
सर्वत्र सङ्गमुत्सृज्य स्वप्नौपम्येन भार्गवी ।
कृष्णे मनः समावेश्य व्यधुनोल्लिङ्गमात्मनः ॥२८॥

sā sannivāsaṁ suhṛdāṁ
prapāyām iva gacchatām
vijñāyeśvara-tantrāṇāṁ
māyā-viracitaṁ prabhoḥ

sarvatra saṅgam utsṛjya
svapnaupamyena bhārgavī
kṛṣṇe manaḥ samāveśya
vyadhunol liṅgam ātmanaḥ

sā—Devayānī; *sannivāsam*—living in the association; *suhṛdām*—of friends and relatives; *prapāyām*—in a place where water is supplied; *iva*—like; *gacchatām*—of tourists on a program for going from one place to another; *vijñāya*—understanding; *īśvara-tantrāṇām*—under the influence of the rigid laws of nature; *māyā-viracitam*—the laws enforced by *māyā,* the illusory energy; *prabhoḥ*—of the Supreme Personality of Godhead; *sarvatra*—everywhere in this material world; *saṅgam*—association; *utsṛjya*—giving up; *svapna-aupamyena*—by the analogy of a dream; *bhārgavī*—Devayānī, the daughter of Śukrācārya; *kṛṣṇe*—unto Lord Kṛṣṇa; *manaḥ*—complete attention; *samāveśya*—fixing; *vyadhunot*—gave up; *liṅgam*—the gross and subtle bodies; *ātmanaḥ*—of the soul.

TRANSLATION

Thereafter, Devayānī, the daughter of Śukrācārya, understood that the materialistic association of husband, friends and relatives is like the association in a hotel full of tourists. The relationships of society, friendship and love are created by the māyā of the Supreme Personality of Godhead, exactly as in a dream. By the grace of Kṛṣṇa, Devayānī gave up her imaginary position in the material world. Completely fixing her mind upon Kṛṣṇa, she achieved liberation from the gross and subtle bodies.

PURPORT

One should be convinced that he is a spirit soul, part and parcel of the Supreme Brahman, Kṛṣṇa, but has somehow or other been entrapped by the material coverings of the gross and subtle bodies, consisting of earth, water, fire, air, ether, mind, intelligence and false ego. One should know that the association of society, friendship, love, nationalism, religion and so on are nothing but creations of *māyā*. One's only business is to become Kṛṣṇa conscious and render service unto Kṛṣṇa as extensively as possible for a living being. In this way one is liberated from material bondage. By the grace of Kṛṣṇa, Devayānī attained this state through the instructions of her husband.

TEXT 29

नमस्तुभ्यं भगवते वासुदेवाय वेधसे ।
सर्वभूताधिवासाय शान्ताय बृहते नमः ॥२९॥

namas tubhyaṁ bhagavate
vāsudevāya vedhase
sarva-bhūtādhivāsāya
śāntāya bṛhate namaḥ

namaḥ—I offer my respectful obeisances; *tubhyam*—unto You; *bhagavate*—the Supreme Personality of Godhead; *vāsudevāya*—Lord Vāsudeva; *vedhase*—the creator of everything; *sarva-bhūta-adhivāsāya*—present everywhere (within the heart of every living entity and within the atom also); *śāntāya*—peaceful, as if completely inactive; *bṛhate*—the greatest of all; *namaḥ*—I offer my respectful obeisances.

TRANSLATION

O Lord Vāsudeva, O Supreme Personality of Godhead, You are the creator of the entire cosmic manifestation. You live as the Supersoul in everyone's heart and are smaller than the smallest, yet You are greater than the greatest and are all-pervading. You appear completely silent, having nothing to do, but this is due to Your all-pervading nature and Your fullness in all opulences. I therefore offer my respectful obeisances unto You.

PURPORT

How Devayānī became self-realized by the grace of her great husband, Mahārāja Yayāti, is described here. Describing such realization is another way of performing the *bhakti* process.

śravaṇaṁ kīrtanaṁ viṣṇoḥ
smaraṇaṁ pāda-sevanam
arcanaṁ vandanaṁ dāsyaṁ
sakhyam ātma-nivedanam

"Hearing and chanting about the transcendental holy name, form, qualities, paraphernalia and pastimes of Lord Viṣṇu, remembering them, serving the lotus feet of the Lord, offering the Lord respectful worship, offering prayers to the Lord, becoming His servant, considering the Lord one's best friend, and surrendering everything unto Him—these nine processes are accepted as pure devotional service." (*Bhāg.* 7.5.23) *Śravaṇaṁ kīrtanam,* hearing and chanting, are especially important. By hearing from her husband about the greatness of Lord Vāsudeva, Devayānī certainly became convinced and surrendered herself unto the lotus feet of the Lord (*oṁ namo bhagavate vāsudevāya*). This is knowledge. *Bahūnāṁ janmanām ante jñānavān māṁ prapadyate.* Surrender to Vāsudeva is the result of hearing about Him for many, many births. As soon as one surrenders unto Vāsudeva, one is liberated immediately. Because of her association with her great husband, Mahārāja Yayāti, Devayānī became purified, adopted the means of *bhakti-yoga,* and thus became liberated.

Thus end the Bhaktivedanta purports of the Ninth Canto, Nineteenth Chapter, of the Śrīmad-Bhāgavatam, *entitled "King Yayāti Achieves Liberation."*

CHAPTER TWENTY

The Dynasty of Pūru

This chapter describes the history of Pūru and his descendant Duṣmanta. The son of Pūru was Janamejaya, and his son was Pracinvān. The sons and grandsons in the line of Pracinvān, one after another, were Pravīra, Manusyu, Cārupada, Sudyu, Bahugava, Saṁyāti, Ahaṁyāti and Raudrāśva. Raudrāśva had ten sons—Ṛteyu, Kakṣeyu, Sthaṇḍileyu, Kṛteyuka, Jaleyu, Sannateyu, Dharmeyu, Satyeyu, Vrateyu and Vaneyu. The son of Ṛteyu was Rantināva, who had three sons—Sumati, Dhruva and Apratiratha. The son of Apratiratha was Kaṇva, and Kaṇva's son was Medhātithi. The sons of Medhātithi, headed by Praskanna, were all *brāhmaṇas*. The son of Rantināva named Sumati had a son named Rebhi, and his son was Duṣmanta.

While hunting in the forest, Duṣmanta once approached the *āśrama* of Mahārṣi Kaṇva, where he saw an extremely beautiful woman and became attracted to her. That woman was the daughter of Viśvāmitra, and her name was Śakuntalā. Her mother was Menakā, who had left her in the forest, where Kaṇva Muni found her. Kaṇva Muni brought her to his *āśrama*, where he raised and maintained her. When Śakuntalā accepted Mahārāja Duṣmanta as her husband, he married her according to the *gāndharva-vidhi*. Śakuntalā later became pregnant by her husband, who left her in the *āśrama* of Kaṇva Muni and returned to his kingdom.

In due course of time, Śakuntalā gave birth to a Vaiṣṇava son, but Duṣmanta, having returned to the capital, forgot what had taken place. Therefore, when Śakuntalā approached him with her newly born child, Mahārāja Duṣmanta refused to accept them as his wife and son. Later, however, after a mysterious omen, the King accepted them. After Mahārāja Duṣmanta's death, Bharata, the son of Śakuntalā, was enthroned. He performed many great sacrifices, in which he gave great riches in charity to the *brāhmaṇas*. This chapter ends by describing the birth of Bharadvāja and how Mahārāja Bharata accepted Bharadvāja as his son.

TEXT 1

श्रीबादरायणिरुवाच
पूरोर्वंशं प्रवक्ष्यामि यत्र जातोऽसि भारत ।
यत्र राजर्षयो वंश्या ब्रह्मवंश्याश्च जज्ञिरे ॥ १ ॥

śrī-bādarāyaṇir uvāca
pūror vaṁśaṁ pravakṣyāmi
yatra jāto 'si bhārata
yatra rājarṣayo vaṁśyā
brahma-vaṁśyāś ca jajñire

śrī-bādarāyaṇiḥ uvāca—Śrī Śukadeva Gosvāmī said; *pūroḥ vaṁśam*—the dynasty of Mahārāja Pūru; *pravakṣyāmi*—now I shall narrate; *yatra*—in which dynasty; *jātaḥ asi*—you were born; *bhārata*—O Mahārāja Parīkṣit, descendant of Mahārāja Bharata; *yatra*—in which dynasty; *rāja-ṛṣayaḥ*—all the kings were saintly; *vaṁśyāḥ*—one after another; *brahma-vaṁśyāḥ*—many *brāhmaṇa* dynasties; *ca*—also; *jajñire*—grew up.

TRANSLATION

Śukadeva Gosvāmī said: O Mahārāja Parīkṣit, descendant of Mahārāja Bharata, I shall now describe the dynasty of Pūru, in which you were born, in which many saintly kings appeared, and from which many dynasties of brāhmaṇas began.

PURPORT

There are many historical instances by which we can understand that from *kṣatriyas* many *brāhmaṇas* have been born and that from *brāhmaṇas* many *kṣatriyas* have been born. The Lord Himself says in *Bhagavad-gītā* (4.13), *cātur-varṇyaṁ mayā sṛṣṭaṁ guṇa-karma-vibhāgaśaḥ:* "According to the three modes of material nature and the work ascribed to them, the four divisions of human society were created by Me." Therefore, regardless of the family in which one takes birth, when one is qualified with the symptoms of a particular section, he is to be described accordingly. *Yal-lakṣaṇaṁ proktam.* One's place in the *varṇa* divisions of society is determined according to one's symptoms or qualities. This is maintained everywhere in the *śāstra*. Birth is a secondary consideration; the first consideration is one's qualities and activities.

TEXT 2

जनमेजयो ह्यभूत् पूरोः प्रचिन्वांस्तत्सुतस्ततः ।
प्रवीरोऽथ मनुस्युर्वै तस्माच्चारुपदोऽभवत् ॥ २ ॥

janamejayo hy abhūt pūroḥ
pracinvāṁs tat-sutas tataḥ
pravīro 'tha manusyur vai
tasmāc cārupado 'bhavat

janamejayaḥ—King Janamejaya; *hi*—indeed; *abhūt*—appeared; *pūroḥ*—from Pūru; *pracinvān*—Pracinvān; *tat*—his (Janamejaya's); *sutaḥ*—son; *tataḥ*—from him (Pracinvān); *pravīraḥ*—Pravīra; *atha*—thereafter; *manusyuḥ*—Pravīra's son Manusyu; *vai*—indeed; *tasmāt*—from him (Manusyu); *cārupadaḥ*—King Cārupada; *abhavat*—appeared.

TRANSLATION

King Janamejaya was born of this dynasty of Pūru. Janamejaya's son was Pracinvān, and his son was Pravīra. Thereafter, Pravīra's son was Manusyu, and from Manusyu came the son named Cārupada.

TEXT 3

तस्य सुद्युरभूत् पुत्रस्तस्माद् बहुगवस्ततः ।
संयातिस्तस्याहंयाती रौद्राश्वस्तत्सुतः स्मृतः ॥ ३ ॥

tasya sudyur abhūt putras
tasmād bahugavas tataḥ
saṁyātis tasyāhaṁyātī
raudrāśvas tat-sutaḥ smṛtaḥ

tasya—of him (Cārupada); *sudyuḥ*—by the name Sudyu; *abhūt*—appeared; *putraḥ*—a son; *tasmāt*—from him (Sudyu); *bahugavaḥ*—a son named Bahugava; *tataḥ*—from him; *saṁyātiḥ*—a son named Saṁyāti; *tasya*—and from him; *ahaṁyātiḥ*—a son named Ahaṁyāti; *raudrāśvaḥ*—Raudrāśva; *tat-sutaḥ*—his son; *smṛtaḥ*—well known.

TRANSLATION

The son of Cārupada was Sudyu, and the son of Sudyu was Bahugava. Bahugava's son was Saṁyāti. From Saṁyāti came a son named Ahaṁyāti, from whom Raudrāśva was born.

TEXTS 4–5

ऋतेयुस्तस्य कक्षेयुः स्थण्डिलेयुः कृतेयुकः ।
जलेयुः सन्नतेयुश्च धर्मसत्यव्रतेयवः ॥ ४ ॥
दशैतेऽप्सरसः पुत्रा वनेयुश्चावमः स्मृतः ।
घृताच्यामिन्द्रियाणीव मुख्यस्य जगदात्मनः ॥ ५ ॥

ṛteyus tasya kakṣeyuḥ
sthaṇḍileyuḥ kṛteyukaḥ
jaleyuḥ sannateyuś ca
dharma-satya-vrateyavaḥ

daśaite 'psarasaḥ putrā
vaneyuś cāvamaḥ smṛtaḥ
ghṛtācyām indriyāṇīva
mukhyasya jagad-ātmanaḥ

ṛteyuḥ—Ṛteyu; *tasya*—of him (Raudrāśva); *kakṣeyuḥ*—Kakṣeyu; *sthaṇḍileyuḥ*—Sthaṇḍileyu; *kṛteyukaḥ*—Kṛteyuka; *jaleyuḥ*—Jaleyu; *sannateyuḥ*—Sannateyu; *ca*—also; *dharma*—Dharmeyu; *satya*—Satyeyu; *vrateyavaḥ*—and Vrateyu; *daśa*—ten; *ete*—all of them; *apsarasaḥ*—born of an Apsarā; *putrāḥ*—sons; *vaneyuḥ*—the son named Vaneyu; *ca*—and; *avamaḥ*—the youngest; *smṛtaḥ*—known; *ghṛtācyām*—Ghṛtācī; *indriyāṇi iva*—exactly like the ten senses; *mukhyasya*—of the living force; *jagat-ātmanaḥ*—the living force of the entire universe.

TRANSLATION

Raudrāśva had ten sons, named Ṛteyu, Kakṣeyu, Sthaṇḍileyu, Kṛteyuka, Jaleyu, Sannateyu, Dharmeyu, Satyeyu, Vrateyu and Vaneyu. Of these ten sons, Vaneyu was the youngest. As the ten senses, which are products of the universal life, act under the control of life, these ten sons of Raudrāśva acted under Raudrāśva's full control. All of them were born of the Apsarā named Ghṛtācī.

TEXT 6

ऋतेयो रन्तिनावोऽभूत् त्रयस्तस्यात्मजा नृप ।
सुमतिर्ध्रुवोऽप्रतिरथः कण्वोऽप्रतिरथात्मजः ॥ ६ ॥

ṛteyo rantināvo 'bhūt
trayas tasyātmajā nṛpa
sumatir dhruvo 'pratirathaḥ
kaṇvo 'pratirathātmajaḥ

ṛteyoḥ—from the son named Ṛteyu; *rantināvaḥ*—the son named Rantināva; *abhūt*—appeared; *trayaḥ*—three; *tasya*—his (Rantināva's); *ātmajāḥ*—sons; *nṛpa*—O King; *sumatiḥ*—Sumati; *dhruvaḥ*—Dhruva; *apratirathaḥ*—Apratiratha; *kaṇvaḥ*—Kaṇva; *apratiratha-ātmajaḥ*—the son of Apratiratha.

TRANSLATION

Ṛteyu had a son named Rantināva, who had three sons, named Sumati, Dhruva and Apratiratha. Apratiratha had only one son, whose name was Kaṇva.

TEXT 7

तस्य मेधातिथिस्तस्मात् प्रस्कन्नाद्या द्विजातयः ।
पुत्रोऽभूत् सुमते रेभिर्दुष्मन्तस्तत्सुतो मतः ॥७॥

tasya medhātithis tasmāt
praskannādyā dvijātayaḥ

putro 'bhūt sumate rebhir
duṣmantas tat-suto mataḥ

tasya—of him (Kaṇva); *medhātithiḥ*—a son named Medhātithi; *tasmāt*—from him (Medhātithi); *praskanna-ādyāḥ*—sons headed by Praskanna; *dvijātayaḥ*—all *brāhmaṇas; putraḥ*—a son; *abhūt*—there was; *sumateḥ*—from Sumati; *rebhiḥ*—Rebhi; *duṣmantaḥ*—Mahārāja Duṣmanta; *tat-sutaḥ*—the son of Rebhi; *mataḥ*—is well-known.

TRANSLATION

The son of Kaṇva was Medhātithi, whose sons, all brāhmaṇas, were headed by Praskanna. The son of Rantināva named Sumati had a son named Rebhi. Mahārāja Duṣmanta is well known as the son of Rebhi.

TEXTS 8–9

दुष्मन्तो मृगयां यातः कण्वाश्रमपदं गतः ।
तत्रासीनां स्वप्रभया मण्डयन्तीं रमामिव ॥ ८ ॥
विलोक्य सद्यो मुमुहे देवमायामिव स्त्रियम् ।
बभाषे तां वरारोहां भटैः कतिपयैर्वृतः ॥ ९ ॥

duṣmanto mṛgayāṁ yātaḥ
kaṇvāśrama-padaṁ gataḥ
tatrāsīnāṁ sva-prabhayā
maṇḍayantīṁ ramām iva

vilokya sadyo mumuhe
deva-māyām iva striyam
babhāṣe tāṁ varārohāṁ
bhaṭaiḥ katipayair vṛtaḥ

duṣmantaḥ—Mahārāja Duṣmanta; *mṛgayām yātaḥ*—when he went hunting; *kaṇva-āśrama-padam*—to the residence of Kaṇva; *gataḥ*—he came; *tatra*—there; *āsīnām*—a woman sitting; *sva-prabhayā*—by her own beauty; *maṇḍyantīm*—illuminating; *ramām iva*—exactly like the goddess of fortune; *vilokya*—by observing; *sadyaḥ*—immediately; *mumuhe*—he became enchanted; *deva-māyām iva*—exactly like the illusory energy of the Lord; *striyam*—a beautiful woman; *babhāṣe*—he addressed; *tām*—her (the woman); *vara-ārohām*—who was the best of beautiful women; *bhaṭaiḥ*—by soldiers; *katipayaiḥ*—a few; *vṛtaḥ*—surrounded.

TRANSLATION

Once when King Duṣmanta went to the forest to hunt and was very much fatigued, he approached the residence of Kaṇva Muni. There he saw a most beautiful woman who looked exactly like the goddess of fortune and who sat there illuminating the entire āśrama by her effulgence. The King was naturally attracted by her beauty, and therefore he approached her, accompanied by some of his soldiers, and spoke to her.

TEXT 10

तद्दर्शनप्रमुदितः संनिवृत्तपरिश्रमः ।
पप्रच्छ कामसन्तप्तः प्रहसञ्श्लक्ष्णया गिरा ॥१०॥

tad-darśana-pramuditaḥ
sannivṛtta-pariśramaḥ
papraccha kāma-santaptaḥ
prahasañ ślakṣṇayā girā

tat-darśana-pramuditaḥ—being very much enlivened by seeing the beautiful woman; *sannivṛtta-pariśramaḥ*—being relieved of the fatigue of the hunting excursion; *papraccha*—he inquired from her; *kāma-santaptaḥ*—being agitated by lusty desires; *prahasan*—in a joking mood; *ślakṣṇayā*—very beautiful and pleasing; *girā*—with words.

TRANSLATION

Seeing the beautiful woman, the King was very much enlivened, and the fatigue of his hunting excursion was relieved. He was of course very much attracted because of lusty desires, and thus he inquired from her as follows, in a joking mood.

TEXT 11

का त्वं कमलपत्राक्षि कस्यासि हृदयङ्गमे ।
किंस्विच्चिकीर्षितं तत्र भवत्या निर्जने वने ॥११॥

kā tvaṁ kamala-patrākṣi
kasyāsi hṛdayaṅ-game
kiṁ svic cikīrṣitaṁ tatra
bhavatyā nirjane vane

kā—who; *tvam*—are you; *kamala-patra-akṣi*—O beautiful woman with eyes like the petals of a lotus; *kasya asi*—with whom are you related; *hṛdayam-game*—O most beautiful one, pleasing to the heart; *kim svit*—what kind of business; *cikīrṣitam*—is being thought of; *tatra*—there; *bhavatyāḥ*—by you; *nirjane*—solitary; *vane*—in the forest.

TRANSLATION

O beautiful lotus-eyed woman, who are you? Whose daughter are you? What purpose do you have in this solitary forest? Why are you staying here?

TEXT 12

व्यक्तं राजन्यतनयां वेद्म्यहं त्वां सुमध्यमे ।
न हि चेतः पौरवाणामधर्मे रमते क्वचित् ॥१२॥

vyaktaṁ rājanya-tanayāṁ
vedmy ahaṁ tvāṁ sumadhyame
na hi cetaḥ pauravāṇām
adharme ramate kvacit

vyaktam—it appears; *rājanya-tanayām*—the daughter of a *kṣatriya;* *vedmi*—can realize; *aham*—I; *tvām*—your good self; *su-madhyame*—O most beautiful; *na*—not; *hi*—indeed; *cetaḥ*—the mind; *pauravāṇām*—of persons who have taken birth in the Pūru dynasty; *adharme*—in irreligion; *ramate*—enjoys; *kvacit*—at any time.

TRANSLATION

O most beautiful one, it appears to my mind that you must be the daughter of a kṣatriya. Because I belong to the Pūru dynasty, my mind never endeavors to enjoy anything irreligiously.

PURPORT

Mahārāja Duṣmanta indirectly expressed his desire to marry Śakuntalā, for she appeared to his mind to be the daughter of some *kṣatriya* king.

TEXT 13

श्रीशकुन्तलोवाच
विश्वामित्रात्मजैवाहं त्यक्ता मेनकया वने ।
वेदैतद् भगवान् कण्वो वीर किं करवाम ते ॥१३॥

śrī-śakuntalovāca
viśvāmitrātmajaivāhaṁ
tyaktā menakayā vane
vedaitad bhagavān kaṇvo
vīra kiṁ karavāma te

śrī-śakuntalā uvāca—Śrī Śakuntalā replied; *viśvāmitra-ātmajā*—the daughter of Viśvāmitra; *eva*—indeed; *aham*—I (am); *tyaktā*—left; *menakayā*—by Menakā; *vane*—in the forest; *veda*—knows; *etat*—all these incidents; *bhagavān*—the most powerful saintly person; *kaṇvaḥ*—Kaṇva Muni; *vīra*—O hero; *kim*—what; *karavāma*—can I do; *te*—for you.

TRANSLATION

Śakuntalā said: I am the daughter of Viśvāmitra. My mother, Menakā, left me in the forest. O hero, the most powerful saint Kaṇva Muni knows all about this. Now let me know, how may I serve you?

PURPORT

Śakuntalā informed Mahārāja Duṣmanta that although she never saw or knew her father or mother, Kaṇva Muni knew everything about her, and she had heard from him that she was the daughter of Viśvāmitra and that her mother was Menakā, who had left her in the forest.

TEXT 14

आस्यतां ह्यरविन्दाक्ष गृह्यतामर्हणं च नः ।
भुज्यतां सन्ति नीवारा उष्यतां यदि रोचते ॥१४॥

āsyatāṁ hy aravindākṣa
gṛhyatām arhaṇaṁ ca naḥ
bhujyatāṁ santi nīvārā
uṣyatāṁ yadi rocate

āsyatām—please come sit here; *hi*—indeed; *aravinda-akṣa*—O great hero with eyes like the petals of a lotus; *gṛhyatām*—please accept; *arhaṇam*—humble reception; *ca*—and; *naḥ*—our; *bhujyatām*—please eat; *santi*—what there is in stock; *nīvārāḥ*—*nīvārā* rice; *uṣyatām*—stay here; *yadi*—if; *rocate*—you so desire.

TRANSLATION

O King with eyes like the petals of a lotus, kindly come sit down and accept whatever reception we can offer. We have a supply of nīvārā rice that you may kindly take. And if you so desire, stay here without hesitation.

TEXT 15

श्रीदुष्मन्त उवाच
उपपन्नमिदं सुभ्रु जातायाः कुशिकान्वये ।
स्वयं हि वृणुते राज्ञां कन्यकाः सदृशं वरम् ॥१५॥

śrī-duṣmanta uvāca
upapannam idaṁ subhru
jātāyāḥ kuśikānvaye
svayaṁ hi vṛṇute rājñāṁ
kanyakāḥ sadṛśaṁ varam

śrī-duṣmantaḥ uvāca—King Duṣmanta replied; *upapannam*—just befitting your position; *idam*—this; *su-bhru*—O Śakuntalā, with beautiful eyebrows; *jātāyāḥ*—because of your birth; *kuśika-anvaye*—in the family of Viśvāmitra; *svayam*—personally; *hi*—indeed; *vṛṇute*—select; *rājñām*—of a royal family; *kanyakāḥ*—daughters; *sadṛśam*—on an equal level; *varam*—husbands.

TRANSLATION

King Duṣmanta replied: O Śakuntalā, with beautiful eyebrows, you have taken your birth in the family of the great saint Viśvāmitra, and your reception is quite worthy of your family. Aside from this, the daughters of a king generally select their own husbands.

PURPORT

In her reception of Mahārāja Duṣmanta, Śakuntalā clearly said, "Your Majesty may stay here, and you may accept whatever reception I can offer." Thus she indicated that she wanted Mahārāja Duṣmanta as her husband. As far as Mahārāja Duṣmanta was concerned, he desired Śakuntalā as his wife from the very beginning, as soon as he saw her, so the agreement to unite as husband and wife was natural. To induce Śakuntalā to accept the marriage, Mahārāja Duṣmanta reminded her that as the daughter of a king she could select her husband in an open assembly. In the history of Āryan civilization there have been many instances in which famous princesses have selected their husbands in open competitions. For example, it was in such a competition that Sītādevī accepted Lord Rāmacandra as her husband and that Draupadī accepted Arjuna, and there are many other instances. So marriage by agreement or by selecting one's own husband in an open competition is allowed. There are eight kinds of marriage, of which marriage by agreement is called *gāndharva* marriage. Generally the parents select the husband or wife for their daughter or son, but *gāndharva* marriage takes place by personal selection. Still, although marriage by personal selection or by agreement took place in the past, we find no such thing as divorce by disagreement. Of course, divorce by disagreement took place among low-class men, but marriage by agreement was found even in the very highest classes, especially in the royal *kṣatriya* families. Mahārāja Duṣmanta's acceptance of Śakuntalā as his wife was sanctioned by Vedic culture. How the marriage took place is described in the next verse.

TEXT 16

ओमित्युक्ते यथाधर्ममुपयेमे शकुन्तलाम् ।
गान्धर्वविधिना राजा देशकालविधानवित् ॥१६॥

om ity ukte yathā-dharmam
upayeme śakuntalām
gāndharva-vidhinā rājā
deśa-kāla-vidhānavit

om iti ukte—by reciting the Vedic *praṇava*, invoking the Supreme Personality of Godhead to witness the marriage; *yathā-dharmam*—exactly according to the principles of religion (because Nārāyaṇa becomes the witness in an ordinary religious marriage also); *upayeme*—he married; *śakuntalām*—the girl Śakuntalā; *gāndharva-vidhinā*—by the regulative principle of the Gandharvas, without deviation from religious principles; *rājā*—Mahārāja Duṣmanta; *deśa-kāla-vidhāna-vit*—completely aware of duties according to time, position and objective.

TRANSLATION

When Śakuntalā responded to Mahārāja Duṣmanta's proposal with silence, the agreement was complete. Then the King, who knew the laws of marriage, immediately married her by chanting the Vedic praṇava [oṁkāra], in accordance with the marriage ceremony as performed among the Gandharvas.

PURPORT

The *oṁkāra, praṇava,* is the Supreme Personality of Godhead represented by letters. *Bhagavad-gītā* says that the letters *a-u-m,* combined together as *oṁ,* represent the Supreme Lord. Religious principles are meant to invoke the blessings and mercy of the Supreme Personality of Godhead, Kṛṣṇa, who says in *Bhagavad-gītā* that He is personally present in sexual desires that are not contrary to religious principles. The word *vidhinā* means, "according to religious principles." The association of men and women according to religious principles is allowed in the Vedic culture. In our Kṛṣṇa consciousness movement we allow marriage on the basis of religious principles, but the sexual combination of men and women as friends is irreligious and is not allowed.

TEXT 17

अमोघवीर्यो राजर्षिर्महिष्यां वीर्यमादधे ।
श्वोभूते स्वपुरं यातः कालेनासूत सा सुतम् ॥१७॥

amogha-vīryo rājarṣir
mahiṣyāṁ vīryam ādadhe
śvo-bhūte sva-puraṁ yātaḥ
kālenāsūta sā sutam

amogha-vīryaḥ—a person who discharges semen without being baffled, or, in other words, who must beget a child; *rāja-ṛṣiḥ*—the saintly King Duṣmanta; *mahiṣyām*—into the Queen, Śakuntalā (after her marriage, Śakuntalā became the Queen); *vīryam*—semen; *ādadhe*—placed; *śvaḥ-bhūte*—in the morning; *sva-puram*—to his own place; *yātaḥ*—returned; *kālena*—in due course of time; *asūta*—gave birth; *sā*—she (Śakuntalā); *sutam*—to a son.

TRANSLATION

King Duṣmanta, who never discharged semen without a result, placed his semen at night in the womb of his Queen, Śakuntalā, and in the morning he returned to his palace. Thereafter, in due course of time, Śakuntalā gave birth to a son.

TEXT 18

कण्वः कुमारस्य वने चक्रे समुचिताः क्रियाः ।
बद्ध्वा मृगेन्द्रंतरसा क्रीडति स्म स बालकः ॥१८॥

kaṇvaḥ kumārasya vane
cakre samucitāḥ kriyāḥ
baddhvā mṛgendraṁ tarasā
krīḍati sma sa bālakaḥ

kaṇvaḥ—Kaṇva Muni; *kumārasya*—of the son born of Śakuntalā; *vane*—in the forest; *cakre*—executed; *samucitāḥ*—prescribed; *kriyāḥ*—ritualistic ceremonies; *baddhvā*—capturing; *mṛga-indram*—a lion; *tarasā*—by force; *krīḍati*—playing; *sma*—in the past; *saḥ*—he; *bālakaḥ*—the child.

TRANSLATION

In the forest, Kaṇva Muni performed all the ritualistic ceremonies concerning the newborn child. Later, the boy became so powerful that he would capture a lion and play with it.

TEXT 19

तं दुरत्ययविक्रान्तमादाय प्रमदोत्तमा ।
हरेरंशांशसम्भूतं भर्तुरन्तिकमागमत् ॥१९॥

taṁ duratyaya-vikrāntam
ādāya pramadottamā
harer aṁśāṁśa-sambhūtaṁ
bhartur antikam āgamat

tam—him; *duratyaya-vikrāntam*—whose strength was insurmountable; *ādāya*—taking with her; *pramadā-uttamā*—the best of women, Śakuntalā; *hareḥ*—of God; *aṁśa-aṁśa-sambhūtam*—a partial plenary incarnation; *bhartuḥ antikam*—unto her husband; *āgamat*—approached.

TRANSLATION

Śakuntalā, the best of beautiful women, along with her son, whose strength was insurmountable and who was a partial expansion of the Supreme Godhead, approached her husband, Duṣmanta.

TEXT 20

यदा न जगृहे राजा भार्यापुत्रावनिन्दितौ ।
शृण्वतां सर्वभूतानां खे वागाहाशरीरिणी ॥२०॥

yadā na jagṛhe rājā
bhāryā-putrāv aninditau
śṛṇvatāṁ sarva-bhūtānāṁ
khe vāg āhāśarīriṇī

yadā—when; *na*—not; *jagṛhe*—accepted; *rājā*—the King (Duṣmanta); *bhāryā-putrau*—his real son and real wife; *aninditau*—not abominable, not accused by anyone; *śṛṇvatām*—while hearing; *sarva-bhūtānām*—all the people; *khe*—in the sky; *vāk*—a sound vibration; *āha*—declared; *aśarīriṇī*—without a body.

TRANSLATION

When the King refused to accept his wife and son, who were both irreproachable, an unembodied voice spoke from the sky as an omen and was heard by everyone present.

PURPORT

Mahārāja Duṣmanta knew that Śakuntalā and the boy were his own wife and son, but because they came from outside and were unknown to the citizens, he at first declined to accept them. Śakuntalā, however, was so chaste that an omen from the sky declared the truth so that others could hear. When everyone heard from the omen that Śakuntalā and her child were truly the King's wife and son, the King gladly accepted them.

TEXT 21

माता भस्त्रा पितुः पुत्रो येन जातः स एव सः ।
भरस्व पुत्रं दुष्मन्त मावमंस्थाः शकुन्तलाम् ॥२१॥

mātā bhastrā pituḥ putro
yena jātaḥ sa eva saḥ

bharasva putraṁ duṣmanta
māvamaṁsthāḥ śakuntalām

mātā—the mother; *bhastrā*—just like the skin of a bellows containing air; *pituḥ*—of the father; *putraḥ*—the son; *yena*—by whom; *jātaḥ*—one is born; *saḥ*—the father; *eva*—indeed; *saḥ*—the son; *bharasva*—just maintain; *putram*—your son; *duṣmanta*—O Mahārāja Duṣmanta; *mā*—do not; *avamaṁsthāḥ*—insult; *śakuntalām*—Śakuntalā.

TRANSLATION

The voice said: O Mahārāja Duṣmanta, a son actually belongs to his father, whereas the mother is only a container, like the skin of a bellows. According to Vedic injunctions, the father is born as the son. Therefore, maintain your own son and do not insult Śakuntalā.

PURPORT

According to the Vedic injunction *ātmā vai putra-nāmāsi*, the father becomes the son. The mother is simply like a storekeeper, because the seed of the child is placed in her womb, but it is the father who is responsible for maintaining the son. In *Bhagavad-gītā* the Lord says that He is the seed-giving father of all living entities (*ahaṁ bīja-pradaḥ pitā*), and therefore He is responsible for maintaining them. This is also confirmed in the *Vedas*. *Eko bahūnāṁ yo vidadhāti kāmān:* although God is one, He maintains all living entities with their necessities for life. The living entities in different forms are sons of the Lord, and therefore the father, the Supreme Lord, supplies them food according to their different bodies. The small ant is supplied a grain of sugar, and the elephant is supplied tons of food, but everyone is able to eat. Therefore there is no question of overpopulation. Because the father, Kṛṣṇa, is fully opulent, there is no scarcity of food, and because there is no scarcity, the propaganda of overpopulation is only a myth. Actually one suffers for want of food when material nature, under the order of the father, refuses to supply him food. It is the living entity's position that determines whether food will be supplied or not. When a diseased person is forbidden to eat, this does not mean that there is a scarcity of food;

rather, the diseased person requires the treatment of not being supplied with food. In *Bhagavad-gītā* (7.10) the Lord also says, *bījaṁ māṁ sarva-bhūtānām:* "I am the seed of all living entities." A particular type of seed is sown within the earth, and then a particular type of tree or plant comes out. The mother resembles the earth, and when a particular type of seed is sown by the father, a particular type of body takes birth.

TEXT 22

रेतोधाः पुत्रो नयति नरदेव यमक्षयात् ।
त्वं चास्य धाता गर्भस्य सत्यमाह शकुन्तला ॥२२॥

reto-dhāḥ putro nayati
naradeva yama-kṣayāt
tvaṁ cāsya dhātā garbhasya
satyam āha śakuntalā

retaḥ-dhāḥ—a person who discharges semen; *putraḥ*—the son; *nayati*—saves; *nara-deva*—O King (Mahārāja Duṣmanta); *yama-kṣayāt*—from punishment by Yamarāja, or from the custody of Yamarāja; *tvam*—your good self; *ca*—and; *asya*—of this child; *dhātā*—the creator; *garbhasya*—of the embryo; *satyam*—truthfully; *āha*—said; *śakuntalā*—your wife, Śakuntalā.

TRANSLATION

O King Duṣmanta, he who discharges semen is the actual father, and his son saves him from the custody of Yamarāja. You are the actual procreator of this child. Indeed, Śakuntalā is speaking the truth.

PURPORT

Upon hearing the omen, Mahārāja Duṣmanta accepted his wife and child. According to Vedic *smṛti:*

pun-nāmno narakād yasmāt
pitaraṁ trāyate sutaḥ

tasmāt putra iti proktaḥ
svayam eva svayambhuvā

Because a son delivers his father from punishment in the hell called *put*, the son is called *putra*. According to this principle, when there is a disagreement between the father and mother, it is the father, not the mother, who is delivered by the son. But if the wife is faithful and firmly adherent to her husband, when the father is delivered the mother is also delivered. Consequently, there is no such thing as divorce in the Vedic literature. A wife is always trained to be chaste and faithful to her husband, for this helps her achieve deliverance from any abominable material condition. This verse clearly says, *putro nayati naradeva yamakṣayāt:* "The son saves his father from the custody of Yamarāja." It never says, *putro nayati mātaram:* "The son saves his mother." The seed-giving father is delivered, not the storekeeper mother. Consequently, husband and wife should not separate under any condition, for if they have a child whom they raise to be a Vaiṣṇava, he can save both the father and mother from the custody of Yamarāja and punishment in hellish life.

TEXT 23

पितर्युपरते सोऽपि चक्रवर्ती महायशाः ।
महिमा गीयते तस्य हरेरंशभुवो भुवि ॥२३॥

pitary uparate so 'pi
cakravartī mahā-yaśāḥ
mahimā gīyate tasya
harer aṁśa-bhuvo bhuvi

pitari—after his father; *uparate*—passed away; *saḥ*—the King's son; *api*—also; *cakravartī*—the emperor; *mahā-yaśāḥ*—very famous; *mahimā*—glories; *gīyate*—are glorified; *tasya*—his; *hareḥ*—of the Supreme Personality of Godhead; *aṁśa-bhuvaḥ*—a partial representation; *bhuvi*—upon this earth.

TRANSLATION

Śukadeva Gosvāmī said: When Mahārāja Duṣmanta passed away from this earth, his son became the emperor of the world, the

proprietor of the seven islands. He is referred to as a partial representation of the Supreme Personality of Godhead in this world.

PURPORT

In *Bhagavad-gītā* (10.41) it is said:

yad yad vibhūtimat sattvaṁ
śrīmad ūrjitam eva vā
tat tad evāvagaccha tvaṁ
mama tejo 'ṁśa-sambhavam

Anyone extraordinarily powerful must be considered a partial representation of the opulence of the Supreme Godhead. Therefore when the son of Mahārāja Duṣmanta became the emperor of the entire world, he was celebrated in this way.

TEXTS 24–26

चक्रं दक्षिणहस्तेऽस्य पद्मकोशोऽस्य पादयोः ।
ईजे महाभिषेकेण सोऽभिषिक्तोऽधिराड् विभुः ॥२४॥
पञ्चपञ्चाशता मेध्यैर्गङ्गायामनु वाजिभिः ।
मामतेयं पुरोधाय यमुनामनु च प्रभुः ॥२५॥
अष्टसप्ततिमेध्याश्वान् बबन्ध प्रददद् वसु ।
भरतस्य हि दौष्मन्तेरग्निः साचीगुणे चितः ।
सहस्रं बद्वशो यस्मिन् ब्राह्मणा गा विभेजिरे ॥२६॥

cakraṁ dakṣiṇa-haste 'sya
padma-kośo 'sya pādayoḥ
īje mahābhiṣekeṇa
so 'bhiṣikto 'dhirāḍ vibhuḥ

pañca-pañcāśatā medhyair
gaṅgāyām anu vājibhiḥ
māmateyaṁ purodhāya
yamunām anu ca prabhuḥ

aṣṭa-saptati-medhyāśvān
babandha pradadad vasu
bharatasya hi dauṣmanter
agniḥ sācī-guṇe citaḥ
sahasraṁ badvaśo yasmin
brāhmaṇā gā vibhejire

cakram—the mark of Kṛṣṇa's disc; *dakṣiṇa-haste*—on the palm of the right hand; *asya*—of him (Bharata); *padma-kośaḥ*—the mark of the whorl of a lotus; *asya*—of him; *pādayoḥ*—on the soles of the feet; *īje*—worshiped the Supreme Personality of Godhead; *mahā-abhiṣekeṇa*—by a grand Vedic ritualistic ceremony; *saḥ*—he (Mahārāja Bharata); *abhiṣiktaḥ*—being promoted; *adhirāṭ*—to the topmost position of a ruler; *vibhuḥ*—the master of everything; *pañca-pañcāśatā*—fifty-five; *medhyaiḥ*—fit for sacrifices; *gaṅgāyām anu*—from the mouth of the Ganges to the source; *vājibhiḥ*—with horses; *māmateyam*—the great sage Bhṛgu; *purodhāya*—making him the great priest; *yamunām*—on the bank of the Yamunā; *anu*—in regular order; *ca*—also; *prabhuḥ*—the supreme master, Mahārāja Bharata; *aṣṭa-saptati*—seventy-eight; *medhya-aśvān*—horses fit for sacrifice; *babandha*—he bound; *pradadat*—gave in charity; *vasu*—riches; *bharatasya*—of Mahārāja Bharata; *hi*—indeed; *dauṣmanteḥ*—the son of Mahārāja Duṣmanta; *agniḥ*—the sacrificial fire; *sācī-guṇe*—on an excellent site; *citaḥ*—established; *sahasram*—thousands; *badvaśaḥ*—by the number of one *badva* (one *badva* equals 13,084); *yasmin*—in which sacrifices; *brāhmaṇāḥ*—all the *brāhmaṇas* present; *gāḥ*—the cows; *vibhejire*—received their respective share.

TRANSLATION

Mahārāja Bharata, the son of Duṣmanta, had the mark of Lord Kṛṣṇa's disc on the palm of his right hand, and he had the mark of a lotus whorl on the soles of his feet. By worshiping the Supreme Personality of Godhead with a grand ritualistic ceremony, he became the emperor and master of the entire world. Then, under the priesthood of Māmateya, Bhṛgu Muni, he performed fifty-five horse sacrifices on the bank of the Ganges, beginning from its mouth and ending at its source, and seventy-eight horse sacrifices

on the bank of the Yamunā, beginning from the confluence at Prayāga and ending at the source. He established the sacrificial fire on an excellent site, and he distributed great wealth to the brāhmaṇas. Indeed, he distributed so many cows that each of thousands of brāhmaṇas had one badva [13,084] as his share.

PURPORT

As indicated here by the words *dauṣmanter agniḥ sācī-guṇe citaḥ*, Bharata, the son of Mahārāja Duṣmanta, arranged for many ritualistic ceremonies all over the world, especially all over India on the banks of the Ganges and Yamunā, from the mouth to the source, and all such sacrifices were performed in very distinguished places. As stated in *Bhagavad-gītā* (3.9), *yajñārthāt karmaṇo 'nyatra loko 'yaṁ karma-bandhanaḥ:* "Work done as a sacrifice for Viṣṇu has to be performed, otherwise work binds one to this material world." Everyone should engage in the performance of *yajña*, and the sacrificial fire should be ignited everywhere, the entire purpose being to make people happy, prosperous and progressive in spiritual life. Of course, these things were possible before the beginning of Kali-yuga because there were qualified *brāhmaṇas* who could perform such *yajñas*. For the present, however, the *Brahma-vaivarta Purāṇa* enjoins:

aśvamedhaṁ gavālambhaṁ
sannyāsaṁ pala-paitṛkam
devareṇa sutotpattiṁ
kalau pañca vivarjayet

"In this age of Kali, five acts are forbidden: offering a horse in sacrifice, offering a cow in sacrifice, accepting the order of *sannyāsa*, offering oblations of flesh to the forefathers, and begetting children in the wife of one's brother." In this age, such *yajñas* as the *aśvamedha-yajña* and *gomedha-yajña* are impossible to perform because there are neither sufficient riches nor qualified *brāhmaṇas*. This verse says, *māmateyaṁ purodhāya:* Mahārāja Bharata engaged the son of Mamatā, Bhṛgu Muni, to take charge of performing this *yajña*. Now, however, such *brāhmaṇas* are impossible to find. Therefore the *śāstras* recommend, *yajñaiḥ saṅkīrtana-prāyair yajanti hi sumedhasaḥ:* those who are intelligent should perform the *saṅkīrtana-yajña* inaugurated by Lord Śrī Caitanya Mahāprabhu.

kṛṣṇa-varṇaṁ tviṣākṛṣṇaṁ
saṅgopāṅgāstra-pārṣadam
yajñaiḥ saṅkīrtana-prāyair
yajanti hi sumedhasaḥ

"In this age of Kali, people endowed with sufficient intelligence will worship the Lord, who is accompanied by His associates, by performance of *saṅkīrtana-yajña.*" (*Bhāg.* 11.5.32) *Yajña* must be performed, for otherwise people will be entangled in sinful activities and will suffer immensely. Therefore the Kṛṣṇa consciousness movement has taken charge of introducing the chanting of Hare Kṛṣṇa all over the world. This Hare Kṛṣṇa movement is also *yajña,* but without the difficulties involved in securing paraphernalia and qualified *brāhmaṇas.* This congregational chanting can be performed anywhere and everywhere. If people somehow or other assemble together and are induced to chant Hare Kṛṣṇa, Hare Kṛṣṇa, Kṛṣṇa Kṛṣṇa, Hare Hare/ Hare Rāma, Hare Rāma, Rāma Rāma, Hare Hare, all the purposes of *yajña* will be fulfilled. The first purpose is that there must be sufficient rain, for without rain there cannot be any produce (*annād bhavanti bhūtāni parjanyād anna-sambhavaḥ*). All our necessities can be produced simply by rainfall (*kāmaṁ vavarṣa parjanyaḥ*), and the earth is the original source of all necessities (*sarva-kāma-dughā mahī*). In conclusion, therefore, in this age of Kali people all over the world should refrain from the four principles of sinful life—illicit sex, meat-eating, intoxication and gambling—and in a pure state of existence should perform the simple *yajña* of chanting the Hare Kṛṣṇa *mahā-mantra.* Then the earth will certainly produce all the necessities for life, and people will be happy economically, politically, socially, religiously and culturally. Everything will be in proper order.

TEXT 27

त्रयस्त्रिंशच्छतं ह्यश्वान् बद्ध्वा विस्मापयन् नृपान् ।
दौष्मन्तिरत्यगान्मायां देवानां गुरुमाययौ ॥२७॥

trayas-triṁśac-chataṁ hy aśvān
baddhvā vismāpayan nṛpān
dauṣmantir atyagān māyāṁ
devānāṁ gurum āyayau

trayaḥ—three; *triṁśat*—thirty; *śatam*—hundred; *hi*—indeed; *aśvān*—horses; *baddhvā*—arresting in the *yajña; vismāpayan*—astonishing; *nṛpān*—all other kings; *dauṣmantiḥ*—the son of Mahārāja Duṣmanta; *atyagāt*—surpassed; *māyām*—material opulences; *devānām*—of the demigods; *gurum*—the supreme spiritual master; *āyayau*—achieved.

TRANSLATION

Bharata, the son of Mahārāja Duṣmanta, bound thirty-three hundred horses for those sacrifices, and thus he astonished all other kings. He surpassed even the opulence of the demigods, for he achieved the supreme spiritual master, Hari.

PURPORT

One who achieves the lotus feet of the Supreme Personality of Godhead certainly surpasses all material wealth, even that of the demigods in the heavenly planets. *Yaṁ labdhvā cāparaṁ lābhaṁ manyate nādhikaṁ tataḥ.* The achievement of the lotus feet of the Supreme Personality of Godhead is the most exalted achievement in life.

TEXT 28

मृगाञ्छुक्लदतः कृष्णान् हिरण्येन परीवृतान् ।
अदात् कर्मणि मष्णारे नियुतानि चतुर्दश ॥२८॥

mṛgāñ chukla-dataḥ kṛṣṇān
hiraṇyena parīvṛtān
adāt karmaṇi maṣṇāre
niyutāni caturdaśa

mṛgān—first-class elephants; *śukla-dataḥ*—with very white tusks; *kṛṣṇān*—with black bodies; *hiraṇyena*—with gold ornaments;

parīvṛtan—completely covered; *adāt*—give in charity; *karmaṇi*—in the sacrifice; *maṣṇāre*—by the name Maṣṇāra, or in the place known as Maṣṇāra; *niyutāni*—*lakhs* (one *lakh* equals one hundred thousand); *caturdaśa*—fourteen.

TRANSLATION

When Mahārāja Bharata performed the sacrifice known as Maṣṇāra [or a sacrifice in the place known as Maṣṇāra], he gave in charity fourteen lakhs of excellent elephants with white tusks and black bodies, completely covered with golden ornaments.

TEXT 29

भरतस्य महत् कर्म न पूर्वे नापरे नृपाः ।
नैवापुर्नैव प्राप्स्यन्ति बाहुभ्यां त्रिदिवं यथा ॥२९॥

bharatasya mahat karma
na pūrve nāpare nṛpāḥ
naivāpur naiva prāpsyanti
bāhubhyāṁ tridivaṁ yathā

bharatasya—of Mahārāja Bharata, the son of Mahārāja Duṣmanta; *mahat*—very great, exalted; *karma*—activities; *na*—neither; *pūrve*—previously; *na*—nor; *apare*—after his time; *nṛpāḥ*—kings as a class; *na*—neither; *eva*—certainly; *āpuḥ*—attained; *na*—nor; *eva*—certainly; *prāpsyanti*—will get; *bāhubhyām*—by the strength of his arms; *tri-divam*—the heavenly planets; *yathā*—as.

TRANSLATION

As one cannot approach the heavenly planets simply by the strength of his arms (for who can touch the heavenly planets with his hands?), one cannot imitate the wonderful activities of Mahārāja Bharata. No one could perform such activities in the past, nor will anyone be able to do so in the future.

TEXT 30

किरातहूणान् यवनानन्ध्रान् कङ्कान् खशाञ्छकान् ।
अब्रह्मण्यनृपांश्चाहन् म्लेच्छान् दिग्विजयेऽखिलान् ॥३०॥

kirāta-hūṇān yavanān
pauṇḍrān kaṅkān khaśāñ chakān
abrahmaṇya-nṛpāṁś cāhan
mlecchān dig-vijaye 'khilān

kirāta—the black people called Kirātas (mostly the Africans); *hūṇān*—the Huns, the tribes from the far north; *yavanān*—the meat-eaters; *pauṇḍrān*—the Pauṇḍras; *kaṅkān*—the Kaṅkas; *khaśān*—the Mongolians; *śakān*—the Śakas; *abrahmaṇya*—against the brahminical culture; *nṛpān*—kings; *ca*—and; *ahan*—he killed; *mlecchān*—such atheists, who had no respect for Vedic civilization; *dik-vijaye*—while conquering all directions; *akhilān*—all of them.

TRANSLATION

When Mahārāja Bharata was on tour, he defeated or killed all the Kirātas, Hūṇas, Yavanas, Pauṇḍras, Kaṅkas, Khaśas, Śakas and the kings who were opposed to the Vedic principles of brahminical culture.

TEXT 31

जित्वा पुरासुरा देवान् ये रसौकांसि भेजिरे ।
देवस्त्रियो रसां नीताः प्राणिभिः पुनराहरत् ॥३१॥

jitvā purāsurā devān
ye rasaukāṁsi bhejire
deva-striyo rasāṁ nītāḥ
prāṇibhiḥ punar āharat

jitvā—conquering; *purā*—formerly; *asurāḥ*—the demons; *devān*—the demigods; *ye*—all who; *rasa-okāṁsi*—in the lower planetary system known as Rasātala; *bhejire*—took shelter; *deva-striyaḥ*—the wives and daughters of the demigods; *rasām*—in the lower planetary system; *nītāḥ*—were brought; *prāṇibhiḥ*—with their own dear associates; *punaḥ*—again; *āharat*—brought back to their original places.

TRANSLATION

Formerly, after conquering the demigods, all the demons had taken shelter in the lower planetary system known as Rasātala and had brought all the wives and daughters of the demigods there also. Mahārāja Bharata, however, rescued all those women, along with their associates, from the clutches of the demons, and he returned them to the demigods.

TEXT 32

सर्वान्कामान् दुदुहतुः प्रजानां तस्य रोदसी ।
समास्त्रिणवसाहस्रीर्दिक्षु चक्रमवर्तयत् ॥३२॥

sarvān kāmān duduhatuḥ
prajānāṁ tasya rodasī
samās tri-ṇava-sāhasrīr
dikṣu cakram avartayat

sarvān kāmān—all necessities or desirable things; *duduhatuḥ*—fulfilled; *prajānām*—of the subjects; *tasya*—his; *rodasī*—this earth and the heavenly planets; *samāḥ*—years; *tri-nava-sāhasrīḥ*—three times nine thousand (that is, twenty-seven thousand); *dikṣu*—in all directions; *cakram*—soldiers or orders; *avartayat*—circulated.

TRANSLATION

Mahārāja Bharata provided all necessities for his subjects, both on this earth and in the heavenly planets, for twenty-seven thousand years. He circulated his orders and distributed his soldiers in all directions.

TEXT 33

स सम्राड् लोकपालाख्यमैश्वर्यमधिराट् श्रियम् ।
चक्रं चास्खलितं प्राणान् मृषेत्युपरराम ह ॥३३॥

sa saṁrāḍ loka-pālākhyam
aiśvaryam adhirāṭ śriyam
cakraṁ cāskhalitaṁ prāṇān
mṛṣety upararāma ha

saḥ—he (Mahārāja Bharata); *saṁrāṭ*—the emperor; *loka-pāla-ākhyam*—known as the ruler of all the *lokas*, or planets; *aiśvaryam*—such opulences; *adhirāṭ*—thoroughly in power; *śriyam*—kingdom; *cakram*—soldiers or orders; *ca*—and; *askhalitam*—without failure; *prāṇān*—life or sons and family; *mṛṣā*—all false; *iti*—thus; *upararāma*—ceased to enjoy; *ha*—in the past.

TRANSLATION

As the ruler of the entire universe, Emperor Bharata had the opulences of a great kingdom and unconquerable soldiers. His sons and family had seemed to him to be his entire life. But finally he thought of all this as an impediment to spiritual advancement, and therefore he ceased from enjoying it.

PURPORT

Mahārāja Bharata had incomparable opulence in sovereignty, soldiers, sons, daughters and everything for material enjoyment, but when he realized that all such material opulences were useless for spiritual advancement, he retired from material enjoyment. The Vedic civilization enjoins that after a certain age, following in the footsteps of Mahārāja Bharata, one should cease to enjoy material opulences and should take the order of *vānaprastha*.

TEXT 34

तस्यासन् नृप वैदर्भ्यः पत्न्यस्तिस्रः सुसम्मताः ।
जघ्नुस्त्यागभयात् पुत्रान् नानुरूपा इतीरिते ॥३४॥

tasyāsan nṛpa vaidarbhyaḥ
patnyas tisraḥ susammatāḥ
jaghnus tyāga-bhayāt putrān
nānurūpā itīrite

tasya—of him (Mahārāja Bharata); *āsan*—there were; *nṛpa*—O King (Mahārāja Parīkṣit); *vaidarbhyaḥ*—daughters of Vidarbha; *patnyaḥ*—wives; *tisraḥ*—three; *su-sammatāḥ*—very pleasing and suitable; *jaghnuḥ*—killed; *tyāga-bhayāt*—fearing rejection; *putrān*—their sons; *na anurūpāḥ*—not exactly like the father; *iti*—like this; *īrite*—considering.

TRANSLATION

O King Parīkṣit, Mahārāja Bharata had three pleasing wives, who were daughters of the King of Vidarbha. When all three of them bore children who did not resemble the King, these wives thought that he would consider them unfaithful queens and reject them, and therefore they killed their own sons.

TEXT 35

तस्यैवं वितथे वंशे तदर्थं यजतः सुतम् ।
मरुत्स्तोमेन मरुतो भरद्वाजमुपाददुः ॥३५॥

tasyaivaṁ vitathe vaṁśe
tad-arthaṁ yajataḥ sutam
marut-stomena maruto
bharadvājam upādaduḥ

tasya—his (Mahārāja Bharata's); *evam*—thus; *vitathe*—being baffled; *vaṁśe*—in generating progeny; *tat-artham*—to get sons; *yajataḥ*—performing sacrifices; *sutam*—a son; *marut-stomena*—by performing a *marut-stoma* sacrifice; *marutaḥ*—the demigods named the Maruts; *bharadvājam*—Bharadvāja; *upādaduḥ*—presented.

TRANSLATION

The King, his attempt for progeny frustrated in this way, performed a sacrifice named marut-stoma to get a son. The demigods known as the Maruts, being fully satisfied with him, then presented him a son named Bharadvāja.

TEXT 36

अन्तर्वत्न्यां भ्रातृपत्न्यां मैथुनाय बृहस्पतिः ।
प्रवृत्तो वारितो गर्भं शप्त्वा वीर्यमुपासृजत् ॥३६॥

antarvatnyāṁ bhrātṛ-patnyāṁ
maithunāya bṛhaspatiḥ
pravṛtto vārito garbhaṁ
śaptvā vīryam upāsṛjat

antaḥ-vatnyām—pregnant; *bhrātṛ-patnyām*—with the brother's wife; *maithunāya*—desiring sexual enjoyment; *bṛhaspatiḥ*—the demigod named Bṛhaspati; *pravṛttaḥ*—so inclined; *vāritaḥ*—when forbidden to do so; *garbham*—the son within the abdomen; *śaptvā*—by cursing; *vīryam*—semen; *upāsṛjat*—discharged.

TRANSLATION

When the demigod named Bṛhaspati was attracted by his brother's wife, Mamatā, who at that time was pregnant, he desired to have sexual relations with her. The son within her womb forbid this, but Bṛhaspati cursed him and forcibly discharged semen into the womb of Mamatā.

PURPORT

The sex impulse is so strong in this material world that even Bṛhaspati, who is supposed to be the priest of the demigods and a very learned scholar, wanted to have a sexual relationship with his brother's pregnant wife. This can happen even in the society of the higher demigods, so what to speak of human society? The sex impulse is so strong that it can agitate even a learned personality like Bṛhaspati.

TEXT 37

तं त्यक्तुकामां ममतां भर्तुस्त्यागविशङ्किताम् ।
नामनिर्वाचनं तस्य श्लोकमेनं सुरा जगुः ॥३७॥

taṁ tyaktu-kāmāṁ mamatāṁ
bhārtus tyāga-viśaṅkitām
nāma-nirvācanaṁ tasya
ślokam enaṁ surā jaguḥ

tam—that newly born baby; *tyaktu-kāmām*—who was trying to avoid; *mamatām*—unto Mamatā; *bhartuḥ tyāga-viśaṅkitām*—very much afraid of being forsaken by her husband because of giving birth to an illegitimate son; *nāma-nirvācanam*—a name-giving ceremony, or *nāma-karaṇa; tasya*—to the child; *ślokam*—verse; *enam*—this; *surāḥ*—the demigods; *jaguḥ*—enunciated.

TRANSLATION

Mamatā very much feared being forsaken by her husband for giving birth to an illegitimate son, and therefore she considered giving up the child. But then the demigods solved the problem by enunciating a name for the child.

PURPORT

According to Vedic scripture, whenever a child is born there are some ceremonies known as *jāta-karma* and *nāma-karaṇa*, in which learned *brāhmaṇas*, immediately after the birth of the child, make a horoscope according to astrological calculations. But the child to which Mamatā gave birth was begotten by Bṛhaspati irreligiously, for although Mamatā was the wife of Utathya, Bṛhaspati made her pregnant by force. Therefore Bṛhaspati became *bhartā.* According to Vedic culture, a wife is considered the property of her husband, and a son born by illicit sex is called *dvāja.* The common word still current in Hindu society for such a son is *doglā*, which refers to a son not begotten by the husband of his mother. In such a situation, it is difficult to give the child a name according to proper regulative principles. Mamatā, therefore, was perplexed, but the demigods gave the child the appropriate name Bharadvāja, which indicated that the child born illegitimately should be maintained by both Mamatā and Bṛhaspati.

TEXT 38

मूढे भर द्वाजमिमं भर द्वाजं बृहस्पते ।
यातौ यदुक्त्वा पितरौ भरद्वाजस्ततस्त्वयम् ॥३८॥

mūḍhe bhara dvājam imaṁ
bhara dvājaṁ bṛhaspate
yātau yad uktvā pitarau
bharadvājas tatas tv ayam

mūḍhe—O foolish woman; *bhara*—just maintain; *dvājam*—although born by an illicit connection between two; *imam*—this child; *bhara*—maintain; *dvājam*—although born by an illicit connection between two; *bṛhaspate*—O Bṛhaspati; *yātau*—left; *yat*—because; *uktvā*—having said; *pitarau*—both the father and mother; *bharadvājaḥ*—by the name Bharadvāja; *tataḥ*—thereafter; *tu*—indeed; *ayam*—this child.

TRANSLATION

Bṛhaspati said to Mamatā, "You foolish woman, although this child was born from the wife of one man through the semen discharged by another, you should maintain him." Upon hearing this, Mamatā replied, "O Bṛhaspati, you maintain him!" After speaking in this way, Bṛhaspati and Mamatā both left. Thus the child was known as Bharadvāja.

TEXT 39

चोद्यमाना सुरैरेवं मत्वा वितथमात्मजम् ।
व्यसृजन् मरुतोऽबिभ्रन् दत्तोऽयं वितथेऽन्वये॥३९॥

codyamānā surair evaṁ
matvā vitatham ātmajam
vyasṛjan maruto 'bibhran
datto 'yaṁ vitathe 'nvaye

codyamānā—although Mamatā was encouraged (to maintain the child); *suraiḥ*—by the demigods; *evam*—in this way; *matvā*—

considering; *vitatham*—purposeless; *ātmajam*—her own child; *vyasṛjat*—rejected; *marutaḥ*—the demigods known as the Maruts; *abibhran*—maintained (the child); *dattaḥ*—the same child was given; *ayam*—this; *vitathe*—was disappointed; *anvaye*—when the dynasty of Mahārāja Bharata.

TRANSLATION

Although encouraged by the demigods to maintain the child, Mamatā considered him useless because of his illicit birth, and therefore she left him. Consequently, the demigods known as the Maruts maintained the child, and when Mahārāja Bharata was disappointed for want of a child, this child was given to him as his son.

PURPORT

From this verse it is understood that those who are rejected from the higher planetary system are given a chance to take birth in the most exalted families on this planet earth.

Thus end the Bhaktivedanta purports of the Ninth Canto, Twentieth Chapter, of the Śrīmad-Bhāgavatam, *entitled "The Dynasty of Pūru."*

CHAPTER TWENTY-ONE

The Dynasty of Bharata

This Twenty-first Chapter describes the dynasty born from Mahārāja Bharata, the son of Mahārāja Duṣmanta, and it also describes the glories of Rantideva, Ajamīḍha and others.

The son of Bharadvāja was Manyu, and Manyu's sons were Bṛhatkṣatra, Jaya, Mahāvīrya, Nara and Garga. Of these five, Nara had a son named Saṅkṛti, who had two sons, named Guru and Rantideva. As an exalted devotee, Rantideva saw every living entity in relationship with the Supreme Personality of Godhead, and therefore he completely engaged his mind, his words and his very self in the service of the Supreme Lord and His devotees. Rantideva was so exalted that he would sometimes give away his own food in charity, and he and his family would fast. Once, after Rantideva spent forty-eight days fasting, not even drinking water, excellent food made with ghee was brought to him, but when he was about to eat it a *brāhmaṇa* guest appeared. Rantideva, therefore, did not eat the food, but instead immediately offered a portion of it to the *brāhmaṇa.* When the *brāhmaṇa* left and Rantideva was just about to eat the remnants of the food, a *śūdra* appeared. Rantideva therefore divided the remnants between the *śūdra* and himself. Again, when he was just about to eat the remnants of the food, another guest appeared. Rantideva therefore gave the rest of the food to the new guest and was about to content himself with drinking the water to quench his thirst, but this also was precluded, for a thirsty guest came and Rantideva gave him the water. This was all ordained by the Supreme Personality of Godhead just to glorify His devotee and show how tolerant a devotee is in rendering service to the Lord. The Supreme Personality of Godhead, being extremely pleased with Rantideva, entrusted him with very confidential service. The special power to render the most confidential service is entrusted by the Supreme Personality of Godhead to a pure devotee, not to ordinary devotees.

Garga, the son of Bharadvāja, had a son named Śini, and Śini's son was Gārgya. Although Gārgya was a *kṣatriya* by birth, his sons became *brāhmaṇas.* The son of Mahāvīrya was Duritakṣaya, whose sons were Trayyāruṇi, Kavi and Puṣkarāruṇi. Although these three sons were born of a *kṣatriya* king, they also achieved the position of *brāhmaṇas.* The son of Bṛhatkṣatra constructed the city of Hastināpura and was known as Hastī. His sons were Ajamīḍha, Dvimīḍha and Purumīḍha.

From Ajamīḍha came Priyamedha and other *brāhmaṇas* and also a son named Bṛhadiṣu. The sons, grandsons and further descendants of Bṛhadiṣu were Bṛhaddhanu, Bṛhatkāya, Jayadratha, Viśada and Syenajit. From Syenajit came four sons—Rucirāśva, Dṛḍhahanu, Kāśya and Vatsa. From Rucirāśva came a son named Pāra, whose sons were Pṛthusena and Nīpa, and from Nīpa came one hundred sons. Another son of Nīpa was Brahmadatta. From Brahmadatta came Viṣvaksena; from Viṣvaksena, Udaksena; and from Udaksena, Bhallāṭa.

The son of Dvimīḍha was Yavīnara, and from Yavīnara came many sons and grandsons, such as Kṛtimān, Satyadhṛti, Dṛḍhanemi, Supārśva, Sumati, Sannatimān, Kṛtī, Nīpa, Udgrāyudha, Kṣemya, Suvīra, Ripuñjaya and Bahuratha. Purumīḍha had no sons, but Ajamīḍha, in addition to his other sons, had a son named Nīla, whose son was Śānti. The descendants of Śānti were Suśānti, Puruja, Arka and Bharmyāśva. Bharmyāśva had five sons, one of whom, Mudgala, begot a dynasty of *brāhmaṇas.* Mudgala had twins—a son, Divodāsa, and a daughter, Ahalyā. From Ahalyā, by her husband, Gautama, Śatānanda was born. The son of Śatānanda was Satyadhṛti, and his son was Śaradvān. Śaradvān's son was known as Kṛpa, and Śaradvān's daughter, known as Kṛpī, became the wife of Droṇācārya.

TEXT 1

श्रीशुक उवाच

वितथस्य सुतान् मन्योर्बृहत्क्षत्रो जयस्ततः ।
महावीर्यो नरो गर्गः सङ्कृतिस्तु नरात्मजः ॥ १ ॥

śrī-śuka uvāca
vitathasya sutān manyor
bṛhatkṣatro jayas tataḥ
mahāvīryo naro gargaḥ
saṅkṛtis tu narātmajaḥ

śrī-śukaḥ uvāca—Śrī Śukadeva Gosvāmī said; *vitathasya*—of Vitatha (Bharadvāja), who was accepted in the family of Mahārāja Bharata under special circumstances of disappointment; *sutāt*—from the son; *manyoḥ*—named Manyu; *bṛhatkṣatraḥ*—Bṛhatkṣatra; *jayaḥ*—Jaya; *tataḥ*—from him; *mahāvīryaḥ*—Mahāvīrya; *naraḥ*—Nara; *gargaḥ*—Garga; *saṅkṛtiḥ*—Saṅkṛti; *tu*—certainly; *nara-ātmajaḥ*—the son of Nara.

TRANSLATION

Śukadeva Gosvāmī said: Because Bharadvāja was delivered by the Marut demigods, he was known as Vitatha. The son of Vitatha was Manyu, and from Manyu came five sons—Bṛhatkṣatra, Jaya, Mahāvīrya, Nara and Garga. Of these five, the one known as Nara had a son named Saṅkṛti.

TEXT 2

गुरुश्च रन्तिदेवश्च सङ्कृतेः पाण्डुनन्दन ।
रन्तिदेवस्य महिमा इहामुत्र च गीयते ॥ २ ॥

guruś ca rantidevaś ca
saṅkṛteḥ pāṇḍu-nandana
rantidevasya mahimā
ihāmutra ca gīyate

guruḥ—a son named Guru; *ca*—and; *rantidevaḥ ca*—and a son named Rantideva; *saṅkṛteḥ*—from Saṅkṛti; *pāṇḍu-nandana*—O Mahārāja Parīkṣit, descendant of Pāṇḍu; *rantidevasya*—of Rantideva; *mahimā*—the glories; *iha*—in this world; *amutra*—and in the next world; *ca*—also; *gīyate*—are glorified.

TRANSLATION

O Mahārāja Parīkṣit, descendant of Pāṇḍu, Saṅkṛti had two sons, named Guru and Rantideva. Rantideva is famous in both this world and the next, for he is glorified not only in human society but also in the society of the demigods.

TEXTS 3–5

वियद्वित्तस्य ददतो लब्धं लब्धं बुभुक्षतः ।
निष्किञ्चनस्य धीरस्य सकुटुम्बस्य सीदतः ॥ ३ ॥
व्यतीयुरष्टचत्वारिंशदहान्यपिबतः किल ।
घृतपायससंयावं तोयं प्रातरुपस्थितम् ॥ ४ ॥
कृच्छ्रप्राप्तकुटुम्बस्य क्षुत्तृड्भ्यां जातवेपथोः ।
अतिथिर्ब्राह्मणः काले भोक्तुकामस्य चागमत् ॥ ५ ॥

viyad-vittasya dadato
labdhaṁ labdhaṁ bubhukṣataḥ
niṣkiñcanasya dhīrasya
sakuṭumbasya sīdataḥ

vyatīyur aṣṭa-catvāriṁśad
ahāny apibataḥ kila
ghṛta-pāyasa-saṁyāvaṁ
toyaṁ prātar upasthitam

kṛcchra-prāpta-kuṭumbasya
kṣut-tṛḍbhyāṁ jāta-vepathoḥ
atithir brāhmaṇaḥ kāle
bhoktu-kāmasya cāgamat

viyat-vittasya—of Rantideva, who received things sent by providence, just as the *cātaka* bird receives water from the sky; *dadataḥ*—who distributed to others; *labdham*—whatever he got; *labdham*—such gains; *bubhukṣataḥ*—he enjoyed; *niṣkiñcanasya*—always penniless; *dhīrasya*—yet very sober; *sa-kuṭumbasya*—even with his family members; *sīdataḥ*—suffering very much; *vyatīyuḥ*—passed by; *aṣṭa-catvāriṁśat*—forty-eight; *ahāni*—days; *apibataḥ*—without even drinking water; *kila*—indeed; *ghṛta-pāyasa*—food prepared with ghee and milk; *saṁyāvam*—varieties of food grains; *toyam*—water; *prātaḥ*—in the morning; *upasthitam*—arrived by chance; *kṛcchra-prāpta*—undergoing suffering; *kuṭumbasya*—whose family members; *kṣut-*

tṛḍbhyām—by thirst and hunger; *jāta*—became; *vepathoḥ*—trembling; *atithiḥ*—a guest; *brāhmaṇaḥ*—a *brāhmaṇa; kāle*—just at that time; *bhoktu-kāmasya*—of Rantideva, who desired to eat something; *ca*—also; *āgamat*—arrived there.

TRANSLATION

Rantideva never endeavored to earn anything. He would enjoy whatever he got by the arrangement of providence, but when guests came he would give them everything. Thus he underwent considerable suffering, along with the members of his family. Indeed, he and his family members shivered for want of food and water, yet Rantideva always remained sober. Once, after fasting for forty-eight days, in the morning Rantideva received some water and some foodstuffs made with milk and ghee, but when he and his family were about to eat, a brāhmaṇa guest arrived.

TEXT 6

तस्मै संव्यभजत् सोऽन्नमादृत्य श्रद्धयान्वितः ।
हरिं सर्वत्र संपश्यन् स भुक्त्वा प्रययौ द्विजः ॥ ६ ॥

tasmai saṁvyabhajat so 'nnam
ādṛtya śraddhayānvitaḥ
hariṁ sarvatra saṁpaśyan
sa bhuktvā prayayau dvijaḥ

tasmai—unto him (the *brāhmaṇa*); *saṁvyabhajat*—after dividing, gave his share; *saḥ*—he (Rantideva); *annam*—the food; *ādṛtya*—with great respect; *śraddhayā anvitaḥ*—and with faith; *harim*—the Supreme Lord; *sarvatra*—everywhere, or in the heart of every living being; *saṁpaśyan*—conceiving; *saḥ*—he; *bhuktvā*—after eating the food; *prayayau*—left that place; *dvijaḥ*—the *brāhmaṇa.*

TRANSLATION

Because Rantideva perceived the presence of the Supreme Godhead everywhere, and in every living entity, he received the guest

with faith and respect and gave him a share of the food. The brāhmaṇa guest ate his share and then went away.

PURPORT

Rantideva perceived the presence of the Supreme Personality of Godhead in every living being, but he never thought that because the Supreme Lord is present in every living being, every living being must be God. Nor did he distinguish between one living being and another. He perceived the presence of the Lord both in the *brāhmaṇa* and in the *caṇḍāla.* This is the true vision of equality, as confirmed by the Lord Himself in *Bhagavad-gītā* (5.18):

vidyā-vinaya-sampanne
brāhmaṇe gavi hastini
śuni caiva śva-pāke ca
paṇḍitāḥ sama-darśinaḥ

"The humble sage, by virtue of true knowledge, sees with equal vision a learned and gentle *brāhmaṇa*, a cow, an elephant, a dog and a dog-eater [outcaste]." A *paṇḍita*, or learned person, perceives the presence of the Supreme Personality of Godhead in every living being. Therefore, although it has now become fashionable to give preference to the so-called *daridra-nārāyaṇa*, or "poor Nārāyaṇa," Rantideva had no reason to give preference to any one person. The idea that because Nārāyaṇa is present in the heart of one who is *daridra*, or poor, the poor man should be called *daridra-nārāyaṇa* is a wrong conception. By such logic, because the Lord is present within the hearts of the dogs and hogs, the dogs and hogs would also be Nārāyaṇa. One should not mistakenly think that Rantideva subscribed to this view. Rather, he saw everyone as part of the Supreme Personality of Godhead (*hari-sambandhi-vastunaḥ*). It is not that everyone is the Supreme Godhead. Such a theory, which is propounded by the Māyāvāda philosophy, is always misleading, and Rantideva would never have accepted it.

TEXT 7

अथान्यो भोक्ष्यमाणस्य विभक्तस्य महीपतेः।
विभक्तं व्यभजत् तस्मै वृषलाय हरिं स्मरन् ॥ ७ ॥

athānyo bhokṣyamāṇasya
vibhaktasya mahīpateḥ
vibhaktaṁ vyabhajat tasmai
vṛṣalāya hariṁ smaran

atha—thereafter; *anyaḥ*—another guest; *bhokṣyamāṇasya*—who was just about to eat; *vibhaktasya*—after setting aside the share for the family; *mahīpateḥ*—of the King; *vibhaktam*—the food allotted for the family; *vyabhajat*—he divided and distributed; *tasmai*—unto him; *vṛṣalāya*—unto a *śūdra; harim*—the Supreme Personality of Godhead; *smaran*—remembering.

TRANSLATION

Thereafter, having divided the remaining food with his relatives, Rantideva was just about to eat his own share when a śūdra guest arrived. Seeing the śūdra in relationship with the Supreme Personality of Godhead, King Rantideva gave him also a share of the food.

PURPORT

Because King Rantideva saw everyone as part of the Supreme Personality of Godhead, he never distinguished between the *brāhmaṇa* and the *śūdra*, the poor and the rich. Such equal vision is called *sama-darśinaḥ* (*paṇḍitāḥ sama-darśinaḥ*). One who has actually realized that the Supreme Personality of Godhead is situated in everyone's heart and that every living being is part of the Lord does not make any distinction between the *brāhmaṇa* and the *śūdra*, the poor (*daridra*) and the rich (*dhanī*). Such a person sees all living beings equally and treats them equally, without discrimination.

TEXT 8

याते शूद्रे तमन्योऽगादतिथिः श्वभिरावृतः ।
राजन् मे दीयतामन्नं सगणाय बुभुक्षते ॥ ८ ॥

yāte śūdre tam anyo 'gād
atithiḥ śvabhir āvṛtaḥ

rājan me dīyatām annaṁ
sagaṇāya bubhukṣate

yāte—when he went away; *śūdre*—the *śūdra* guest; *tam*—unto the King; *anyaḥ*—another; *agāt*—arrived there; *atithiḥ*—guest; *śvabhiḥ āvṛtaḥ*—accompanied by dogs; *rājan*—O King; *me*—unto me; *dīyatām*—deliver; *annam*—eatables; *sa-gaṇāya*—with my company of dogs; *bubhukṣate*—hankering for food.

TRANSLATION

When the śūdra went away, another guest arrived, surrounded by dogs, and said, "O King, I and my company of dogs are very hungry. Please give us something to eat."

TEXT 9

स आदृत्यावशिष्टं यद् बहुमानपुरस्कृतम् ।
तच्च दत्त्वा नमश्चक्रे श्वभ्यः श्वपतये विभुः ॥ ९ ॥

sa ādṛtyāvaśiṣṭaṁ yad
bahu-māna-puraskṛtam
tac ca dattvā namaścakre
śvabhyaḥ śva-pataye vibhuḥ

saḥ—he (King Rantideva); *ādṛtya*—after honoring them; *avaśiṣṭam*—the food that remained after the *brāhmaṇa* and *śūdra* were fed; *yat*—whatever there was; *bahu-māna-puraskṛtam*—offering him much respect; *tat*—that; *ca*—also; *dattvā*—giving away; *namaḥ-cakre*—offered obeisances; *śvabhyaḥ*—unto the dogs; *śva-pataye*—unto the master of the dogs; *vibhuḥ*—the all-powerful King.

TRANSLATION

With great respect, King Rantideva offered the balance of the food to the dogs and the master of the dogs, who had come as guests. The King offered them all respects and obeisances.

TEXT 10

पानीयमात्रमुच्छेषं तच्चैकपरितर्पणम् ।
पास्यतः पुल्कसोऽभ्यागादपो देह्यशुभाय मे ॥१०॥

pānīya-mātram ucchesaṁ
tac caika-paritarpaṇam
pāsyataḥ pulkaso 'bhyāgād
apo dehy aśubhāya me

pānīya-mātram—only the drinking water; *ucchesam*—what remained of the food; *tat ca*—that also; *eka*—for one; *paritarpaṇam*—satisfying; *pāsyataḥ*—when the King was about to drink; *pulkasaḥ*—a *caṇḍāla; abhyāgāt*—came there; *apaḥ*—water; *dehi*—please give; *aśubhāya*—although I am a lowborn *caṇḍāla; me*—to me.

TRANSLATION

Thereafter, only the drinking water remained, and there was only enough to satisfy one person, but when the King was just about to drink it, a caṇḍāla appeared and said, "O King, although I am lowborn, kindly give me some drinking water."

TEXT 11

तस्य तां करुणां वाचं निशम्य विपुलश्रमाम् ।
कृपया भृशसन्तप्त इदमाहामृतं वचः ॥११॥

tasya tāṁ karuṇāṁ vācaṁ
niśamya vipula-śramām
kṛpayā bhṛśa-santapta
idam āhāmṛtaṁ vacaḥ

tasya—of him (the *caṇḍāla*); *tām*—those; *karuṇām*—pitiable; *vācam*—words; *niśamya*—hearing; *vipula*—very much; *śramām*—fatigued; *kṛpayā*—out of compassion; *bhṛśa-santaptaḥ*—very much aggrieved; *idam*—these; *āha*—spoke; *amṛtam*—very sweet; *vacaḥ*—words.

TRANSLATION

Aggrieved at hearing the pitiable words of the poor fatigued caṇḍāla, Mahārāja Rantideva spoke the following nectarean words.

PURPORT

Mahārāja Rantideva's words were like *amṛta*, or nectar, and therefore, aside from rendering bodily service to an aggrieved person, by his words alone the King could save the life of anyone who might hear him.

TEXT 12

न कामयेऽहं गतिमीश्वरात् परा-
मष्टर्द्धियुक्तामपुनर्भवं वा ।
आर्तिं प्रपद्येऽखिलदेहभाजा-
मन्तःस्थितो येन भवन्त्यदुःखाः ॥१२॥

na kāmaye 'haṁ gatim īśvarāt parām
aṣṭarddhi-yuktām apunar-bhavaṁ vā
ārtiṁ prapadye 'khila-deha-bhājām
antaḥ-sthito yena bhavanty aduḥkhāḥ

na—not; *kāmaye*—desire; *aham*—I; *gatim*—destination; *īśvarāt*—from the Supreme Personality of Godhead; *parām*—great; *aṣṭa-ṛddhi-yuktām*—composed of the eight kinds of mystic perfection; *apunaḥ-bhavam*—cessation of repeated birth (liberation, salvation); *vā*—either; *ārtim*—sufferings; *prapadye*—I accept; *akhila-deha-bhājām*—of all living entities; *antaḥ-sthitaḥ*—staying among them; *yena*—by which; *bhavanti*—they become; *aduḥkhāḥ*—without distress.

TRANSLATION

I do not pray to the Supreme Personality of Godhead for the eight perfections of mystic yoga, nor for salvation from repeated

birth and death. I want only to stay among all the living entities and suffer all distresses on their behalf, so that they may be freed from suffering.

PURPORT

Vāsudeva Datta made a similar statement to Śrī Caitanya Mahāprabhu, requesting the Lord to liberate all living entities in His presence. Vāsudeva Datta submitted that if they were unfit to be liberated, he himself would take all their sinful reactions and suffer personally so that the Lord might deliver them. A Vaiṣṇava is therefore described as being *para-duḥkha-duḥkhī*, very much aggrieved by the sufferings of others. As such, a Vaiṣṇava engages in activities for the real welfare of human society.

TEXT 13

क्षुत्तृट्श्रमो गात्रपरिभ्रमश्च
दैन्यं क्लमः शोकविषादमोहाः ।
सर्वे निवृत्ताः कृपणस्य जन्तो-
र्जिजीविषोर्जीवजलार्पणान्मे ॥१३॥

kṣut-tṛṭ-śramo gātra-paribhramaś ca
dainyaṁ klamaḥ śoka-viṣāda-mohāḥ
sarve nivṛttāḥ kṛpaṇasya jantor
jijīviṣor jīva-jalārpaṇān me

kṣut—from hunger; *tṛṭ*—and thirst; *śramaḥ*—fatigue; *gātra-paribhramaḥ*—trembling of the body; *ca*—also; *dainyam*—poverty; *klamaḥ*—distress; *śoka*—lamentation; *viṣāda*—moroseness; *mohāḥ*—and bewilderment; *sarve*—all of them; *nivṛttāḥ*—finished; *kṛpaṇasya*—of the poor; *jantoḥ*—living entity (the *caṇḍāla*); *jijīviṣoḥ*—desiring to live; *jīva*—maintaining life; *jala*—water; *arpaṇāt*—by delivering; *me*—mine.

TRANSLATION

By offering my water to maintain the life of this poor caṇḍāla, who is struggling to live, I have been freed from all hunger, thirst,

fatigue, trembling of the body, moroseness, distress, lamentation and illusion.

TEXT 14

इति प्रभाष्य पानीयं म्रियमाणः पिपासया ।
पुल्कसायाददाद्धीरो निसर्गकरुणो नृपः ॥१४॥

iti prabhāṣya pānīyaṁ
mriyamāṇaḥ pipāsayā
pulkasāyādadād dhīro
nisarga-karuṇo nṛpaḥ

iti—thus; *prabhāṣya*—giving his statement; *pānīyam*—drinking water; *mriyamāṇaḥ*—although on the verge of death; *pipāsayā*—because of thirst; *pulkasāya*—unto the low-class *caṇḍāla; adadāt*—delivered; *dhīraḥ*—sober; *nisarga-karuṇaḥ*—by nature very kind; *nṛpaḥ*—the King.

TRANSLATION

Having spoken thus, King Rantideva, although on the verge of death because of thirst, gave his own portion of water to the caṇḍāla without hesitation, for the King was naturally very kind and sober.

TEXT 15

तस्य त्रिभुवनाधीशाः फलदाः फलमिच्छताम् ।
आत्मानं दर्शयाञ्चक्रुर्माया विष्णुविनिर्मिताः ॥१५॥

tasya tribhuvanādhīśāḥ
phaladāḥ phalam icchatām
ātmānaṁ darśayāṁ cakrur
māyā viṣṇu-vinirmitāḥ

tasya—before him (King Rantideva); *tri-bhuvana-adhīśāḥ*—the controllers of the three worlds (demigods like Brahmā and Śiva); *phala-*

dāḥ—who can bestow all fruitive results; *phalam icchatām*—of persons who desire material benefit; *ātmānam*—their own identities; *darśayām cakruḥ*—manifested; *māyāḥ*—the illusory energy; *viṣṇu*—by Lord Viṣṇu; *vinirmitāḥ*—created.

TRANSLATION

Demigods like Lord Brahmā and Lord Śiva, who can satisfy all materially ambitious men by giving them the rewards they desire, then manifested their own identities before King Rantideva, for it was they who had presented themselves as the brāhmaṇa, śūdra, caṇḍāla and so on.

TEXT 16

स वै तेभ्यो नमस्कृत्य निःसङ्गो विगतस्पृहः ।
वासुदेवे भगवति भक्त्या चक्रे मनः परम् ॥१६॥

sa vai tebhyo namaskṛtya
niḥsaṅgo vigata-spṛhaḥ
vāsudeve bhagavati
bhaktyā cakre manaḥ param

saḥ—he (King Rantideva); *vai*—indeed; *tebhyaḥ*—unto Lord Brahmā, Lord Śiva and the other demigods; *namaḥ-kṛtya*—offering obeisances; *niḥsaṅgaḥ*—with no ambition to take any benefit from them; *vigata-spṛhaḥ*—completely free from desires for material possessions; *vāsudeve*—unto Lord Vāsudeva; *bhagavati*—the Supreme Lord; *bhaktyā*—by devotional service; *cakre*—fixed; *manaḥ*—the mind; *param*—as the ultimate goal of life.

TRANSLATION

King Rantideva had no ambition to enjoy material benefits from the demigods. He offered them obeisances, but because he was factually attached to Lord Viṣṇu, Vāsudeva, the Supreme Personality of Godhead, he fixed his mind at Lord Viṣṇu's lotus feet.

PURPORT

Śrīla Narottama dāsa Ṭhākura has sung:

anya devāśraya nāi, tomāre kahinu bhāi,
ei bhakti parama karaṇa

If one wants to become a pure devotee of the Supreme Lord, one should not hanker to take benedictions from the demigods. As stated in *Bhagavad-gītā* (7.20), *kāmais tais tair hṛta-jñānāḥ prapadyante 'nya-devatāḥ:* those befooled by the illusion of the material energy worship gods other than the Supreme Personality of Godhead. Therefore, although Rantideva was personally able to see Lord Brahmā and Lord Śiva, he did not hanker to take material benefits from them. Rather, he fixed his mind upon Lord Vāsudeva and rendered devotional service unto Him. This is the sign of a pure devotee, whose heart is not adulterated by material desires.

anyābhilāṣitā-śūnyaṁ
jñāna-karmādy-anāvṛtam
ānukūlyena kṛṣṇānu-
śīlanaṁ bhaktir uttamā

"One should render transcendental loving service to the Supreme Lord Kṛṣṇa favorably and without desire for material profit or gain through fruitive activities or philosophical speculation. That is called pure devotional service."

TEXT 17

ईश्वरालम्बनं चित्तं कुर्वतोऽनन्यराधसः ।
माया गुणमयी राजन् स्वप्नवत् प्रत्यलीयत ॥१७॥

īśvarālambanaṁ cittaṁ
kurvato 'nanya-rādhasaḥ
māyā guṇamayī rājan
svapnavat pratyalīyata

īśvara-ālambanam—completely taking shelter at the lotus feet of the Supreme Lord; *cittam*—his consciousness; *kurvataḥ*—fixing; *ananya-*

rādhasaḥ—for Rantideva, who was undeviating and desired nothing other than to serve the Supreme Lord; *māyā*—the illusory energy; *guṇa-mayī*—consisting of the three modes of nature; *rājan*—O Mahārāja Parīkṣit; *svapna-vat*—like a dream; *pratyalīyata*—merged.

TRANSLATION

O Mahārāja Parīkṣit, because King Rantideva was a pure devotee, always Kṛṣṇa conscious and free from all material desires, the Lord's illusory energy, māyā, could not exhibit herself before him. On the contrary, for him māyā entirely vanished, exactly like a dream.

PURPORT

As it is said:

kṛṣṇa——sūrya-sama; māyā haya andhakāra
yāhāṅ kṛṣṇa, tāhāṅ nāhi māyāra adhikāra

Just as there is no chance that darkness can exist in the sunshine, in a pure Kṛṣṇa conscious person there can be no existence of *māyā*. The Lord Himself says in *Bhagavad-gītā* (7.14):

daivī hy eṣā guṇamayī
mama māyā duratyayā
mām eva ye prapadyante
māyām etāṁ taranti te

"This divine energy of Mine, consisting of the three modes of material nature, is difficult to overcome. But those who have surrendered unto Me can easily cross beyond it." If one wants to be free from the influence of *māyā*, the illusory energy, one must become Kṛṣṇa conscious and always keep Kṛṣṇa prominent within the core of his heart. In *Bhagavad-gītā* (9.34) the Lord advises that one always think of Him (*man-manā bhava mad-bhakto mad-yājī māṁ namaskuru*). In this way, by always being Kṛṣṇa-minded or Kṛṣṇa conscious, one can surpass the influence of *māyā* (*māyām etāṁ taranti te*). Because Rantideva was Kṛṣṇa conscious, he was not under the influence of the illusory energy. The word *svapnavat* is significant in this connection. Because in the material world the mind is absorbed in materialistic activities, when one is asleep many contradictory activities appear in one's dreams. When one awakens, however, these activities automatically merge into the mind. Similarly, as long as one is under the influence of the material energy he makes many plans and schemes, but when one is Kṛṣṇa conscious such dreamlike plans automatically disappear.

TEXT 18

तत्प्रसङ्गानुभावेन रन्तिदेवानुवर्तिनः ।
अभवन् योगिनः सर्वे नारायणपरायणाः ॥१८॥

tat-prasaṅgānubhāvena
rantidevānuvartinaḥ
abhavan yoginaḥ sarve
nārāyaṇa-parāyaṇāḥ

tat-prasaṅga-anubhāvena—because of associating with King Rantideva (when talking with him about *bhakti-yoga*); *rantideva-anuvartinaḥ*—the followers of King Rantideva (that is, his servants, his family members, his friends and others); *abhavan*—became; *yoginaḥ*—first-class mystic *yogīs*, or *bhakti-yogīs; sarve*—all of them; *nārāyaṇa-parāyaṇāḥ*—devotees of the Supreme Personality of Godhead, Nārāyaṇa.

TRANSLATION

All those who followed the principles of King Rantideva were totally favored by his mercy and became pure devotees, attached to the Supreme Personality of Godhead, Nārāyaṇa. Thus they all became the best of yogīs.

PURPORT

The best *yogīs* or mystics are the devotees, as confirmed by the Lord Himself in *Bhagavad-gītā* (6.47):

yoginām api sarveṣāṁ
mad-gatenāntarātmanā

śraddhāvān bhajate yo māṁ
sa me yuktatamo mataḥ

"Of all *yogīs*, he who always abides in Me with great faith, worshiping Me in transcendental loving service, is most intimately united with Me in *yoga* and is the highest of all." The best *yogī* is he who constantly thinks of the Supreme Personality of Godhead within the core of the heart. Because Rantideva was the king, the chief executive in the state, all the residents of the state became devotees of the Supreme Personality of Godhead, Nārāyaṇa, by the king's transcendental association. This is the influence of a pure devotee. If there is one pure devotee, his association can create hundreds and thousands of pure devotees. Śrīla Bhaktivinoda Ṭhākura has said that a Vaiṣṇava is meritorious in proportion to the number of devotees he has created. A Vaiṣṇava becomes superior not simply by jugglery of words but by the number of devotees he has created for the Lord. Here the word *rantidevānuvartinaḥ* indicates that Rantideva's officers, friends, relatives and subjects all became first-class Vaiṣṇavas by his association. In other words, Rantideva is confirmed herein to be a first-class devotee, or *mahā-bhāgavata. Mahat-sevāṁ dvāram āhur vimukteḥ:* one should render service to such *mahātmās*, for then one will automatically achieve the goal of liberation. Śrīla Narottama dāsa Ṭhākura has also said, *chāḍiyā vaiṣṇava-sevā nistāra pāyeche kebā:* one cannot be liberated by his own effort, but if one becomes subordinate to a pure Vaiṣṇava, the door to liberation is open.

TEXTS 19–20

गर्गाच्छिनिस्ततो गार्ग्यः क्षत्राद् ब्रह्म ह्यवर्तत ।
दुरितक्षयो महावीर्यात् तस्य त्रय्यारुणिः कविः ॥१९॥
पुष्करारुणिरित्यत्र ये ब्राह्मणगतिं गताः ।
बृहत्क्षत्रस्य पुत्रोऽभूद्धस्ती यद्धास्तिनापुरम् ॥२०॥

gargāc chinis tato gārgyaḥ
kṣatrād brahma hy avartata
duritakṣayo mahāvīryāt
tasya trayyāruṇiḥ kaviḥ

puṣkarāruṇir ity atra
ye brāhmaṇa-gatiṁ gatāḥ
bṛhatkṣatrasya putro 'bhūd
dhastī yad-dhastināpuram

gargāt—from Garga (another grandson of Bharadvāja); *śiniḥ*—a son named Śini; *tataḥ*—from him (Śini); *gārgyaḥ*—a son named Gārgya; *kṣatrāt*—although he was a *kṣatriya; brahma*—the *brāhmaṇas; hi*—indeed; *avartata*—became possible; *duritakṣayaḥ*—a son named Duritakṣaya; *mahāvīryāt*—from Mahāvīrya (another grandson of Bharadvāja); *tasya*—his; *trayyāruṇiḥ*—the son named Trayyāruṇi; *kaviḥ*—a son named Kavi; *puṣkarāruṇiḥ*—a son named Puṣkarāruṇi; *iti*—thus; *atra*—therein; *ye*—all of them; *brāhmaṇa-gatim*—the position of *brāhmaṇas; gatāḥ*—achieved; *bṛhatkṣatrasya*—of the grandson of Bharadvāja named Bṛhatkṣatra; *putraḥ*—the son; *abhūt*—became; *hastī*—Hastī; *yat*—from whom; *hastināpuram*—the city of Hastināpura (New Delhi) was established.

TRANSLATION

From Garga came a son named Śini, and his son was Gārgya. Although Gārgya was a kṣatriya, there came from him a generation of brāhmaṇas. From Mahāvīrya came a son named Duritakṣaya, whose sons were Trayyāruṇi, Kavi and Puṣkarāruṇi. Although these sons of Duritakṣaya took birth in a dynasty of kṣatriyas, they too attained the position of brāhmaṇas. Bṛhatkṣatra had a son named Hastī, who established the city of Hastināpura [now New Delhi].

TEXT 21

अजमीढो द्विमीढश्च पुरुमीढश्च हस्तिनः ।
अजमीढस्य वंश्याः स्युः प्रियमेधादयो द्विजाः ॥२१॥

ajamīḍho dvimīḍhaś ca
purumīḍhaś ca hastinaḥ
ajamīḍhasya vaṁśyāḥ syuḥ
priyamedhādayo dvijāḥ

ajamīḍhaḥ—Ajamīḍha; *dvimīḍhaḥ*—Dvimīḍha; *ca*—also; *purumīḍhaḥ*—Purumīḍha; *ca*—also; *hastinaḥ*—became the sons of Hastī; *ajamīḍhasya*—of Ajamīḍha; *vaṁśyāḥ*—descendants; *syuḥ*—are; *priyamedha-ādayaḥ*—headed by Priyamedha; *dvijāḥ*—*brāhmaṇas.*

TRANSLATION

From King Hastī came three sons, named Ajamīḍha, Dvimīḍha and Purumīḍha. The descendants of Ajamīḍha, headed by Priyamedha, all achieved the position of brāhmaṇas.

PURPORT

This verse gives evidence confirming the statement of *Bhagavad-gītā* that the orders of society—*brāhmaṇa, kṣatriya, vaiśya* and *śūdra*—are calculated in terms of qualities and activities (*guṇa-karma-vibhāgaśaḥ*). All the descendants of Ajamīḍha, who was a *kṣatriya,* became *brāhmaṇas.* This was certainly because of their qualities and activities. Similarly, sometimes the sons of *brāhmaṇas* or *kṣatriyas* become *vaiśyas* (*brāhmaṇā vaiśyatāṁ gatāḥ*). When a *kṣatriya* or *brāhmaṇa* adopts the occupation or duty of a *vaiśya* (*kṛṣi-gorakṣya-vāṇijyam*), he is certainly counted as a *vaiśya.* On the other hand, if one is born a *vaiśya,* by his activities he can become a *brāhmaṇa.* This is confirmed by Nārada Muni. *Yasya yal-lakṣaṇaṁ proktam.* The members of the *varṇas,* or social orders—*brāhmaṇa, kṣatriya, vaiśya* and *śūdra*—must be ascertained by their symptoms, not by birth. Birth is immaterial; quality is essential.

TEXT 22

अजमीढाद् बृहदिषुस्तस्य पुत्रो बृहद्धनुः ।
बृहत्कायस्ततस्तस्य पुत्र आसीज्जयद्रथः ॥२२॥

ajamīḍhād bṛhadiṣus
tasya putro bṛhaddhanuḥ
bṛhatkāyas tatas tasya
putra āsīj jayadrathaḥ

ajamīḍhāt—from Ajamīḍha; *bṛhadiṣuḥ*—a son named Bṛhadiṣu; *tasya*—his; *putraḥ*—son; *bṛhaddhanuḥ*—Bṛhaddhanu; *bṛhatkāyaḥ*—Bṛhatkāya; *tataḥ*—thereafter; *tasya*—his; *putraḥ*—son; *āsīt*—was; *jayadrathaḥ*—Jayadratha.

TRANSLATION

From Ajamīḍha came a son named Bṛhadiṣu, from Bṛhadiṣu came a son named Bṛhaddhanu, from Bṛhaddhanu a son named Bṛhatkāya, and from Bṛhatkāya a son named Jayadratha.

TEXT 23

तत्सुतो विशदस्तस्य स्येनजित् समजायत ।
रुचिराश्वो दृढहनुः काश्यो वत्सश्च तत्सुताः ॥२३॥

tat-suto viśadas tasya
syenajit samajāyata
rucirāśvo dṛḍhahanuḥ
kāśyo vatsaś ca tat-sutāḥ

tat-sutaḥ—the son of Jayadratha; *viśadaḥ*—Viśada; *tasya*—the son of Viśada; *syenajit*—Syenajit; *samajāyata*—was born; *rucirāśvaḥ*—Rucirāśva; *dṛḍhahanuḥ*—Dṛḍhahanu; *kāśyaḥ*—Kāśya; *vatsaḥ*—Vatsa; *ca*—also; *tat-sutāḥ*—sons of Syenajit.

TRANSLATION

The son of Jayadratha was Viśada, and his son was Syenajit. The sons of Syenajit were Rucirāśva, Dṛḍhahanu, Kāśya and Vatsa.

TEXT 24

रुचिराश्वसुतः पारः पृथुसेनस्तदात्मजः ।
पारस्य तनयो नीपस्तस्य पुत्रशतं त्वभूत् ॥२४॥

rucirāśva-sutaḥ pāraḥ
pṛthusenas tad-ātmajaḥ

pārasya tanayo nīpas
tasya putra-śataṁ tv abhūt

rucirāśva-sutaḥ—the son of Rucirāśva; *pāraḥ*—Pāra; *pṛthusenaḥ*—Pṛthusena; *tat*—his; *ātmajaḥ*—son; *pārasya*—from Pāra; *tanayaḥ*—a son; *nīpaḥ*—Nīpa; *tasya*—his; *putra-śatam*—one hundred sons; *tu*—indeed; *abhūt*—generated.

TRANSLATION

The son of Rucirāśva was Pāra, and the sons of Pāra were Pṛthusena and Nīpa. Nīpa had one hundred sons.

TEXT 25

स कृत्व्यां शुककन्यायां ब्रह्मदत्तमजीजनत् ।
योगी स गवि भार्यायां विष्वक्सेनमधात् सुतम् ॥२५॥

sa kṛtvyāṁ śuka-kanyāyāṁ
brahmadattam ajījanat
yogī sa gavi bhāryāyāṁ
viṣvaksenam adhāt sutam

saḥ—he (King Nīpa); *kṛtvyām*—in his wife, Kṛtvī; *śuka-kanyāyām*—who was the daughter of Śuka; *brahmadattam*—a son named Brahmadatta; *ajījanat*—begot; *yogī*—a mystic *yogī; saḥ*—that Brahmadatta; *gavi*—by the name Gau or Sarasvatī; *bhāryāyām*—in the womb of his wife; *viṣvaksenam*—Viṣvaksena; *adhāt*—begot; *sutam*—a son.

TRANSLATION

King Nīpa begot a son named Brahmadatta through the womb of his wife, Kṛtvī, who was the daughter of Śuka. And Brahmadatta, who was a great yogī, begot a son named Viṣvaksena through the womb of his wife, Sarasvatī.

PURPORT

The Śuka mentioned here is different from the Śukadeva Gosvāmī who spoke *Śrīmad-Bhāgavatam.* Śukadeva Gosvāmī, the son of

Vyāsadeva, is described in great detail in the *Brahma-vaivarta Purāṇa*. There it is said that Vyāsadeva maintained the daughter of Jābāli as his wife and that after they performed penances together for many years, he placed his seed in her womb. The child remained in the womb of his mother for twelve years, and when the father asked the son to come out, the son replied that he would not come out unless he were completely liberated from the influence of *māyā*. Vyāsadeva then assured the child that he would not be influenced by *māyā*, but the child did not believe his father, for the father was still attached to his wife and children. Vyāsadeva then went to Dvārakā and informed the Personality of Godhead about his problem, and the Personality of Godhead, at Vyāsadeva's request, went to Vyāsadeva's cottage, where He assured the child in the womb that he would not be influenced by *māyā*. Thus assured, the child came out, but he immediately went away as a *parivrājakācārya*. When the father, very much aggrieved, began to follow his saintly boy, Śukadeva Gosvāmī, the boy created a duplicate Śukadeva, who later entered family life. Therefore, the *śuka-kanyā*, or daughter of Śukadeva, mentioned in this verse is the daughter of the duplicate or imitation Śukadeva. The original Śukadeva was a lifelong *brahmacārī*.

TEXT 26

जैगीषव्योपदेशेन योगतन्त्रं चकार ह ।
उदक्सेनस्ततस्तस्माद् भल्लाटो बार्हदीषवाः ॥२६॥

jaigīṣavyopadeśena
yoga-tantraṁ cakāra ha
udaksenas tatas tasmād
bhallāṭo bārhadīṣavāḥ

jaigīṣavya—of the great *ṛṣi* named Jaigīṣavya; *upadeśena*—by the instruction; *yoga-tantram*—an elaborate description of the mystic *yoga* system; *cakāra*—compiled; *ha*—in the past; *udaksenaḥ*—Udaksena; *tataḥ*—from him (Viṣvaksena); *tasmāt*—from him (Udaksena); *bhallāṭaḥ*—a son named Bhallāṭa; *bārhadīṣavāḥ*—(all of these are known as) descendants of Bṛhadiṣu.

TRANSLATION

Following the instructions of the great sage Jaigīṣavya, Viṣvaksena compiled an elaborate description of the mystic yoga system. From Viṣvaksena, Udaksena was born, and from Udaksena, Bhallāṭa. All these sons are known as descendants of Bṛhadiṣu.

TEXT 27

यवीनरो द्विमीढस्य कृतिमांस्तत्सुतः स्मृतः ।
नाम्ना सत्यधृतिस्तस्य दृढनेमिः सुपार्श्वकृत् ॥२७॥

yavīnaro dvimīḍhasya
kṛtimāṁs tat-sutaḥ smṛtaḥ
nāmnā satyadhṛtis tasya
dṛḍhanemiḥ supārśvakṛt

yavīnaraḥ—Yavīnara; *dvimīḍhasya*—the son of Dvimīḍha; *kṛtimān*—Kṛtimān; *tat-sutaḥ*—the son of Yavīnara; *smṛtaḥ*—is well known; *nāmnā*—by name; *satyadhṛtiḥ*—Satyadhṛti; *tasya*—of him (Satyadhṛti); *dṛḍhanemiḥ*—Dṛḍhanemi; *supārśva-kṛt*—the father of Supārśva.

TRANSLATION

The son of Dvimīḍha was Yavīnara, whose son was Kṛtimān. The son of Kṛtimān was well known as Satyadhṛti. From Satyadhṛti came a son named Dṛḍhanemi, who became the father of Supārśva.

TEXTS 28–29

सुपार्श्वात् सुमतिस्तस्य पुत्रः सन्नतिमांस्ततः ।
कृती हिरण्यनाभाद् यो योगं प्राप्य जगौ स्म षट्॥२८॥
संहिताः प्राच्यसाम्नां वै नीपो ह्युद्ग्रायुधस्ततः ।
तस्य क्षेम्यः सुवीरोऽथ सुवीरस्य रिपुञ्जयः ॥२९॥

supārśvāt sumatis tasya
putraḥ sannatimāṁs tataḥ

kṛtī hiraṇyanābhād yo
yogaṁ prāpya jagau sma ṣaṭ

saṁhitāḥ prācyasāmnāṁ vai
nīpo hy udgrāyudhas tataḥ
tasya kṣemyaḥ suvīro 'tha
suvīrasya ripuñjayaḥ

supārśvāt—from Supārśva; *sumatiḥ*—a son named Sumati; *tasya putraḥ*—his son (Sumati's son); *sannatimān*—Sannatimān; *tataḥ*—from him; *kṛtī*—a son named Kṛtī; *hiraṇyanābhāt*—from Lord Brahmā; *yaḥ*—he who; *yogam*—mystic power; *prāpya*—getting; *jagau*—taught; *sma*—in the past; *ṣaṭ*—six; *saṁhitāḥ*—descriptions; *prācyasāmnām*—of the Prācyasāma verses of the *Sāma Veda; vai*—indeed; *nīpaḥ*—Nīpa; *hi*—indeed; *udgrāyudhaḥ*—Udgrāyudha; *tataḥ*—from him; *tasya*—his; *kṣemyaḥ*—Kṣemya; *suvīraḥ*—Suvīra; *atha*—thereafter; *suvīrasya*—of Suvīra; *ripuñjayaḥ*—a son named Ripuñjaya.

TRANSLATION

From Supārśva came a son named Sumati, from Sumati came Sannatimān, and from Sannatimān came Kṛtī, who achieved mystic power from Brahmā and taught six saṁhitās of the Prācyasāma verses of the Sāma Veda. The son of Kṛtī was Nīpa; the son of Nīpa, Udgrāyudha; the son of Udgrāyudha, Kṣemya; the son of Kṣemya, Suvīra; and the son of Suvīra, Ripuñjaya.

TEXT 30

ततो बहुरथो नाम पुरुमीढोऽप्रजोऽभवत् ।
नलिन्यामजमीढस्य नीलः शान्तिस्तु तत्सुतः ॥३०॥

tato bahuratho nāma
purumīḍho 'prajo 'bhavat
nalinyām ajamīḍhasya
nīlaḥ śāntis tu tat-sutaḥ

tataḥ—from him (Ripuñjaya); *bahurathaḥ*—Bahuratha; *nāma*—named; *purumīḍhaḥ*—Purumīḍha, the younger brother of Dvimīḍha; *aprajaḥ*—sonless; *abhavat*—became; *nalinyām*—through Nalinī; *ajamīḍhasya*—of Ajamīḍha; *nīlaḥ*—Nīla; *śāntiḥ*—Śānti; *tu*—then; *tat-sutaḥ*—the son of Nīla.

TRANSLATION

From Ripuñjaya came a son named Bahuratha. Purumīḍha was sonless. Ajamīḍha had a son named Nīla by his wife known as Nalinī, and the son of Nīla was Śānti.

TEXTS 31–33

शान्तेः सुशान्तिस्तत्पुत्रः पुरुजोऽर्कस्ततोऽभवत् ।
भर्म्याश्वस्तनयस्तस्य पञ्चासन्मुद्गलादयः ॥३१॥
यवीनरो बृहद्विश्वः काम्पिल्लः संजयः सुताः ।
भर्म्याश्वः प्राह पुत्रा मे पञ्चानां रक्षणाय हि ॥३२॥
विषयाणामलमिमे इति पञ्चालसंज्ञिताः ।
मुद्गलाद् ब्रह्म निर्वृत्तं गोत्रं मौद्गल्यसंज्ञितम् ॥३३॥

śānteḥ suśāntis tat-putraḥ
purujo 'rkas tato 'bhavat
bharmyāśvas tanayas tasya
pañcāsan mudgalādayaḥ

yavīnaro bṛhadviśvaḥ
kāmpillaḥ sañjayaḥ sutāḥ
bharmyāśvaḥ prāha putrā me
pañcānāṁ rakṣaṇāya hi

viṣayāṇām alam ime
iti pañcāla-saṁjñitāḥ
mudgalād brahma-nirvṛttaṁ
gotraṁ maudgalya-saṁjñitam

śānteḥ—of Śānti; *suśāntiḥ*—Suśānti; *tat-putraḥ*—his son; *purujaḥ*—Puruja; *arkaḥ*—Arka; *tataḥ*—from him; *abhavat*—generated; *bharmyāśvaḥ*—Bharmyāśva; *tanayaḥ*—son; *tasya*—of him; *pañca*—five sons; *āsan*—were; *mudgala-ādayaḥ*—headed by Mudgala; *yavīnaraḥ*—Yavīnara; *bṛhadviśvaḥ*—Bṛhadviśva; *kāmpillaḥ*—Kāmpilla; *sañjayaḥ*—Sañjaya; *sutāḥ*—sons; *bharmyāśvaḥ*—Bharmyāśva; *prāha*—said; *putrāḥ*—sons; *me*—my; *pañcānām*—of five; *rakṣaṇāya*—for protection; *hi*—indeed; *viṣayāṇām*—of different states; *alam*—competent; *ime*—all of them; *iti*—thus; *pañcāla*—Pañcāla; *saṁjñitāḥ*—designated; *mudgalāt*—from Mudgala; *brahma-nirvṛttam*—consisting of *brāhmaṇas; gotram*—a dynasty; *maudgalya*—Maudgalya; *saṁjñitam*—so designated.

TRANSLATION

The son of Śānti was Suśānti, the son of Suśānti was Puruja, and the son of Puruja was Arka. From Arka came Bharmyāśva, and from Bharmyāśva came five sons—Mudgala, Yavīnara, Bṛhadviśva, Kāmpilla and Sañjaya. Bharmyāśva prayed to his sons, "O my sons, please take charge of my five states, for you are quite competent to do so." Thus his five sons were known as the Pañcālas. From Mudgala came a dynasty of brāhmaṇas known as Maudgalya.

TEXT 34

मिथुनं मुद्गलाद् भार्म्याद् दिवोदासः पुमानभूत् ।
अहल्या कन्यका यस्यां शतानन्दस्तु गौतमात् ॥३४॥

mithunaṁ mudgalād bhārmyād
divodāsaḥ pumān abhūt
ahalyā kanyakā yasyāṁ
śatānandas tu gautamāt

mithunam—twins, one male and one female; *mudgalāt*—from Mudgala; *bhārmyāt*—the son of Bharmyāśva; *divodāsaḥ*—Divodāsa; *pumān*—the male one; *abhūt*—generated; *ahalyā*—Ahalyā; *kanyakā*—the female; *yasyām*—through whom; *śatānandaḥ*—Śatānanda; *tu*—indeed; *gautamāt*—generated by her husband, Gautama.

TRANSLATION

Mudgala, the son of Bharmyāśva, had twin children, one male and the other female. The male child was named Divodāsa, and the female child was named Ahalyā. From the womb of Ahalyā by the semen of her husband, Gautama, came a son named Śatānanda.

TEXT 35

तस्य सत्यधृतिः पुत्रो धनुर्वेदविशारदः ।
शरद्वांस्तत्सुतो यस्मादुर्वशीदर्शनात् किल ।
शरस्तम्बेऽपतद् रेतो मिथुनं तदभूच्छुभम् ॥३५॥

tasya satyadhṛtiḥ putro
dhanur-veda-viśāradaḥ
śaradvāṁs tat-suto yasmād
urvaśī-darśanāt kila
śara-stambe 'patad reto
mithunaṁ tad abhūc chubham

tasya—of him (Śatānanda); *satyadhṛtiḥ*—Satyadhṛti; *putraḥ*—a son; *dhanuḥ-veda-viśāradaḥ*—very expert in the art of archery; *śaradvān*—Śaradvān; *tat-sutaḥ*—the son of Satyadhṛti; *yasmāt*—from whom; *urvaśī-darśanāt*—simply by seeing the celestial Urvaśī; *kila*—indeed; *śara-stambe*—on a clump of *śara* grass; *apatat*—fell; *retaḥ*—semen; *mithunam*—a male and female; *tat abhūt*—there were born; *śubham*—all-auspicious.

TRANSLATION

The son of Śatānanda was Satyadhṛti, who was expert in archery, and the son of Satyadhṛti was Śaradvān. When Śaradvān met Urvaśī, he discharged semen, which fell on a clump of śara grass. From this semen were born two all-auspicious babies, one male and the other female.

TEXT 36

तद् दृष्ट्वा कृपयागृह्णाच्छान्तनुर्मृगयां चरन् ।
कृपः कुमारः कन्या च द्रोणपत्न्यभवत् कृपी ॥३६॥

tad dṛṣṭvā kṛpayāgṛhṇāc
chāntanur mṛgayāṁ caran
kṛpaḥ kumāraḥ kanyā ca
droṇa-patny abhavat kṛpī

tat—those twin male and female babies; *dṛṣṭvā*—seeing; *kṛpayā*—out of compassion; *agṛhṇāt*—took; *śāntanuḥ*—King Śāntanu; *mṛgayām*—while hunting in the forest; *caran*—wandering in that way; *kṛpaḥ*—Kṛpa; *kumāraḥ*—the male child; *kanyā*—the female child; *ca*—also; *droṇa-patnī*—the wife of Droṇācārya; *abhavat*—became; *kṛpī*—named Kṛpī.

TRANSLATION

While Mahārāja Śāntanu was on a hunting excursion, he saw the male and female children lying in the forest, and out of compassion he took them home. Consequently, the male child was known as Kṛpa, and the female child was named Kṛpī. Kṛpī later became the wife of Droṇācārya.

Thus end the Bhaktivedanta purports of the Ninth Canto, Twenty-first Chapter, of the Śrīmad-Bhāgavatam, *entitled "The Dynasty of Bharata."*

CHAPTER TWENTY-TWO

The Descendants of Ajamīḍha

This chapter describes the descendants of Divodāsa. It also describes Jarāsandha, who belonged to the Ṛkṣa dynasty, as well as Duryodhana, Arjuna and others.

The son of Divodāsa was Mitrāyu, who had four sons, one after another—Cyavana, Sudāsa, Sahadeva and Somaka. Somaka had one hundred sons, of whom the youngest was Pṛṣata, from whom Drupada was born. Drupada's daughter was Draupadī, and his sons were headed by Dhṛṣṭadyumna. Dhṛṣṭadyumna's son was Dhṛṣṭaketu.

Another son of Ajamīḍha was named Ṛkṣa. From Ṛkṣa came a son named Saṁvaraṇa, and from Saṁvaraṇa came Kuru, the king of Kurukṣetra. Kuru had four sons—Parīkṣi, Sudhanu, Jahnu and Niṣadha. Among the descendants in the dynasty from Sudhanu were Suhotra, Cyavana, Kṛtī and Uparicara Vasu. The sons of Uparicara Vasu, including Bṛhadratha, Kuśāmba, Matsya, Pratyagra and Cedipa, became kings of the Cedi state. In the dynasty from Bṛhadratha came Kuśāgra, Ṛṣabha, Satyahita, Puṣpavān and Jahu, and from Bṛhadratha through the womb of another wife came Jarāsandha, who was followed by Sahadeva, Somāpi and Śrutaśravā. Parīkṣi, the son of Kuru, had no sons. Among the descendants of Jahnu were Suratha, Vidūratha, Sārvabhauma, Jayasena, Rādhika, Ayutāyu, Akrodhana, Devātithi, Ṛkṣa, Dilīpa and Pratīpa.

The sons of Pratīpa were Devāpi, Śāntanu and Bāhlīka. When Devāpi retired to the forest, his younger brother Śāntanu became the king. Although Śāntanu, being younger, was not eligible to occupy the throne, he disregarded his elder brother. Consequently, there was no rainfall for twelve years. Following the advice of the *brāhmaṇas*, Śāntanu was ready to return the kingdom to Devāpi, but by the intrigue of Śāntanu's minister, Devāpi became unfit to be king. Therefore Śāntanu resumed charge of the kingdom, and rain fell properly during his regime. By mystic power, Devāpi still lives in the village known as Kalāpa-grāma. In this Kali-yuga, when the descendants of Soma known as the *candra-vaṁśa* (the lunar dynasty) die out, Devāpi, at the beginning of

Satya-yuga, will reestablish the dynasty of the moon. The wife of Śāntanu named Gaṅgā gave birth to Bhīṣma, one of the twelve authorities. Two sons named Citrāṅgada and Vicitravīrya were also born from the womb of Satyavatī by the semen of Śāntanu, and Vyāsadeva was born from Satyavatī by the semen of Parāśara. Vyāsadeva instructed the history of the *Bhāgavatam* to his son Śukadeva. Through the womb of the two wives and the maidservant of Vicitravīrya, Vyāsadeva begot Dhṛtarāṣṭra, Pāṇḍu and Vidura.

Dhṛtarāṣṭra had one hundred sons, headed by Duryodhana, and one daughter named Duḥśalā. Pāṇḍu had five sons, headed by Yudhiṣṭhira, and each of these five sons had one son from Draupadī. The names of these sons of Draupadī were Prativindhya, Śrutasena, Śrutakīrti, Śatānīka and Śrutakarmā. Besides these five sons, by other wives the Pāṇḍavas had many other sons, such as Devaka, Ghaṭotkaca, Sarvagata, Suhotra, Naramitra, Irāvān, Babhruvāhana and Abhimanyu. From Abhimanyu, Mahārāja Parīkṣit was born, and Mahārāja Parīkṣit had four sons—Janamejaya, Śrutasena, Bhīmasena and Ugrasena.

Next Śukadeva Gosvāmī described the future sons of the Pāṇḍu family. From Janamejaya, he said, would come a son named Śatānīka, and following in the dynasty would be Sahasrānīka, Aśvamedhaja, Asīmakṛṣṇa, Nemicakra, Citraratha, Śuciratha, Vṛṣṭimān, Suṣeṇa, Sunītha, Nṛcakṣu, Sukhīnala, Pariplava, Sunaya, Medhāvī, Nṛpañjaya, Dūrva, Timi, Bṛhadratha, Sudāsa, Śatānīka, Durdamana, Mahīnara, Daṇḍapāṇi, Nimi and Kṣemaka.

Śukadeva Gosvāmī then predicted the kings of the *māgadha-vaṁśa*, or Māgadha dynasty. Sahadeva, the son of Jarāsandha, would beget Mārjāri, and from him would come Śrutaśravā. Subsequently taking birth in the dynasty will be Yutāyu, Niramitra, Sunakṣatra, Bṛhatsena, Karmajit, Sutañjaya, Vipra, Śuci, Kṣema, Suvrata, Dharmasūtra, Sama, Dyumatsena, Sumati, Subala, Sunītha, Satyajit, Viśvajit and Ripuñjaya.

TEXT 1

श्रीशुक उवाच

मित्रायुश्च दिवोदासाच्च्यवनस्तत्सुतो नृप ।
सुदासः सहदेवोऽथ सोमको जन्तुजन्मकृत् ॥ १ ॥

śrī-śuka uvāca
mitrāyuś ca divodāsāc
cyavanas tat-suto nṛpa
sudāsaḥ sahadevo 'tha
somako jantu-janmakṛt

śrī-śukaḥ uvāca—Śrī Śukadeva Gosvāmī said; *mitrāyuḥ*—Mitrāyu; *ca*—and; *divodāsāt*—was born from Divodāsa; *cyavanaḥ*—Cyavana; *tat-sutaḥ*—the son of Mitrāyu; *nṛpa*—O King; *sudāsaḥ*—Sudāsa; *sahadevaḥ*—Sahadeva; *atha*—thereafter; *somakaḥ*—Somaka; *jantu-janma-kṛt*—the father of Jantu.

TRANSLATION

Śukadeva Gosvāmī said: O King, the son of Divodāsa was Mitrāyu, and from Mitrāyu came four sons, named Cyavana, Sudāsa, Sahadeva and Somaka. Somaka was the father of Jantu.

TEXT 2

तस्य पुत्रशतं तेषां यवीयान् पृषतः सुतः ।
स तस्माद् द्रुपदो जज्ञे सर्वसम्पत्समन्वितः॥ २ ॥

tasya putra-śataṁ teṣāṁ
yavīyān pṛṣataḥ sutaḥ
sa tasmād drupado jajñe
sarva-sampat-samanvitaḥ

tasya—of him (Somaka); *putra-śatam*—one hundred sons; *teṣām*—of all of them; *yavīyān*—the youngest; *pṛṣataḥ*—Pṛṣata; *sutaḥ*—the son; *saḥ*—he; *tasmāt*—from him (Pṛṣata); *drupadaḥ*—Drupada; *jajñe*—was born; *sarva-sampat*—with all opulences; *samanvitaḥ*—decorated.

TRANSLATION

Somaka had one hundred sons, of whom the youngest was Pṛṣata. From Pṛṣata was born King Drupada, who was opulent in all supremacy.

TEXT 3

द्रुपदाद् द्रौपदी तस्य धृष्टद्युम्नादयः सुताः ।
धृष्टद्युम्नाद् धृष्टकेतुर्भार्म्याः पाञ्चालका इमे ॥ ३ ॥

drupadād draupadī tasya
dhṛṣṭadyumnādayaḥ sutāḥ
dhṛṣṭadyumnād dhṛṣṭaketur
bhārmyāḥ pāñcālakā ime

drupadāt—from Drupada; *draupadī*—Draupadī, the famous wife of the Pāṇḍavas; *tasya*—of him (Drupada); *dhṛṣṭadyumna-ādayaḥ*—headed by Dhṛṣṭadyumna; *sutāḥ*—sons; *dhṛṣṭadyumnāt*—from Dhṛṣṭadyumna; *dhṛṣṭaketuḥ*—the son named Dhṛṣṭaketu; *bhārmyāḥ*—all descendants of Bharmyāśva; *pāñcālakāḥ*—they are known as the Pāñcālakas; *ime*—all of these.

TRANSLATION

From Mahārāja Drupada, Draupadī was born. Mahārāja Drupada also had many sons, headed by Dhṛṣṭadyumna. From Dhṛṣṭadyumna came a son named Dhṛṣṭaketu. All these personalities are known as descendants of Bharmyāśva or as the dynasty of Pāñcāla.

TEXTS 4–5

योऽजमीढसुतो ह्यन्य ऋक्षः संवरणस्ततः ।
तपत्यां सूर्यकन्यायां कुरुक्षेत्रपतिः कुरुः ॥ ४ ॥
परीक्षिः सुधनुर्जह्नुर्निषधश्च कुरोः सुताः ।
सुहोत्रोऽभूत् सुधनुषश्च्यवनोऽथ ततः कृती ॥ ५ ॥

yo 'jamīḍha-suto hy anya
ṛkṣaḥ saṁvaraṇas tataḥ
tapatyāṁ sūrya-kanyāyāṁ
kurukṣetra-patiḥ kuruḥ

parīkṣiḥ sudhanur jahnur
niṣadhaś ca kuroḥ sutāḥ
suhotro 'bhūt sudhanuṣaś
cyavano 'tha tataḥ kṛtī

yaḥ—who; *ajamīḍha-sutaḥ*—was a son born from Ajamīḍha; *hi*—indeed; *anyaḥ*—another; *ṛkṣaḥ*—Ṛkṣa; *saṁvaraṇaḥ*—Saṁvaraṇa; *tataḥ*—from him (Ṛkṣa); *tapatyām*—Tapatī; *sūrya-kanyāyām*—in the womb of the daughter of the sun-god; *kurukṣetra-patiḥ*—the King of Kurukṣetra; *kuruḥ*—Kuru was born; *parīkṣiḥ sudhanuḥ jahnuḥ niṣadhaḥ ca*—Parīkṣi, Sudhanu, Jahnu and Niṣadha; *kuroḥ*—of Kuru; *sutāḥ*—the sons; *suhotraḥ*—Suhotra; *abhūt*—was born; *sudhanuṣaḥ*—from Sudhanu; *cyavanaḥ*—Cyavana; *atha*—from Suhotra; *tataḥ*—from him (Cyavana); *kṛtī*—a son named Kṛtī.

TRANSLATION

Another son of Ajamīḍha was known as Ṛkṣa. From Ṛkṣa came a son named Saṁvaraṇa, and from Saṁvaraṇa through the womb of his wife, Tapatī, the daughter of the sun-god, came Kuru, the King of Kurukṣetra. Kuru had four sons—Parīkṣi, Sudhanu, Jahnu and Niṣadha. From Sudhanu, Suhotra was born, and from Suhotra, Cyavana. From Cyavana, Kṛtī was born.

TEXT 6

वसुस्तस्योपरिचरो बृहद्रथमुखास्ततः ।
कुशाम्बमत्स्यप्रत्यग्रचेदिपाद्याश्च चेदिपाः ॥ ६ ॥

vasus tasyoparicaro
bṛhadratha-mukhās tataḥ
kuśāmba-matsya-pratyagra-
cedipādyāś ca cedipāḥ

vasuḥ—a son named Vasu; *tasya*—of him (Kṛtī); *uparicaraḥ*—the surname of Vasu; *bṛhadratha-mukhāḥ*—headed by Bṛhadratha; *tataḥ*—from him (Vasu); *kuśāmba*—Kuśāmba; *matsya*—Matsya; *pratyagra*—

Pratyagra; *cedipa-ādyāḥ*—Cedipa and others; *ca*—also; *cedi-pāḥ*—all of them became rulers of the Cedi state.

TRANSLATION

The son of Kṛtī was Uparicara Vasu, and among his sons, headed by Bṛhadratha, were Kuśāmba, Matsya, Pratyagra and Cedipa. All the sons of Uparicara Vasu became rulers of the Cedi state.

TEXT 7

बृहद्रथात् कुशाग्रोऽभूदृषभस्तस्य तत्सुतः ।
जज्ञे सत्यहितोऽपत्यं पुष्पवांस्तत्सुतो जहुः ॥ ७ ॥

bṛhadrathāt kuśāgro 'bhūd
ṛṣabhas tasya tat-sutaḥ
jajñe satyahito 'patyaṁ
puṣpavāṁs tat-suto jahuḥ

bṛhadrathāt—from Bṛhadratha; *kuśāgraḥ*—Kuśāgra; *abhūt*—a son was born; *ṛṣabhaḥ*—Ṛṣabha; *tasya*—of him (Kuśāgra); *tat-sutaḥ*—his (Ṛṣabha's) son; *jajñe*—was born; *satyahitaḥ*—Satyahita; *apatyam*—offspring; *puṣpavān*—Puṣpavān; *tat-sutaḥ*—his (Puṣpavān's) son; *jahuḥ*—Jahu.

TRANSLATION

From Bṛhadratha, Kuśāgra was born; from Kuśāgra, Ṛṣabha; and from Ṛṣabha, Satyahita. The son of Satyahita was Puṣpavān, and the son of Puṣpavān was Jahu.

TEXT 8

अन्यस्यामपि भार्यायां शकले द्वे बृहद्रथात् ।
ये मात्रा बहिरुत्सृष्टे जरया चाभिसन्धिते ।
जीव जीवेति क्रीडन्त्या जरासन्धोऽभवत् सुतः ॥ ८ ॥

anyasyām api bhāryāyāṁ
śakale dve bṛhadrathāt
ye mātrā bahir utsṛṣṭe
jarayā cābhisandhite
jīva jīveti krīḍantyā
jarāsandho 'bhavat sutaḥ

anyasyām—in another; *api*—also; *bhāryāyām*—wife; *śakale*—parts; *dve*—two; *bṛhadrathāt*—from Bṛhadratha; *ye*—which two parts; *mātrā*—by the mother; *bahiḥ utsṛṣṭe*—because of rejection; *jarayā*—by the demoness named Jarā; *ca*—and; *abhisandhite*—when they were joined together; *jīva jīva iti*—O living entity, be alive; *krīḍantyā*—playing like that; *jarāsandhaḥ*—Jarāsandha; *abhavat*—was generated; *sutaḥ*—a son.

TRANSLATION

Through the womb of another wife, Bṛhadratha begot two halves of a son. When the mother saw those two halves she rejected them, but later a she-demon named Jarā playfully joined them and said, "Come to life, come to life!" Thus the son named Jarāsandha was born.

TEXT 9

ततश्च सहदेवोऽभूत् सोमापिर्यच्छ्रुतश्रवाः ।
परीक्षिरनपत्योऽभूत् सुरथो नाम जाह्नवः ॥ ९ ॥

tataś ca sahadevo 'bhūt
somāpir yac chrutaśravāḥ
parīkṣir anapatyo 'bhūt
suratho nāma jāhnavaḥ

tataḥ ca—and from him (Jarāsandha); *sahadevaḥ*—Sahadeva; *abhūt*—was born; *somāpiḥ*—Somāpi; *yat*—of him (Somāpi); *śrutaśravāḥ*—a son named Śrutaśravā; *parīkṣiḥ*—the son of Kuru named Parīkṣi; *anapatyaḥ*—without any son; *abhūt*—became; *surathaḥ*—Suratha; *nāma*—named; *jāhnavaḥ*—was the son of Jahnu.

TRANSLATION

From Jarāsandha came a son named Sahadeva; from Sahadeva, Somāpi; and from Somāpi, Śrutaśravā. The son of Kuru called Parīkṣi had no sons, but the son of Kuru called Jahnu had a son named Suratha.

TEXT 10

ततो विदूरथस्तस्मात् सार्वभौमस्ततोऽभवत् ।
जयसेनस्तत्तनयो राधिकोऽतोऽयुताय्वभूत् ॥१०॥

tato vidūrathas tasmāt
sārvabhaumas tato 'bhavat
jayasenas tat-tanayo
rādhiko 'to 'yutāyv abhūt

tataḥ—from him (Suratha); *vidūrathaḥ*—a son named Vidūratha; *tasmāt*—from him (Vidūratha); *sārvabhaumaḥ*—a son named Sārvabhauma; *tataḥ*—from him (Sārvabhauma); *abhavat*—was born; *jayasenaḥ*—Jayasena; *tat-tanayaḥ*—the son of Jayasena; *rādhikaḥ*—Rādhika; *ataḥ*—and from him (Rādhika); *ayutāyuḥ*—Ayutāyu; *abhūt*—was born.

TRANSLATION

From Suratha came a son named Vidūratha, from whom Sārvabhauma was born. From Sārvabhauma came Jayasena; from Jayasena, Rādhika; and from Rādhika, Ayutāyu.

TEXT 11

ततश्चाक्रोधनस्तस्माद् देवातिथिरमुष्य च ।
ऋक्षस्तस्य दिलीपोऽभूत् प्रतीपस्तस्य चात्मजः ॥११॥

tataś cākrodhanas tasmād
devātithir amuṣya ca
ṛkṣas tasya dilīpo 'bhūt
pratīpas tasya cātmajaḥ

tataḥ—from him (Ayutāyu); *ca*—and; *akrodhanaḥ*—a son named Akrodhana; *tasmāt*—from him (Akrodhana); *devātithiḥ*—a son named Devātithi; *amuṣya*—of him (Devātithi); *ca*—also; *ṛkṣaḥ*—Ṛkṣa; *tasya*—of him (Ṛkṣa); *dilīpaḥ*—a son named Dilīpa; *abhūt*—was born; *pratīpaḥ*—Pratīpa; *tasya*—of him (Dilīpa); *ca*—and; *ātma-jaḥ*—the son.

TRANSLATION

From Ayutāyu came a son named Akrodhana, and his son was Devātithi. The son of Devātithi was Ṛkṣa, the son of Ṛkṣa was Dilīpa, and the son of Dilīpa was Pratīpa.

TEXTS 12–13

देवापिः शान्तनुस्तस्य बाह्लीक इति चात्मजाः ।
पितृराज्यं परित्यज्य देवापिस्तु वनं गतः ॥१२॥
अभवच्छान्तनू राजा प्राङ्महाभिषसंज्ञितः ।
यं यं कराभ्यां स्पृशति जीर्णं यौवनमेति सः ॥१३॥

devāpiḥ śāntanus tasya
bāhlīka iti cātmajāḥ
pitṛ-rājyaṁ parityajya
devāpis tu vanaṁ gataḥ

abhavac chāntanū rājā
prāṅ mahābhiṣa-saṁjñitaḥ
yaṁ yaṁ karābhyāṁ spṛśati
jīrṇaṁ yauvanam eti saḥ

devāpiḥ—Devāpi; *śāntanuḥ*—Śāntanu; *tasya*—of him (Pratīpa); *bāhlīkaḥ*—Bāhlīka; *iti*—thus; *ca*—also; *ātma-jāḥ*—the sons; *pitṛ-rājyam*—the father's property, the kingdom; *parityajya*—rejecting; *devāpiḥ*—Devāpi, the eldest; *tu*—indeed; *vanam*—to the forest; *gataḥ*—left; *abhavat*—was; *śāntanuḥ*—Śāntanu; *rājā*—the king; *prāk*—before; *mahābhiṣa*—Mahābhiṣa; *saṁjñitaḥ*—most celebrated; *yam yam*—whomever; *karābhyām*—with his hands; *spṛśati*—touched; *jīrṇam*—although very old; *yauvanam*—youth; *eti*—attained; *saḥ*—he.

TRANSLATION

The sons of Pratīpa were Devāpi, Śāntanu and Bāhlīka. Devāpi left the kingdom of his father and went to the forest, and therefore Śāntanu became the king. Śāntanu, who in his previous birth was known as Mahābhiṣa, had the ability to transform anyone from old age to youth simply by touching that person with his hands.

TEXTS 14–15

शान्तिमाप्नोति चैवाग्र्यां कर्मणा तेन शान्तनुः।
समा द्वादश तद्राज्ये न ववर्ष यदा विभुः ॥१४॥
शान्तनुर्ब्राह्मणैरुक्तः परिवेत्तायमग्रभुक् ।
राज्यं देह्यग्रजायाशु पुरराष्ट्रविवृद्धये ॥१५॥

śāntim āpnoti caivāgryāṁ
karmaṇā tena śāntanuḥ
samā dvādaśa tad-rājye
na vavarṣa yadā vibhuḥ

śāntanur brāhmaṇair uktaḥ
parivettāyam agrabhuk
rājyaṁ dehy agrajāyāśu
pura-rāṣṭra-vivṛddhaye

śāntim—youthfulness for sense gratification; *āpnoti*—one gets; *ca*—also; *eva*—indeed; *agryām*—principally; *karmaṇā*—by the touch of his hand; *tena*—because of this; *śāntanuḥ*—known as Śāntanu; *samāḥ*—years; *dvādaśa*—twelve; *tat-rājye*—in his kingdom; *na*—not; *vavarṣa*—sent rain; *yadā*—when; *vibhuḥ*—the controller of the rain, namely the King of heaven, Indra; *śāntanuḥ*—Śāntanu; *brāhmaṇaiḥ*—by the learned *brāhmaṇas; uktaḥ*—when advised; *parivettā*—faulty because of being a usurper; *ayam*—this; *agra-bhuk*—enjoying in spite of your elder brother's being present; *rājyam*—the kingdom; *dehi*—give; *agrajāya*—to your elder brother; *āśu*—immediately; *pura-rāṣṭra*—of your home and the kingdom; *vivṛddhaye*—for elevation.

TRANSLATION

Because the King was able to make everyone happy for sense gratification, primarily by the touch of his hand, his name was Sāntanu. Once, when there was no rainfall in the kingdom for twelve years and the King consulted his learned brahminical advisors, they said, "You are faulty for enjoying the property of your elder brother. For the elevation of your kingdom and home, you should return the kingdom to him."

PURPORT

One cannot enjoy sovereignty or perform an *agnihotra-yajña* in the presence of one's elder brother, or else one becomes a usurper, known as *parivettā.*

TEXTS 16–17

एवमुक्तो द्विजैर्ज्येष्ठं छन्दयामास सोऽब्रवीत् ।
तन्मन्त्रिप्रहितैर्विप्रैर्वेदाद् विभ्रंशितो गिरा ॥१६॥
वेदवादातिवादान् वै तदा देवो ववर्ष ह ।
देवापिर्योगमास्थाय कलापग्राममाश्रितः ॥१७॥

evam ukto dvijair jyeṣṭhaṁ
chandayām āsa so 'bravīt
tan-mantri-prahitair viprair
vedād vibhraṁśito girā

veda-vādātivādān vai
tadā devo vavarṣa ha
devāpir yogam āsthāya
kalāpa-grāmam āśritaḥ

evam—thus (as above mentioned); *uktaḥ*—being advised; *dvijaiḥ*—by the *brāhmaṇas; jyeṣṭham*—unto his eldest brother, Devāpi; *chandayām āsa*—requested to take charge of the kingdom; *saḥ*—he (Devāpi); *abravīt*—said; *tat-mantri*—by Śāntanu's minister; *prahitaiḥ*—instigated; *vipraiḥ*—by the *brāhmaṇas; vedāt*—from the principles of the *Vedas; vibhraṁśitaḥ*—fallen; *girā*—by such words; *veda-vāda-ativādān*—words blaspheming the Vedic injunctions; *vai*—indeed; *tadā*—at that time; *devaḥ*—the demigod; *vavarṣa*—showered rains; *ha*—in the past; *devāpiḥ*—Devāpi; *yogam āsthāya*—accepting the process of mystic *yoga; kalāpa-grāmam*—the village known as Kalāpa; *āśritaḥ*—took shelter of (and is living in even now).

TRANSLATION

When the brāhmaṇas said this, Mahārāja Śāntanu went to the forest and requested his elder brother Devāpi to take charge of the kingdom, for it is the duty of a king to maintain his subjects. Previously, however, Śāntanu's minister Aśvavāra had instigated some brāhmaṇas to induce Devāpi to transgress the injunctions of the Vedas and thus make himself unfit for the post of ruler. The brāhmaṇas deviated Devāpi from the path of the Vedic principles, and therefore when asked by Śāntanu he did not agree to accept the post of ruler. On the contrary, he blasphemed the Vedic principles and therefore became fallen. Under the circumstances, Śāntanu again became the king, and Indra, being pleased, showered rains. Devāpi later took to the path of mystic yoga to control his mind and senses and went to the village named Kalāpagrāma, where he is still living.

TEXTS 18–19

सोमवंशे कलौ नष्टे कृतादौ स्थापयिष्यति ।
बाह्लीकात् सोमदत्तोऽभूद् भूरिर्भूरिश्रवास्ततः ॥१८॥
शलश्च शान्तनोरासीद् गङ्गायां भीष्म आत्मवान् ।
सर्वधर्मविदां श्रेष्ठो महाभागवतः कविः ॥१९॥

soma-vaṁśe kalau naṣṭe
kṛtādau sthāpayiṣyati
bāhlīkāt somadatto 'bhūd
bhūrir bhūriśravās tataḥ

śalaś ca śāntanor āsīd
gaṅgāyāṁ bhīṣma ātmavān
sarva-dharma-vidāṁ śreṣṭho
mahā-bhāgavataḥ kaviḥ

soma-vaṁśe—when the dynasty of the moon-god; *kalau*—in this age of Kali; *naṣṭe*—being lost; *kṛta-ādau*—at the beginning of the next Satya-yuga; *sthāpayiṣyati*—will reestablish; *bāhlīkāt*—from Bāhlīka; *somadattaḥ*—Somadatta; *abhūt*—generated; *bhūriḥ*—Bhūri; *bhūri-śravāḥ*—Bhūriśravā; *tataḥ*—thereafter; *śalaḥ ca*—a son named Śala; *śāntanoḥ*—from Śāntanu; *āsīt*—generated; *gaṅgāyām*—in the womb of Gaṅgā, the wife of Śāntanu; *bhīṣmaḥ*—a son named Bhīṣma; *ātmavān*—self-realized; *sarva-dharma-vidām*—of all religious persons; *śreṣṭhaḥ*—the best; *mahā-bhāgavataḥ*—an exalted devotee; *kaviḥ*—and a learned scholar.

TRANSLATION

After the dynasty of the moon-god comes to an end in this age of Kali, Devāpi, in the beginning of the next Satya-yuga, will reestablish the Soma dynasty in this world. From Bāhlīka [the brother of Śāntanu] came a son named Somadatta, who had three sons, named Bhūri, Bhūriśravā and Śala. From Śāntanu, through the womb of his wife named Gaṅgā, came Bhīṣma, the exalted, self-realized devotee and learned scholar.

TEXT 20

वीरयूथाग्रणीर्येन रामोऽपि युधि तोषितः ।
शान्तनोर्दासकन्यायां जज्ञे चित्राङ्गदः सुतः ॥२०॥

vīra-yūthāgraṇīr yena
rāmo 'pi yudhi toṣitaḥ
śāntanor dāsa-kanyāyāṁ
jajñe citrāṅgadaḥ sutaḥ

vīra-yūtha-agraṇīḥ—Bhīṣmadeva, the foremost of all warriors; *yena*—by whom; *rāmaḥ api*—even Paraśurāma, the incarnation of God;

yudhi—in a fight; *toṣitaḥ*—was satisfied (when defeated by Bhīṣmadeva); *śāntanoḥ*—by Śāntanu; *dāsa-kanyāyām*—in the womb of Satyavatī, who was known as the daughter of a *śūdra; jajñe*—was born; *citrāṅgadaḥ*—Citrāṅgada; *sutaḥ*—a son.

TRANSLATION

Bhīṣmadeva was the foremost of all warriors. When he defeated Lord Paraśurāma in a fight, Lord Paraśurāma was very satisfied with him. By the semen of Śāntanu in the womb of Satyavatī, the daughter of a fisherman, Citrāṅgada took birth.

PURPORT

Satyavatī was actually the daughter of Uparicara Vasu by the womb of a fisherwoman known as Matsyagarbhā. Later, Satyavatī was raised by a fisherman.

The fight between Paraśurāma and Bhīṣmadeva concerns three daughters of Kaśīrāja—Ambikā, Ambālikā and Ambā—who were forcibly abducted by Bhīṣmadeva, acting on behalf of his brother Vicitravīrya. Ambā thought that Bhīṣmadeva would marry her and became attached to him, but Bhīṣmadeva refused to marry her, for he had taken the vow of *brahmacarya.* Ambā therefore approached Bhīṣmadeva's military spiritual master, Paraśurāma, who instructed Bhīṣma to marry her. Bhīṣmadeva refused, and therefore Paraśurāma fought with him to force him to accept the marriage. But Paraśurāma was defeated, and he was pleased with Bhīṣma.

TEXTS 21–24

विचित्रवीर्यश्चावरजो नाम्ना चित्राङ्गदो हतः ।
यस्यां पराशरात् साक्षादवतीर्णो हरेः कला ॥२१॥
वेदगुप्तो मुनिः कृष्णो यतोऽहमिदमध्यगाम् ।
हित्वा स्वशिष्यान् पैलादीन् भगवान् बादरायणः॥ २२॥
मह्यं पुत्राय शान्ताय परं गुह्यमिदं जगौ ।
विचित्रवीर्योऽथोवाह काशीराजसुते बलात् ॥२३॥

स्वयंवरादुपानीते अम्बिकाम्बालिके उभे ।
तयोरासक्तहृदयो गृहीतो यक्ष्मणा मृतः ॥२४॥

vicitravīryaś cāvarajo
nāmnā citrāṅgado hataḥ
yasyāṁ parāśarāt sākṣād
avatīrṇo hareḥ kalā

veda-gupto muniḥ kṛṣṇo
yato 'ham idam adhyagām
hitvā sva-śiṣyān pailādīn
bhagavān bādarāyaṇaḥ

mahyaṁ putrāya śāntāya
paraṁ guhyam idaṁ jagau
vicitravīryo 'thovāha
kāśīrāja-sute balāt

svayaṁvarād upānīte
ambikāmbālike ubhe
tayor āsakta-hṛdayo
gṛhīto yakṣmaṇā mṛtaḥ

vicitravīryaḥ—Vicitravīrya, the son of Śāntanu; *ca*—and; *avarajaḥ*—the younger brother; *nāmnā*—by a Gandharva named Citrāṅgada; *citrāṅgadaḥ*—Citrāṅgada; *hataḥ*—was killed; *yasyām*—in the womb of Satyavatī previous to her marriage to Śāntanu; *parāśarāt*—by the semen of Parāśara Muni; *sākṣāt*—directly; *avatīrṇaḥ*—incarnated; *hareḥ*—of the Supreme Personality of Godhead; *kalā*—expansion; *veda-guptaḥ*—the protector of the *Vedas; muniḥ*—the great sage; *kṛṣṇaḥ*—Kṛṣṇa Dvaipāyana; *yataḥ*—from whom; *aham*—I (Śukadeva Gosvāmī); *idam*—this (*Śrīmad-Bhāgavatam*); *adhyagām*—studied thoroughly; *hitvā*—rejecting; *sva-śiṣyān*—his disciples; *paila-ādīn*—headed by Paila; *bhagavān*—the incarnation of the Lord; *bādarāyaṇaḥ*—Vyāsadeva; *mahyam*—unto me; *putrāya*—a son; *śāntāya*—who was truly controlled from sense gratification; *param*—the supreme;

guhyam—the most confidential; *idam*—this Vedic literature (*Śrīmad-Bhāgavatam*); *jagau*—instructed; *vicitravīryaḥ*—Vicitravīrya; *atha*—thereafter; *uvāha*—married; *kāśīrāja-sute*—two daughters of Kāśīrāja; *balāt*—by force; *svayaṁvarāt*—from the arena of the *svayaṁvara; upānīte*—being brought; *ambikā-ambālike*—Ambikā and Ambālikā; *ubhe*—both of them; *tayoḥ*—unto them; *āsakta*—being too attached; *hṛdayaḥ*—his heart; *gṛhītaḥ*—being contaminated; *yakṣmaṇā*—by tuberculosis; *mṛtaḥ*—he died.

TRANSLATION

Citrāṅgada, of whom Vicitravīrya was the younger brother, was killed by a Gandharva who was also named Citrāṅgada. Satyavatī, before her marriage to Śāntanu, gave birth to the master authority of the Vedas, Vyāsadeva, known as Kṛṣṇa Dvaipāyana, who was begotten by Parāśara Muni. From Vyāsadeva, I [Śukadeva Gosvāmī] was born, and from him I studied this great work of literature, Śrīmad-Bhāgavatam. The incarnation of Godhead Vedavyāsa, rejecting his disciples, headed by Paila, instructed Śrīmad-Bhāgavatam to me because I was free from all material desires. After Ambikā and Ambālikā, the two daughters of Kāśīrāja, were taken away by force, Vicitravīrya married them, but because he was too attached to these two wives, he had a heart attack and died of tuberculosis.

TEXT 25

क्षेत्रेऽप्रजस्य वै भ्रातुर्मात्रोक्तो बादरायणः ।
धृतराष्ट्रं च पाण्डुं च विदुरं चाप्यजीजनत् ॥२५॥

kṣetre 'prajasya vai bhrātur
mātrokto bādarāyaṇaḥ
dhṛtarāṣṭraṁ ca pāṇḍuṁ ca
viduraṁ cāpy ajījanat

kṣetre—in the wives and maidservant; *aprajasya*—of Vicitravīrya, who had no progeny; *vai*—indeed; *bhrātuḥ*—of the brother; *mātrā uktaḥ*—being ordered by the mother; *bādarāyaṇaḥ*—Vedavyāsa;

dhṛtarāṣṭram—a son named Dhṛtarāṣṭra; *ca*—and; *pāṇḍum*—a son named Pāṇḍu; *ca*—also; *viduram*—a son named Vidura; *ca*—also; *api*—indeed; *ajījanat*—begot.

TRANSLATION

Bādarāyaṇa, Śrī Vyāsadeva, following the order of his mother, Satyavatī, begot three sons, two by the womb of Ambikā and Ambālikā, the two wives of his brother Vicitravīrya, and the third by Vicitravīrya's maidservant. These sons were Dhṛtarāṣṭra, Pāṇḍu and Vidura.

PURPORT

Vicitravīrya died of tuberculosis, and his wives, Ambikā and Ambālikā, had no issue. Therefore, after Vicitravīrya's death, his mother, Satyavatī, who was also the mother of Vyāsadeva, asked Vyāsadeva to beget children through the wives of Vicitravīrya. In those days, the brother of the husband could beget children through the womb of his sister-in-law. This was known as *devareṇa sutotpatti.* If the husband was somehow unable to beget children, his brother could do so through the womb of his sister-in-law. This *devareṇa sutotpatti* and the sacrifices of *aśvamedha* and *gomedha* are forbidden in the age of Kali.

aśvamedhaṁ gavālambhaṁ
sannyāsaṁ pala-paitṛkam
devareṇa sutotpattiṁ
kalau pañca vivarjayet

"In this age of Kali, five acts are forbidden: the offering of a horse in sacrifice, the offering of a cow in sacrifice, the acceptance of the order of *sannyāsa*, the offering of oblations of flesh to the forefathers, and a man's begetting children in his brother's wife." (*Brahma-vaivarta Purāṇa*).

TEXT 26

गान्धार्यां धृतराष्ट्रस्य जज्ञे पुत्रशतं नृप ।
तत्र दुर्योधनो ज्येष्ठो दुःशला चापि कन्यका ॥२६॥

gāndhāryāṁ dhṛtarāṣṭrasya
jajñe putra-śataṁ nṛpa
tatra duryodhano jyeṣṭho
duḥśalā cāpi kanyakā

gāndhāryām—in the womb of Gāndhārī; *dhṛtarāṣṭrasya*—of Dhṛtarāṣṭra; *jajñe*—were born; *putra-śatam*—one hundred sons; *nṛpa*—O King Parīkṣit; *tatra*—among the sons; *duryodhanaḥ*—the son named Duryodhana; *jyeṣṭhaḥ*—the eldest; *duḥśalā*—Duḥśalā; *ca api*—also; *kanyakā*—one daughter.

TRANSLATION

Dhṛtarāṣṭra's wife, Gāndhārī, gave birth to one hundred sons and one daughter, O King. The oldest of the sons was Duryodhana, and the daughter's name was Duḥśalā.

TEXTS 27–28

शापान्मैथुनरुद्धस्य पाण्डोः कुन्त्यां महारथाः ।
जाता धर्मानिलेन्द्रेभ्यो युधिष्ठिरमुखास्त्रयः ॥२७॥
नकुलः सहदेवश्च माद्र्यां नासत्यदस्रयोः ।
द्रौपद्यां पञ्च पञ्चभ्यः पुत्रास्ते पितरोऽभवन् ॥२८॥

śāpān maithuna-ruddhasya
pāṇḍoḥ kuntyāṁ mahā-rathāḥ
jātā dharmānilendrebhyo
yudhiṣṭhira-mukhās trayaḥ

nakulaḥ sahadevaś ca
mādryāṁ nāsatya-dasrayoḥ
draupadyāṁ pañca pañcabhyaḥ
putrās te pitaro 'bhavan

śāpāt—due to being cursed; *maithuna-ruddhasya*—who had to restrain sexual life; *pāṇḍoḥ*—of Pāṇḍu; *kuntyām*—in the womb of Kuntī; *mahā-rathāḥ*—great heroes; *jātāḥ*—took birth; *dharma*—by

Mahārāja Dharma, or Dharmarāja; *anila*—by the demigod controlling the wind; *indrebhyaḥ*—and by the demigod Indra, the controller of rain; *yudhiṣṭhira*—Yudhiṣṭhira; *mukhāḥ*—headed by; *trayaḥ*—three sons (Yudhiṣṭhira, Bhīma and Arjuna); *nakulaḥ*—Nakula; *sahadevaḥ*—Sahadeva; *ca*—also; *mādryām*—in the womb of Mādrī; *nāsatya-dasrayoḥ*—by Nāsatya and Dasra, the Aśvinī-kumāras; *draupadyām*—in the womb of Draupadī; *pañca*—five; *pañcabhyaḥ*—from the five brothers (Yudhiṣṭhira, Bhīma, Arjuna, Nakula and Sahadeva); *putrāḥ*—sons; *te*—they; *pitaraḥ*—uncles; *abhavan*—became.

TRANSLATION

Pāṇḍu was restrained from sexual life because of having been cursed by a sage, and therefore his three sons Yudhiṣṭhira, Bhīma and Arjuna were begotten through the womb of his wife, Kuntī, by Dharmarāja, by the demigod controlling the wind, and by the demigod controlling the rain. Pāṇḍu's second wife, Mādrī, gave birth to Nakula and Sahadeva, who were begotten by the two Aśvinī-kumāras. The five brothers, headed by Yudhiṣṭhira, begot five sons through the womb of Draupadī. These five sons were your uncles.

TEXT 29

युधिष्ठिरात् प्रतिविन्ध्यः श्रुतसेनो वृकोदरात् ।
अर्जुनाच्छ्रुतकीर्तिस्तु शतानीकस्तु नाकुलिः ॥२९॥

yudhiṣṭhirāt prativindhyaḥ
śrutaseno vṛkodarāt
arjunāc chrutakīrtis tu
śatānīkas tu nākuliḥ

yudhiṣṭhirāt—from Mahārāja Yudhiṣṭhira; *prativindhyaḥ*—a son named Prativindhya; *śrutasenaḥ*—Śrutasena; *vṛkodarāt*—begotten by Bhīma; *arjunāt*—from Arjuna; *śrutakīrtiḥ*—a son named Śrutakīrti; *tu*—indeed; *śatānīkaḥ*—a son named Śatānīka; *tu*—indeed; *nākuliḥ*—of Nakula.

TRANSLATION

From Yudhiṣṭhira came a son named Prativindhya, from Bhīma a son named Śrutasena, from Arjuna a son named Śrutakīrti, and from Nakula a son named Śatānīka.

TEXTS 30–31

सहदेवसुतो राजञ्छ्रुतकर्मा तथापरे ।
युधिष्ठिरात् तु पौरव्यां देवकोऽथ घटोत्कचः ॥३०॥
भीमसेनाद्धिडिम्बायां काल्यां सर्वगतस्ततः ।
सहदेवात् सुहोत्रं तु विजयासूत पार्वती ॥३१॥

sahadeva-suto rājañ
chrutakarmā tathāpare
yudhiṣṭhirāt tu pauravyāṁ
devako 'tha ghaṭotkacaḥ

bhīmasenād dhiḍimbāyāṁ
kālyāṁ sarvagatas tataḥ
sahadevāt suhotraṁ tu
vijayāsūta pārvatī

sahadeva-sutaḥ—the son of Sahadeva; *rājan*—O King; *śrutakarmā*—Śrutakarmā; *tathā*—as well as; *apare*—others; *yudhiṣṭhirāt*—from Yudhiṣṭhira; *tu*—indeed; *pauravyām*—in the womb of Pauravī; *devakaḥ*—a son named Devaka; *atha*—as well as; *ghaṭotkacaḥ*—Ghaṭotkaca; *bhīmasenāt*—from Bhīmasena; *hiḍimbāyām*—in the womb of Hiḍimbā; *kālyām*—in the womb of Kālī; *sarvagataḥ*—Sarvagata; *tataḥ*—thereafter; *sahadevāt*—from Sahadeva; *suhotram*—Suhotra; *tu*—indeed; *vijayā*—Vijayā; *asūta*—gave birth to; *pārvatī*—the daughter of the Himalayan king.

TRANSLATION

O King, the son of Sahadeva was Śrutakarmā. Furthermore, Yudhiṣṭhira and his brothers begot other sons in other wives. Yudhiṣṭhira begot a son named Devaka through the womb of

Pauravī, and Bhīmasena begot a son named Ghaṭotkaca through his wife Hiḍimbā and a son named Sarvagata through his wife Kālī. Similarly, Sahadeva had a son named Suhotra through his wife named Vijayā, who was the daughter of the king of the mountains.

TEXT 32

करेणुमत्यां नकुलो नरमित्रं तथार्जुनः ।
इरावन्तमुलुप्यां वै सुतायां बभ्रुवाहनम् ।
मणिपुरपतेः सोऽपि तत्पुत्रः पुत्रिकासुतः ॥३२॥

kareṇumatyāṁ nakulo
naramitraṁ tathārjunaḥ
irāvantam ulupyāṁ vai
sutāyāṁ babhruvāhanam
maṇipura-pateḥ so 'pi
tat-putraḥ putrikā-sutaḥ

kareṇumatyām—in the wife named Kareṇumatī; *nakulaḥ*—Nakula; *naramitram*—a son named Naramitra; *tathā*—also; *arjunaḥ*—Arjuna; *irāvantam*—Irāvān; *ulupyām*—in the womb of the Nāga-kanyā named Ulupī; *vai*—indeed; *sutāyām*—in the daughter; *babhruvāhanam*—a son named Babhruvāhana; *maṇipura-pateḥ*—of the king of Maṇipura; *saḥ*—he; *api*—although; *tat-putraḥ*—the son of Arjuna; *putrikā-sutaḥ*—the son of his maternal grandfather.

TRANSLATION

Nakula begot a son named Naramitra through his wife named Kareṇumatī. Similarly, Arjuna begot a son named Irāvān through his wife known as Ulupī, the daughter of the Nāgas, and a son named Babhruvāhana by the womb of the princess of Maṇipura. Babhruvāhana became the adopted son of the king of Maṇipura.

PURPORT

It is to be understood that Pārvatī is the daughter of the king of the very, very old mountainous country known as the Maṇipura state.

Five thousand years ago, therefore, when the Pāṇḍavas ruled, Maṇipura existed, as did its king. Therefore this kingdom is a very old, aristocratic Vaiṣṇava kingdom. If this kingdom is organized as a Vaiṣṇava state, this revitalization will be a great success because for five thousand years this state has maintained its identity. If the Vaiṣṇava spirit is revived there, it will be a wonderful place, renowned throughout the entire world. Maṇipuri Vaiṣṇavas are very famous in Vaiṣṇava society. In Vṛndāvana and Navadvīpa there are many temples constructed by the king of Maṇipura. Some of our devotees belong to the Maṇipura state. The Kṛṣṇa consciousness movement, therefore, can be well spread in the state of Maṇipura by the cooperative efforts of the Kṛṣṇa conscious devotees.

TEXT 33

तव तातः सुभद्रायामभिमन्युरजायत ।
सर्वातिरथजिद् वीर उत्तरायां ततो भवान् ॥३३॥

tava tātaḥ subhadrāyām
abhimanyur ajāyata
sarvātirathajid vīra
uttarāyāṁ tato bhavān

tava—your; *tātaḥ*—father; *subhadrāyām*—in the womb of Subhadrā; *abhimanyuḥ*—Abhimanyu; *ajāyata*—was born; *sarva-atiratha-jit*—a great fighter who could defeat the *atirathas; vīraḥ*—a great hero; *uttarāyām*—in the womb of Uttarā; *tataḥ*—from Abhimanyu; *bhavān*—your good self.

TRANSLATION

My dear King Parīkṣit, your father, Abhimanyu, was born from the womb of Subhadrā as the son of Arjuna. He was the conqueror of all atirathas [those who could fight with one thousand charioteers]. From him, by the womb of Uttarā, the daughter of Virāḍrāja, you were born.

TEXT 34

परिक्षीणेषु कुरुषु द्रौणेर्ब्रह्मास्त्रतेजसा ।
त्वं च कृष्णानुभावेन सजीवो मोचितोऽन्तकात् ॥३४॥

parikṣīṇeṣu kuruṣu
drauṇer brahmāstra-tejasā
tvaṁ ca kṛṣṇānubhāvena
sajīvo mocito 'ntakāt

parikṣīṇeṣu—because of being annihilated in the Kurukṣetra war; *kuruṣu*—the members of the Kuru dynasty, such as Duryodhana; *drauṇeḥ*—Aśvatthāmā, the son of Droṇācārya; *brahmāstra-tejasā*—because of the heat of the *brahmāstra* nuclear weapon; *tvam ca*—your good self also; *kṛṣṇa-anubhāvena*—because of the mercy of Lord Kṛṣṇa; *sa-jīvaḥ*—with your life; *mocitaḥ*—released; *antakāt*—from death.

TRANSLATION

After the Kuru dynasty was annihilated in the Battle of Kurukṣetra, you also were about to be destroyed by the brahmāstra atomic weapon released by the son of Droṇācārya, but by the mercy of the Supreme Personality of Godhead, Kṛṣṇa, you were saved from death.

TEXT 35

तवेमे तनयास्तात जनमेजयपूर्वकाः ।
श्रुतसेनो भीमसेन उग्रसेनश्च वीर्यवान् ॥३५॥

taveme tanayās tāta
janamejaya-pūrvakāḥ
śrutaseno bhīmasena
ugrasenaś ca vīryavān

tava—your; *ime*—all these; *tanayāḥ*—sons; *tāta*—my dear King Parīkṣit; *janamejaya*—Janamejaya; *pūrvakāḥ*—headed by;

śrutasenaḥ—Śrutasena; *bhīmasenaḥ*—Bhīmasena; *ugrasenaḥ*—Ugrasena; *ca*—also; *vīryavān*—all very powerful.

TRANSLATION

My dear King, your four sons—Janamejaya, Śrutasena, Bhīmasena and Ugrasena—are very powerful. Janamejaya is the eldest.

TEXT 36

जनमेजयस्त्वां विदित्वा तक्षकान्निधनं गतम् ।
सर्पान् वै सर्पयागाग्नौ स होष्यति रुषान्वितः ॥३६॥

janamejayas tvāṁ viditvā
takṣakān nidhanaṁ gatam
sarpān vai sarpa-yāgāgnau
sa hoṣyati ruṣānvitaḥ

janamejayaḥ—the eldest son; *tvām*—about you; *viditvā*—knowing; *takṣakāt*—by the Takṣaka serpent; *nidhanam*—death; *gatam*—undergone; *sarpān*—the snakes; *vai*—indeed; *sarpa-yāga-agnau*—in the fire of the sacrifice for killing all the snakes; *saḥ*—he (Janamejaya); *hoṣyati*—will offer as a sacrifice; *ruṣā-anvitaḥ*—because of being very angry.

TRANSLATION

Because of your death by the Takṣaka snake, your son Janamejaya will be very angry and will perform a sacrifice to kill all the snakes in the world.

TEXT 37

कालषेयं पुरोधाय तुरं तुरगमेधषाट् ।
समन्तात् पृथिवीं सर्वां जित्वा यक्ष्यति चाध्वरैः ॥३७॥

kālaṣeyaṁ purodhāya
turaṁ turaga-medhaṣāṭ

samantāt pṛthivīṁ sarvāṁ
jitvā yakṣyati cādhvaraiḥ

kālaṣeyam—the son of Kalaṣa; *purodhāya*—accepting as the priest; *turam*—Tura; *turaga-medhaṣāṭ*—he will be known as Turaga-medhaṣāṭ (a performer of many horse sacrifices); *samantāt*—including all parts; *pṛthivīm*—the world; *sarvām*—everywhere; *jitvā*—conquering; *yakṣyati*—will execute sacrifices; *ca*—and; *adhvaraiḥ*—by performing *aśvamedha-yajñas.*

TRANSLATION

After conquering throughout the world and after accepting Tura, the son of Kalaṣa, as his priest, Janamejaya will perform aśvamedha-yajñas, for which he will be known as Turaga-medhaṣāṭ.

TEXT 38

तस्य पुत्रः शतानीको याज्ञवल्क्यात् त्रयीं पठन् ।
अस्त्रज्ञानं क्रियाज्ञानं शौनकात् परमेष्यति ॥३८॥

tasya putraḥ śatānīko
yājñavalkyāt trayīṁ paṭhan
astra-jñānaṁ kriyā-jñānaṁ
śaunakāt param eṣyati

tasya—of Janamejaya; *putraḥ*—the son; *śatānīkaḥ*—Śatānīka; *yājñavalkyāt*—from the great sage known as Yājñavalkya; *trayīm*—the three *Vedas* (*Sāma, Yajur* and *Ṛg*); *paṭhan*—studying thoroughly; *astra-jñānam*—the art of military administration; *kriyā-jñānam*—the art of performing ritualistic ceremonies; *śaunakāt*—from Śaunaka Ṛṣi; *param*—transcendental knowledge; *eṣyati*—will achieve.

TRANSLATION

The son of Janamejaya known as Śatānīka will learn from Yājñavalkya the three Vedas and the art of performing ritualistic ceremonies. He will also learn the military art from Kṛpācārya and the transcendental science from the sage Śaunaka.

TEXT 39

सहस्रानीकस्तत्पुत्रस्ततश्चैवाश्वमेधजः ।
असीमकृष्णस्तस्यापि नेमिचक्रस्तु तत्सुतः ॥३९॥

sahasrānīkas tat-putras
tataś caivāśvamedhajaḥ
asīmakṛṣṇas tasyāpi
nemicakras tu tat-sutaḥ

sahasrānīkaḥ—Sahasrānīka; *tat-putraḥ*—the son of Śatānīka; *tataḥ*—from him (Sahasrānīka); *ca*—also; *eva*—indeed; *aśvamedha-jaḥ*—Aśvamedhaja; *asīmakṛṣṇaḥ*—Asīmakṛṣṇa; *tasya*—from him (Aśvamedhaja); *api*—also; *nemicakraḥ*—Nemicakra; *tu*—indeed; *tat-sutaḥ*—his son.

TRANSLATION

The son of Śatānīka will be Sahasrānīka, and from him will come the son named Aśvamedhaja. From Aśvamedhaja will come Asīmakṛṣṇa, and his son will be Nemicakra.

TEXT 40

गजाह्वये हृते नद्या कौशाम्ब्यां साधु वत्स्यति ।
उक्तस्ततश्चित्ररथस्तस्माच्छुचिरथः सुतः ॥४०॥

gajāhvaye hṛte nadyā
kauśāmbyāṁ sādhu vatsyati
uktas tataś citrarathas
tasmāc chucirathaḥ sutaḥ

gajāhvaye—on the town of Hastināpura (New Delhi); *hṛte*—being inundated; *nadyā*—by the river; *kauśāmbyām*—in the place known as Kauśāmbī; *sādhu*—duly; *vatsyati*—will live there; *uktaḥ*—celebrated; *tataḥ*—thereafter; *citrarathaḥ*—Citraratha; *tasmāt*—from him; *śucirathaḥ*—Śuciratha; *sutaḥ*—the son.

TRANSLATION

When the town of Hastināpura [New Delhi] is inundated by the river, Nemicakra will live in the place known as Kauśāmbī. His son will be celebrated as Citraratha, and the son of Citraratha will be Śuciratha.

TEXT 41

तस्माच्च वृष्टिमांस्तस्य सुषेणोऽथ महीपतिः ।
सुनीथस्तस्य भविता नृचक्षुर्यत् सुखीनलः ॥४१॥

tasmāc ca vṛṣṭimāṁs tasya
suṣeṇo 'tha mahīpatiḥ
sunīthas tasya bhavitā
nṛcakṣur yat sukhīnalaḥ

tasmāt—from him (Śuciratha); *ca*—also; *vṛṣṭimān*—the son known as Vṛṣṭimān; *tasya*—his (son); *suṣeṇaḥ*—Suṣeṇa; *atha*—thereafter; *mahī-patiḥ*—the emperor of the whole world; *sunīthaḥ*—Sunītha; *tasya*—his; *bhavitā*—will be; *nṛcakṣuḥ*—his son, Nṛcakṣu; *yat*—from him; *sukhīnalaḥ*—Sukhīnala.

TRANSLATION

From Śuciratha will come the son named Vṛṣṭimān, and his son, Suṣeṇa, will be the emperor of the entire world. The son of Suṣeṇa will be Sunītha, his son will be Nṛcakṣu, and from Nṛcakṣu will come a son named Sukhīnala.

TEXT 42

परिप्लवः सुतस्तस्मान्मेधावी सुनयात्मजः ।
नृपञ्जयस्ततो दूर्वस्तिमिस्तस्माज्जनिष्यति ॥४२॥

pariplavaḥ sutas tasmān
medhāvī sunayātmajaḥ
nṛpañjayas tato dūrvas
timis tasmāj janiṣyati

pariplavaḥ—Pariplava; *sutaḥ*—the son; *tasmāt*—from him (Pariplava); *medhāvī*—Medhāvī; *sunaya-ātmajaḥ*—the son of Sunaya; *nṛpañjayaḥ*—Nṛpañjaya; *tataḥ*—from him; *dūrvaḥ*—Dūrva; *timiḥ*—Timi; *tasmāt*—from him; *janiṣyati*—will take birth.

TRANSLATION

The son of Sukhīnala will be Pariplava, and his son will be Sunaya. From Sunaya will come a son named Medhāvī; from Medhāvī, Nṛpañjaya; from Nṛpañjaya, Dūrva; and from Dūrva, Timi.

TEXT 43

तिमेर्बृहद्रथस्तस्माच्छतानीकः सुदासजः ।
शतानीकाद् दुर्दमनस्तस्यापत्यं महीनरः ॥४३॥

timer bṛhadrathas tasmāc
chatānīkaḥ sudāsajaḥ
śatānīkād durdamanas
tasyāpatyaṁ mahīnaraḥ

timeḥ—of Timi; *bṛhadrathaḥ*—Bṛhadratha; *tasmāt*—from him (Bṛhadratha); *śatānīkaḥ*—Śatānīka; *sudāsa-jaḥ*—the son of Sudāsa; *śatānīkāt*—from Śatānīka; *durdamanaḥ*—a son named Durdamana; *tasya apatyam*—his son; *mahīnaraḥ*—Mahīnara.

TRANSLATION

From Timi will come Bṛhadratha; from Bṛhadratha, Sudāsa; and from Sudāsa, Śatānīka. From Śatānīka will come Durdamana, and from him will come a son named Mahīnara.

TEXTS 44–45

दण्डपाणिर्निमिस्तस्य क्षेमको भविता यतः ।
ब्रह्मक्षत्रस्य वै योनिर्वंशो देवर्षिसत्कृतः ॥४४॥
क्षेमकं प्राप्य राजानं संस्थां प्राप्स्यति वै कलौ ।
अथ मागधराजानो भविनो ये वदामि ते ॥४५॥

daṇḍapāṇir nimis tasya
kṣemako bhavitā yataḥ
brahma-kṣatrasya vai yonir
vaṁśo devarṣi-satkṛtaḥ

kṣemakaṁ prāpya rājānaṁ
saṁsthāṁ prāpsyati vai kalau
atha māgadha-rājāno
bhāvino ye vadāmi te

daṇḍapāṇiḥ—Daṇḍapāṇi; *nimiḥ*—Nimi; *tasya*—from him (Mahīnara); *kṣemakaḥ*—a son named Kṣemaka; *bhavitā*—will take birth; *yataḥ*—from whom (Nimi); *brahma-kṣatrasya*—of *brāhmaṇas* and *kṣatriyas; vai*—indeed; *yoniḥ*—the source; *vaṁśaḥ*—the dynasty; *deva-ṛṣi-satkṛtaḥ*—respected by great saintly persons and demigods; *kṣemakam*—King Kṣemaka; *prāpya*—up to this point; *rājānam*—the monarch; *saṁsthām*—an end to them; *prāpsyati*—there will be; *vai*—indeed; *kalau*—in this Kali-yuga; *atha*—thereafter; *māgadha-rājānaḥ*—the kings in the Māgadha dynasty; *bhāvinaḥ*—the future; *ye*—all those who; *vadāmi*—I shall explain; *te*—unto you.

TRANSLATION

The son of Mahīnara will be Daṇḍapāṇi, and his son will be Nimi, from whom King Kṣemaka will be born. I have now described to you the moon-god's dynasty, which is the source of brāhmaṇas and kṣatriyas and is worshiped by demigods and great saints. In this Kali-yuga, Kṣemaka will be the last monarch. Now I shall describe to you the future of the Māgadha dynasty. Please listen.

TEXTS 46–48

भविता सहदेवस्य मार्जारिर्यच्छ्रुतश्रवाः ।
ततो युतायुस्तस्यापि निरमित्रोऽथ तत्सुतः ॥४६॥
सुनक्षत्रः सुनक्षत्राद् बृहत्सेनोऽथ कर्मजित् ।
ततः सुतञ्जयाद् विप्रः शुचिस्तस्य भविष्यति ॥४७॥

क्षेमोऽथ सुव्रतस्तस्माद् धर्मसूत्रः समस्ततः ।
द्युमत्सेनोऽथ सुमतिः सुबलो जनिता ततः ॥४८॥

bhavitā sahadevasya
mārjārir yac chrutaśravāḥ
tato yutāyus tasyāpi
niramitro 'tha tat-sutaḥ

sunakṣatraḥ sunakṣatrād
bṛhatseno 'tha karmajit
tataḥ sutañjayād vipraḥ
śucis tasya bhaviṣyati

kṣemo 'tha suvratas tasmād
dharmasūtraḥ samas tataḥ
dyumatseno 'tha sumatiḥ
subalo janitā tataḥ

bhavitā—will take birth; *sahadevasya*—the son of Sahadeva; *mārjāriḥ*—Mārjāri; *yat*—his son; *śrutaśravāḥ*—Śrutaśravā; *tataḥ*—from him; *yutāyuḥ*—Yutāyu; *tasya*—his son; *api*—also; *niramitraḥ*—Niramitra; *atha*—thereafter; *tat-sutaḥ*—his son; *sunakṣatraḥ*—Sunakṣatra; *sunakṣatrāt*—from Sunakṣatra; *bṛhatsenaḥ*—Bṛhatsena; *atha*—from him; *karmajit*—Karmajit; *tataḥ*—from him; *sutañjayāt*—from Sutañjaya; *vipraḥ*—Vipra; *śuciḥ*—a son named Śuci; *tasya*—from him; *bhaviṣyati*—will take birth; *kṣemaḥ*—a son named Kṣema; *atha*—thereafter; *suvrataḥ*—a son named Suvrata; *tasmāt*—from him; *dharmasūtraḥ*—Dharmasūtra; *samaḥ*—Sama; *tataḥ*—from him; *dyumatsenaḥ*—Dyumatsena; *atha*—thereafter; *sumatiḥ*—Sumati; *subalaḥ*—Subala; *janitā*—will take birth; *tataḥ*—thereafter.

TRANSLATION

Sahadeva, the son of Jarāsandha, will have a son named Mārjāri. From Mārjāri will come Śrutaśravā; from Śrutaśravā, Yutāyu; and from Yutāyu, Niramitra. The son of Niramitra will be Sunakṣatra, from Sunakṣatra will come Bṛhatsena, and from Bṛhatsena,

Karmajit. The son of Karmajit will be Sutañjaya, the son of Sutañjaya will be Vipra, and his son will be Śuci. The son of Śuci will be Kṣema, the son of Kṣema will be Suvrata, and the son of Suvrata will be Dharmasūtra. From Dharmasūtra will come Sama; from Sama, Dyumatsena; from Dyumatsena, Sumati; and from Sumati, Subala.

TEXT 49

सुनीथः सत्यजिदथ विश्वजिद् यद् रिपुञ्जयः ।
बार्हद्रथाश्च भूपाला भाव्याः साहस्रवत्सरम् ॥४९॥

sunīthaḥ satyajid atha
viśvajid yad ripuñjayaḥ
bārhadrathāś ca bhūpālā
bhāvyāḥ sāhasra-vatsaram

sunīthaḥ—from Subala will come Sunītha; *satyajit*—Satyajit; *atha*—from him; *viśvajit*—from Viśvajit; *yat*—from whom; *ripuñjayaḥ*—Ripuñjaya; *bārhadrathāḥ*—all in the line of Bṛhadratha; *ca*—also; *bhūpālāḥ*—all those kings; *bhāvyāḥ*—will take birth; *sāhasra-vatsaram*—continuously for one thousand years.

TRANSLATION

From Subala will come Sunītha; from Sunītha, Satyajit; from Satyajit, Viśvajit; and from Viśvajit, Ripuñjaya. All of these personalities will belong to the dynasty of Bṛhadratha, which will rule the world for one thousand years.

PURPORT

This is the history of a monarchy that began with Jarāsandha and continues for one thousand years as the above-mentioned kings appear on the surface of the globe.

Thus end the Bhaktivedanta purports of the Ninth Canto, Twenty-second Chapter, of the Śrīmad-Bhāgavatam, *entitled "The Descendants of Ajamīḍha."*

CHAPTER TWENTY-THREE

The Dynasties of the Sons of Yayāti

In this Twenty-third Chapter the dynasties of Anu, Druhyu, Turvasu and Yadu, as well as the story of Jyāmagha, are described.

The sons of Yayāti's fourth son, Anu, were Sabhānara, Cakṣu and Pareṣṇu. Of these three, the sons and grandsons of Sabhānara were, in succession, Kālanara, Sṛñjaya, Janamejaya, Mahāśāla and Mahāmanā. The sons of Mahāmanā were Uśīnara and Titikṣu. Uśīnara had four sons, namely Śibi, Vara, Kṛmi and Dakṣa. Śibi also had four sons—Vṛṣādarbha, Sudhīra, Madra and Kekaya. The son of Titikṣu was Ruṣadratha, who begot a son named Homa. From Homa came Sutapā and from Sutapā, Bali. In this way the dynasty continued. Begotten by Dīrghatamā in the womb of the wife of Bali were Aṅga, Vaṅga, Kaliṅga, Suhma, Puṇḍra and Oḍra, all of whom became kings.

From Aṅga came Khalapāna, whose dynasty included Diviratha, Dharmaratha and Citraratha, also called Romapāda, one after another. Mahārāja Daśaratha gave in charity one of his daughters, by the name Śāntā, to his friend Romapāda because Romapāda had no sons. Romapāda accepted Śāntā as his daughter, and the great sage Ṛṣyaśṛṅga married her. By the mercy of Ṛṣyaśṛṅga, Romapāda had a son named Caturaṅga. The son of Caturaṅga was Pṛthulākṣa, who had three sons—Bṛhadratha, Bṛhatkarmā and Bṛhadbhānu. From Bṛhadratha came a son named Bṛhadmanā, whose sons and grandsons in succession were Jayadratha, Vijaya, Dhṛti, Dhṛtavrata, Satkarmā and Adhiratha. Adhiratha accepted the son rejected by Kuntī, namely Karṇa, and Karṇa's son was Vṛṣasena.

The son of Yayāti's third son, Druhyu, was Babhru, whose son and grandsons were Setu, Ārabdha, Gāndhāra, Dharma, Dhṛta, Durmada and Pracetā.

The son of Yayāti's second son, Turvasu, was Vahni, whose seminal dynasty included Bharga, Bhānumān, Tribhānu, Karandhama and Maruta. The childless Maruta accepted Duṣmanta, who belonged to the Pūru dynasty, as his adopted son. Mahārāja Duṣmanta was anxious to have his kingdom returned, and so he went back to the Pūru-vaṁśa.

Of the four sons of Yadu, Sahasrajit was the eldest. The son of Sahasrajit was named Śatajit. He had three sons, of whom one was Haihaya. The sons and grandsons in the dynasty of Haihaya were Dharma, Netra, Kunti, Sohañji, Mahiṣmān, Bhadrasenaka, Dhanaka, Kṛtavīrya, Arjuna, Jayadhvaja, Tālajaṅgha and Vītihotra.

The son of Vītihotra was Madhu, whose eldest son was Vṛṣṇi. Because of Yadu, Madhu and Vṛṣṇi, their dynasties are known as Yādava, Mādhava and Vṛṣṇi. Another son of Yadu was Kroṣṭā, and from him came Vṛjinavān, Svāhita, Viṣadgu, Citraratha, Śaśabindu, Pṛthuśravā, Dharma, Uśanā and Rucaka. Rucaka had five sons, one of whom was known as Jyāmagha. Jyāmagha was sonless, but by the mercy of the demigods his childless wife gave birth to a son named Vidarbha.

TEXT 1

श्रीशुक उवाच

अनोः सभानरश्चक्षुः परेष्णुश्च त्रयः सुताः ।
सभानरात् कालनरः सृञ्जयस्तत्सुतस्ततः ॥ १ ॥

śrī-śuka uvāca
anoḥ sabhānaraś cakṣuḥ
pareṣṇuś ca trayaḥ sutāḥ
sabhānarāt kālanaraḥ
sṛñjayas tat-sutas tataḥ

śrī-śukaḥ uvāca—Śrī Śukadeva Gosvāmī said; *anoḥ*—of Anu, the fourth of the four sons of Yayāti; *sabhānaraḥ*—Sabhānara; *cakṣuḥ*—Cakṣu; *pareṣṇuḥ*—Pareṣṇu; *ca*—also; *trayaḥ*—three; *sutāḥ*—sons; *sabhānarāt*—from Sabhānara; *kālanaraḥ*—Kālanara; *sṛñjayaḥ*—Sṛñjaya; *tat-sutaḥ*—son of Kālanara; *tataḥ*—thereafter.

TRANSLATION

Śukadeva Gosvāmī said: Anu, the fourth son of Yayāti, had three sons, named Sabhānara, Cakṣu and Pareṣṇu. O King, from

Sabhānara came a son named Kālanara, and from Kālanara came a son named Sṛñjaya.

TEXT 2

जनमेजयस्तस्य पुत्रो महाशालो महामनाः ।
उशीनरस्तितिक्षुश्च महामनस आत्मजौ ॥ २ ॥

janamejayas tasya putro
mahāśālo mahāmanāḥ
uśīnaras titikṣuś ca
mahāmanasa ātmajau

janamejayaḥ—Janamejaya; *tasya*—of him (Janamejaya); *putraḥ*—a son; *mahāśālaḥ*—Mahāśāla; *mahāmanāḥ*—(from Mahāśāla) a son named Mahāmanā; *uśīnaraḥ*—Uśīnara; *titikṣuḥ*—Titikṣu; *ca*—and; *mahāmanasaḥ*—from Mahāmanā; *ātmajau*—two sons.

TRANSLATION

From Sṛñjaya came a son named Janamejaya. From Janamejaya came Mahāśāla; from Mahāśāla, Mahāmanā; and from Mahāmanā two sons, named Uśīnara and Titikṣu.

TEXTS 3–4

शिबिर्वरः कृमिर्दक्षश्चत्वारोशीनरात्मजाः ।
वृषादर्भः सुधीरश्च मद्रः केकय आत्मवान् ॥ ३ ॥
शिबेश्चत्वार एवासंस्तितिक्षोश्च रुशद्रथः ।
ततो होमोऽथ सुतपा बलिः सुतपसोऽभवत् ॥ ४ ॥

śibir varaḥ kṛmir dakṣaś
catvārośīnarātmajāḥ
vṛṣādarbhaḥ sudhīraś ca
madraḥ kekaya ātmavān

śibeś catvāra evāsaṁs
titikṣoś ca ruṣadrathaḥ

tato homo 'tha sutapā
baliḥ sutapaso 'bhavat

śibiḥ—Śibi; *varaḥ*—Vara; *kṛmiḥ*—Kṛmi; *dakṣaḥ*—Dakṣa; *catvāraḥ*—four; *uśīnara-ātmajāḥ*—the sons of Uśīnara; *vṛṣādarbhaḥ*—Vṛṣādarbha; *sudhīraḥ ca*—as well as Sudhīra; *madraḥ*—Madra; *kekayaḥ*—Kekaya; *ātmavān*—self-realized; *śibeḥ*—of Śibi; *catvāraḥ*—four; *eva*—indeed; *āsan*—there were; *titikṣoḥ*—of Titikṣu; *ca*—also; *ruṣadrathaḥ*—a son named Ruṣadratha; *tataḥ*—from him (Ruṣadratha); *homaḥ*—Homa; *atha*—from him (Homa); *sutapāḥ*—Sutapā; *baliḥ*—Bali; *sutapasaḥ*—of Sutapā; *abhavat*—there was.

TRANSLATION

The four sons of Uśīnara were Śibi, Vara, Kṛmi and Dakṣa, and from Śibi again came four sons, named Vṛṣādarbha, Sudhīra, Madra and ātma-tattva-vit Kekaya. The son of Titikṣu was Ruṣadratha. From Ruṣadratha came Homa; from Homa, Sutapā; and from Sutapā, Bali.

TEXT 5

अङ्गवङ्गकलिङ्गाद्याः सुह्मपुण्ड्रौड्रसंज्ञिताः ।
जज्ञिरे दीर्घतमसो बलेः क्षेत्रे महीक्षितः ॥ ५ ॥

aṅga-vaṅga-kaliṅgādyāḥ
suhma-puṇḍrauḍra-saṁjñitāḥ
jajñire dīrghatamaso
baleḥ kṣetre mahīkṣitaḥ

aṅga—Aṅga; *vaṅga*—Vaṅga; *kaliṅga*—Kaliṅga; *ādyāḥ*—headed by; *suhma*—Suhma; *puṇḍra*—Puṇḍra; *oḍra*—Oḍra; *saṁjñitāḥ*—known as such; *jajñire*—were born; *dīrghatamasaḥ*—by the semen of Dīrghatamā; *baleḥ*—of Bali; *kṣetre*—in the wife; *mahī-kṣitaḥ*—of the king of the world.

TRANSLATION

By the semen of Dīrghatamā in the wife of Bali, the emperor of the world, six sons took birth, namely Aṅga, Vaṅga, Kaliṅga, Suhma, Puṇḍra and Oḍra.

TEXT 6

चक्रुः स्वनाम्ना विषयान् षडिमान् प्राच्यकांश्च ते ।
खलपानोऽङ्गतो जज्ञे तस्माद् दिविरथस्ततः ॥ ६ ॥

cakruḥ sva-nāmnā viṣayān
ṣaḍ imān prācyakāṁś ca te
khalapāno 'ṅgato jajñe
tasmād divirathas tataḥ

cakruḥ—they created; *sva-nāmnā*—by their own names; *viṣayān*—different states; *ṣaṭ*—six; *imān*—all these; *prācyakān ca*—on the eastern side (of India); *te*—those (six kings); *khalapānaḥ*—Khalapāna; *aṅgataḥ*—from King Aṅga; *jajñe*—took birth; *tasmāt*—from him (Khalapāna); *divirathaḥ*—Diviratha; *tataḥ*—thereafter.

TRANSLATION

These six sons, headed by Aṅga, later became kings of six states in the eastern side of India. These states were known according to the names of their respective kings. From Aṅga came a son named Khalapāna, and from Khalapāna came Diviratha.

TEXTS 7–10

सुतो धर्मरथो यस्य जज्ञे चित्ररथोऽप्रजाः ।
रोमपाद इति ख्यातस्तस्मै दशरथः सखा ॥ ७ ॥
शान्तां स्वकन्यां प्रायच्छदृष्यशृङ्ग उवाह याम् ।
देवेऽवर्षति यं रामा आनिन्युर्हरिणीसुतम् ॥ ८ ॥
नाट्यसङ्गीतवादित्रैर्विभ्रमालिङ्गनार्हणैः ।
स तु राज्ञोऽनपत्यस्य निरूप्येष्टिं मरुत्वते ॥ ९ ॥
प्रजामदाद् दशरथो येन लेभेऽप्रजाः प्रजाः ।
चतुरङ्गो रोमपादात् पृथुलाक्षस्तु तत्सुतः ॥१०॥

suto dharmaratho yasya
jajñe citraratho 'prajāḥ

romapāda iti khyātas
tasmai daśarathaḥ sakhā

śāntāṁ sva-kanyāṁ prāyacchad
ṛṣyaśṛṅga uvāha yām
deve 'varṣati yaṁ rāmā
āninyur hariṇī-sutam

nāṭya-saṅgīta-vāditrair
vibhramāliṅganārhaṇaiḥ
sa tu rājño 'napatyasya
nirūpyeṣṭiṁ marutvate

prajām adād daśaratho
yena lebhe 'prajāḥ prajāḥ
caturaṅgo romapādāt
pṛthulākṣas tu tat-sutaḥ

sutaḥ—a son; *dharmarathaḥ*—Dharmaratha; *yasya*—of whom (Diviratha); *jajñe*—was born; *citrarathaḥ*—Citraratha; *aprajāḥ*—without any sons; *romapādaḥ*—Romapāda; *iti*—thus; *khyātaḥ*—celebrated; *tasmai*—unto him; *daśarathaḥ*—Daśaratha; *sakhā*—friend; *śāntām*—Śāntā; *sva-kanyām*—Daśaratha's own daughter; *prāyacchat*—delivered; *ṛṣyaśṛṅgaḥ*—Ṛṣyaśṛṅga; *uvāha*—married; *yām*—unto her (Śāntā); *deve*—the demigod in charge of rainfall; *avarṣati*—did not shower any rain; *yam*—unto whom (Ṛṣyaśṛṅga); *rāmāḥ*—prostitutes; *āninyuḥ*—brought; *hariṇī-sutam*—that Ṛṣyaśṛṅga, who was the son of a doe; *nāṭya-saṅgīta-vāditraiḥ*—by dancing, by singing and by a musical display; *vibhrama*—bewildering; *āliṅgana*—by embracing; *arhaṇaiḥ*—by worshiping; *saḥ*—he (Ṛṣyaśṛṅga); *tu*—indeed; *rājñaḥ*—from Mahārāja Daśaratha; *anapatyasya*—who was without issue; *nirūpya*—after establishing; *iṣṭim*—a sacrifice; *marutvate*—of the demigod named Marutvān; *prajām*—issue; *adāt*—delivered; *daśarathaḥ*—Daśaratha; *yena*—by which (as a result of the *yajña*); *lebhe*—achieved; *aprajāḥ*—although he had no sons; *prajāḥ*—sons; *caturaṅgaḥ*—Caturaṅga; *romapādāt*—from Citraratha; *pṛthulākṣaḥ*—Pṛthulākṣa; *tu*—indeed; *tat-sutaḥ*—the son of Caturaṅga.

TRANSLATION

From Diviratha came a son named Dharmaratha, and his son was Citraratha, who was celebrated as Romapāda. Romapāda, however, was without issue, and therefore his friend Mahārāja Daśaratha gave him his own daughter, named Śāntā. Romapāda accepted her as his daughter, and thereafter she married Ṛṣyaśṛṅga. When the demigods from the heavenly planets failed to shower rain, Ṛṣyaśṛṅga was appointed the priest for performing a sacrifice, after being brought from the forest by the allurement of prostitutes, who danced, staged theatrical performances accompanied by music, and embraced and worshiped him. After Ṛṣyaśṛṅga came, the rain fell. Thereafter, Ṛṣyaśṛṅga performed a son-giving sacrifice on behalf of Mahārāja Daśaratha, who had no issue, and then Mahārāja Daśaratha had sons. From Romapāda, by the mercy of Ṛṣyaśṛṅga, Caturaṅga was born, and from Caturaṅga came Pṛthulākṣa.

TEXT 11

बृहद्रथो बृहत्कर्मा बृहद्भानुश्च तत्सुताः ।
आद्याद् बृहन्मनास्तस्माज्जयद्रथ उदाहृतः ॥११॥

bṛhadratho bṛhatkarmā
bṛhadbhānuś ca tat-sutāḥ
ādyād bṛhanmanās tasmāj
jayadratha udāhṛtaḥ

bṛhadrathaḥ—Bṛhadratha; *bṛhatkarmā*—Bṛhatkarmā; *bṛhadbhānuḥ*—Bṛhadbhānu; *ca*—also; *tat-sutāḥ*—the sons of Pṛthulākṣa; *ādyāt*—from the eldest (Bṛhadratha); *bṛhanmanāḥ*—Bṛhanmanā was born; *tasmāt*—from him (Bṛhanmanā); *jayadrathaḥ*—a son named Jayadratha; *udāhṛtaḥ*—celebrated as his son.

TRANSLATION

The sons of Pṛthulākṣa were Bṛhadratha, Bṛhatkarmā and Bṛhadbhānu. From the eldest, Bṛhadratha, came a son named Bṛhanmanā, and from Bṛhanmanā came a son named Jayadratha.

TEXT 12

विजयस्तस्य सम्भूत्यां ततो धृतिरजायत ।
ततो धृतव्रतस्तस्य सत्कर्माधिरथस्ततः ॥१२॥

vijayas tasya sambhūtyāṁ
tato dhṛtir ajāyata
tato dhṛtavratas tasya
satkarmādhirathas tataḥ

vijayaḥ—Vijaya; *tasya*—of him (Jayadratha); *sambhūtyām*—in the womb of the wife; *tataḥ*—thereafter (from Vijaya); *dhṛtiḥ*—Dhṛti; *ajāyata*—took birth; *tataḥ*—from him (Dhṛti); *dhṛtavrataḥ*—a son named Dhṛtavrata; *tasya*—of him (Dhṛtavrata); *satkarmā*—Satkarmā; *adhirathaḥ*—Adhiratha; *tataḥ*—from him (Satkarmā).

TRANSLATION

The son of Jayadratha, by the womb of his wife Sambhūti, was Vijaya, and from Vijaya, Dhṛti was born. From Dhṛti came Dhṛtavrata; from Dhṛtavrata, Satkarmā; and from Satkarmā, Adhiratha.

TEXT 13

योऽसौ गङ्गातटे क्रीडन् मञ्जूषान्तर्गतं शिशुम् ।
कुन्त्यापविद्धं कानीनमनपत्योऽकरोत् सुतम् ॥१३॥

yo 'sau gaṅgā-taṭe krīḍan
mañjūṣāntargataṁ śiśum
kuntyāpaviddhaṁ kānīnam
anapatyo 'karot sutam

yaḥ asau—one who (Adhiratha); *gaṅgā-taṭe*—on the bank of the Ganges; *krīḍan*—while playing; *mañjūṣa-antaḥgatam*—packed in a basket; *śiśum*—a baby was found; *kuntyā apaviddham*—this baby had been abandoned by Kuntī; *kānīnam*—because the baby was born during her maiden state, before her marriage; *anapatyaḥ*—this Adhiratha, being sonless; *akarot*—accepted the baby; *sutam*—as his son.

TRANSLATION

While playing on the bank of the Ganges, Adhiratha found a baby wrapped up in a basket. The baby had been left by Kuntī because he was born before she was married. Because Adhiratha had no sons, he raised this baby as his own. [This son was later known as Karṇa.]

TEXT 14

वृषसेनः सुतस्तस्य कर्णस्य जगतीपते ।
द्रुह्योश्च तनयो बभ्रुः सेतुस्तस्यात्मजस्ततः ॥१४॥

vṛṣasenaḥ sutas tasya
karṇasya jagatīpate
druhyoś ca tanayo babhruḥ
setus tasyātmajas tataḥ

vṛṣasenaḥ—Vṛṣasena; *sutaḥ*—a son; *tasya karṇasya*—of that same Karṇa; *jagatī pate*—O Mahārāja Parīkṣit; *druyoḥ ca*—of Druhyu, the third son of Yayāti; *tanayaḥ*—a son; *babhruḥ*—Babhru; *setuḥ*—Setu; *tasya*—of him (Babhru); *ātmajaḥ tataḥ*—a son thereafter.

TRANSLATION

O King, the only son of Karṇa was Vṛṣasena. Druhyu, the third son of Yayāti, had a son named Babhru, and the son of Babhru was known as Setu.

TEXT 15

आरब्धस्तस्य गान्धारस्तस्य धर्मस्ततो धृतः ।
धृतस्य दुर्मदस्तस्मात् प्रचेताः प्राचेतसः शतम् ॥१५॥

ārabdhas tasya gāndhāras
tasya dharmas tato dhṛtaḥ
dhṛtasya durmadas tasmāt
pracetāḥ prācetasaḥ śatam

ārabdhaḥ—Ārabdha (was the son of Setu); *tasya*—of him (Ārabdha); *gāndhāraḥ*—a son named Gāndhāra; *tasya*—of him (Gāndhāra);

dharmaḥ—a son known as Dharma; *tataḥ*—from him (Dharma); *dhṛtaḥ*—a son named Dhṛta; *dhṛtasya*—of Dhṛta; *durmadaḥ*—a son named Durmada; *tasmāt*—from him (Durmada); *pracetāḥ*—a son named Pracetā; *prācetasaḥ*—of Pracetā; *śatam*—there were one hundred sons.

TRANSLATION

The son of Setu was Ārabdha, Ārabdha's son was Gāndhāra, and Gāndhāra's son was Dharma. Dharma's son was Dhṛta, Dhṛta's son was Durmada, and Durmada's son was Pracetā, who had one hundred sons.

TEXT 16

म्लेच्छाधिपतयोऽभूवन्नुदीचीं दिशमाश्रिताः ।
तुर्वसोश्च सुतो वह्निर्वह्नेर्भर्गोऽथ भानुमान् ॥१६॥

mlecchādhipatayo 'bhūvann
udīcīṁ diśam āśritāḥ
turvasoś ca suto vahnir
vahner bhargo 'tha bhānumān

mleccha—of the lands known as Mlecchadeśa (where Vedic civilization was not present); *adhipatayaḥ*—the kings; *abhūvan*—became; *udīcīm*—on the northern side of India; *diśam*—the direction; *āśritāḥ*—accepting as the jurisdiction; *turvasoḥ ca*—of Turvasu, the second son of Mahārāja Yayāti; *sutaḥ*—the son; *vahniḥ*—Vahni; *vahneḥ*—of Vahni; *bhargaḥ*—the son named Bharga; *atha*—thereafter, his son; *bhānumān*—Bhānumān.

TRANSLATION

The Pracetās [the sons of Pracetā] occupied the northern side of India, which was devoid of Vedic civilization, and became kings there. Yayāti's second son was Turvasu. The son of Turvasu was Vahni; the son of Vahni, Bharga; the son of Bharga, Bhānumān.

TEXT 17

त्रिभानुस्तत्सुतोऽस्यापि करन्धम उदारधीः ।
मरुत्तस्तत्सुतोऽपुत्रः पुत्रं पौरवमन्वभूत् ॥१७॥

tribhānus tat-suto 'syāpi
karandhama udāra-dhīḥ
marutas tat-suto 'putraḥ
putraṁ pauravam anvabhūt

tribhānuḥ—Tribhānu; *tat-sutaḥ*—the son of Bhānumān; *asya*—of him (Tribhānu); *api*—also; *karandhamaḥ*—Karandhama; *udāra-dhīḥ*—who was very magnanimous; *marutaḥ*—Maruta; *tat-sutaḥ*—the son of Karandhama; *aputraḥ*—being without issue; *putram*—as his son; *pauravam*—a son of the Pūru dynasty, Mahārāja Duṣmanta; *anvabhūt*—adopted.

TRANSLATION

The son of Bhānumān was Tribhānu, and his son was the magnanimous Karandhama. Karandhama's son was Maruta, who had no sons and who therefore adopted a son of the Pūru dynasty [Mahārāja Duṣmanta] as his own.

TEXTS 18–19

दुष्मन्तः स पुनर्भेजे स्ववंशं राज्यकामुकः ।
ययातेर्ज्येष्ठपुत्रस्य यदोर्वंशं नरर्षभ ॥१८॥
वर्णयामि महापुण्यं सर्वपापहरं नृणाम् ।
यदोर्वंशं नरः श्रुत्वा सर्वपापैः प्रमुच्यते ॥१९॥

duṣmantaḥ sa punar bheje
sva-vaṁśaṁ rājya-kāmukaḥ
yayāter jyeṣṭha-putrasya
yador vaṁśaṁ nararṣabha

varṇayāmi mahā-puṇyaṁ
sarva-pāpa-haraṁ nṛṇām
yador vaṁśaṁ naraḥ śrutvā
sarva-pāpaiḥ pramucyate

duṣmantaḥ—Mahārāja Duṣmanta; *saḥ*—he; *punaḥ bheje*—again accepted; *sva-vaṁśam*—his original dynasty (the Pūru dynasty);

rājya-kāmukaḥ—because of desiring the royal throne; *yayāteḥ*—of Mahārāja Yayāti; *jyeṣṭha-putrasya*—of the first son, Yadu; *yadoḥ vaṁśam*—the dynasty of Yadu; *nara-ṛṣabha*—O best of human beings, Mahārāja Parīkṣit; *varṇayāmi*—I shall describe; *mahā-puṇyam*—supremely pious; *sarva-pāpa-haram*—vanquishes the reactions of sinful activities; *nṛṇām*—of human society; *yadoḥ vaṁśam*—the description of the dynasty of Yadu; *naraḥ*—any person; *śrutvā*—simply by hearing; *sarva-pāpaiḥ*—from all reactions of sinful activities; *pramucyate*—is freed.

TRANSLATION

Mahārāja Duṣmanta, desiring to occupy the throne, returned to his original dynasty [the Pūru dynasty], even though he had accepted Maruta as his father. O Mahārāja Parīkṣit, let me now describe the dynasty of Yadu, the eldest son of Mahārāja Yayāti. This description is supremely pious, and it vanquishes the reactions of sinful activities in human society. Simply by hearing this description, one is freed from all sinful reactions.

TEXTS 20–21

यत्रावतीर्णो भगवान् परमात्मा नराकृतिः ।
यदोः सहस्रजित्क्रोष्टा नलो रिपुरिति श्रुताः ॥२०॥
चत्वारः सूनवस्तत्र शतजित् प्रथमात्मजः ।
महाहयो रेणुहयो हैहयश्चेति तत्सुताः ॥२१॥

yatrāvatīrṇo bhagavān
paramātmā narākṛtiḥ
yadoḥ sahasrajit kroṣṭā
nalo ripur iti śrutāḥ

catvāraḥ sūnavas tatra
śatajit prathamātmajaḥ
mahāhayo reṇuhayo
haihayaś ceti tat-sutāḥ

yatra—wherein, in which dynasty; *avatīrṇaḥ*—descended; *bhagavān*—the Supreme Personality of Godhead, Kṛṣṇa; *paramātmā*—who is the Supersoul of all living entities; *nara-ākṛtiḥ*—a person, exactly resembling a human being; *yadoḥ*—of Yadu; *sahasrajit*—Sahasrajit; *kroṣṭā*—Kroṣṭā; *nalaḥ*—Nala; *ripuḥ*—Ripu; *iti śrutāḥ*—thus they are celebrated; *catvāraḥ*—four; *sūnavaḥ*—sons; *tatra*—therein; *śatajit*—Śatajit; *prathama-ātmajaḥ*—of the first sons; *mahāhayaḥ*—Mahāhaya; *reṇuhayaḥ*—Reṇuhaya; *haihayaḥ*—Haihaya; *ca*—and; *iti*—thus; *tat-sutāḥ*—his sons (the sons of Śatajit).

TRANSLATION

The Supreme Personality of Godhead, Kṛṣṇa, the Supersoul in the hearts of all living entities, descended in His original form as a human being in the dynasty or family of Yadu. Yadu had four sons, named Sahasrajit, Kroṣṭā, Nala and Ripu. Of these four, the eldest, Sahasrajit, had a son named Śatajit, who had three sons, named Mahāhaya, Reṇuhaya and Haihaya.

PURPORT

As confirmed in *Śrīmad-Bhāgavatam* (1.2.11):

vadanti tat tattva-vidas
tattvaṁ yaj jñānam advayam
brahmeti paramātmeti
bhagavān iti śabdyate

"Learned transcendentalists who know the Absolute Truth call this non-dual substance Brahman, Paramātmā or Bhagavān." The majority of transcendentalists understand only the impersonal Brahman or localized Paramātmā, for the Personality of Godhead is very difficult to understand. As the Lord says in *Bhagavad-gītā* (7.3):

manuṣyāṇāṁ sahasreṣu
kaścid yatati siddhaye
yatatām api siddhānāṁ
kaścin māṁ vetti tattvataḥ

"Out of many thousands among men, one may endeavor for perfection, and of those who have achieved perfection, hardly one knows Me in truth." The *yogīs* and *jñānīs*—that is, the mystic *yogīs* and the impersonalists—can understand the Absolute Truth as impersonal or localized, but although such realized souls are above ordinary human beings, they cannot understand how the Supreme Absolute Truth can be a person. Therefore it is said that out of many *siddhas*, the souls who have already realized the Absolute Truth, one may understand Kṛṣṇa, who exactly resembles a human being (*narākṛti*). This human form was explained by Kṛṣṇa Himself after He manifested the *virāṭ-rūpa*. The *virāṭ-rūpa* is not the original form of the Lord; the Lord's original form is Dvibhuja-śyāmasundara, Muralīdhara, the Lord with two hands, playing a flute (*yaṁ śyāmasundaram acintya-guṇa-svarūpam*). The Lord's forms are proof of His inconceivable qualities. Although the Lord maintains innumerable universes within the period of His breath, He is dressed with a form exactly like that of a human being. That does not mean, however, that He is a human being. This is His original form, but because He looks like a human being, those with a poor fund of knowledge consider Him an ordinary man. The Lord says:

avajānanti māṁ mūḍhā
mānuṣīṁ tanum āśritam
paraṁ bhāvam ajānanto
mama bhūta-maheśvaram

"Fools deride Me when I descend in the human form. They do not know My transcendental nature and My supreme dominion over all that be." (Bg. 9.11) By the Lord's *paraṁ bhāvam*, or transcendental nature, He is the all-pervading Paramātmā living in the core of the hearts of all living entities, yet He looks like a human being. Māyāvāda philosophy says that the Lord is originally impersonal but assumes a human form and many other forms when He descends. Actually, however, He is originally like a human being, and the impersonal Brahman consists of the rays of His body (*yasya prabhā prabhavato jagad-aṇḍa-koṭi*).

TEXT 22

धर्मस्तु हैहयसुतो नेत्रः कुन्तेः पिता ततः ।
सोहञ्जिरभवत् कुन्तेर्महिष्मान् भद्रसेनकः ॥२२॥

dharmas tu haihaya-suto
netraḥ kunteḥ pitā tataḥ
sohañjir abhavat kunter
mahiṣmān bhadrasenakaḥ

dharmaḥ tu—Dharma, however; *haihaya-sutaḥ*—became the son of Haihaya; *netraḥ*—Netra; *kunteḥ*—of Kunti; *pitā*—the father; *tataḥ*—from him (Dharma); *sohañjiḥ*—Sohañji; *abhavat*—became; *kunteḥ*—the son of Kunti; *mahiṣmān*—Mahiṣmān; *bhadrasenakaḥ*—Bhadrasenaka.

TRANSLATION

The son of Haihaya was Dharma, and the son of Dharma was Netra, the father of Kunti. From Kunti came a son named Sohañji, from Sohañji came Mahiṣmān, and from Mahiṣmān, Bhadrasenaka.

TEXT 23

दुर्मदो भद्रसेनस्य धनकः कृतवीर्यसूः ।
कृताग्निः कृतवर्मा च कृतौजा धनकात्मजाः ॥२३॥

durmado bhadrasenasya
dhanakaḥ kṛtavīryasūḥ
kṛtāgniḥ kṛtavarmā ca
kṛtaujā dhanakātmajāḥ

durmadaḥ—Durmada; *bhadrasenasya*—of Bhadrasena; *dhanakaḥ*—Dhanaka; *kṛtavīrya-sūḥ*—giving birth to Kṛtavīrya; *kṛtāgniḥ*—by the name Kṛtāgni; *kṛtavarmā*—Kṛtavarmā; *ca*—also; *kṛtaujāḥ*—Kṛtaujā; *dhanaka-ātmajāḥ*—sons of Dhanaka.

TRANSLATION

The sons of Bhadrasena were known as Durmada and Dhanaka. Dhanaka was the father of Kṛtavīrya and also of Kṛtāgni, Kṛtavarmā and Kṛtaujā.

TEXT 24

अर्जुनः कृतवीर्यस्य सप्तद्वीपेश्वरोऽभवत् ।
दत्तात्रेयाद्धरेरंशात् प्राप्तयोगमहागुणः ॥२४॥

arjunaḥ kṛtavīryasya
sapta-dvīpeśvaro 'bhavat
dattātreyād dharer aṁśāt
prāpta-yoga-mahāguṇaḥ

arjunaḥ—Arjuna; *kṛtavīryasya*—of Kṛtavīrya; *sapta-dvīpa*—of the seven islands (the whole world); *īśvaraḥ abhavat*—became the emperor; *dattātreyāt*—from Dattātreya; *hareḥ aṁśāt*—from he who was the incarnation of the Supreme Personality of Godhead; *prāpta*—obtained; *yoga-mahāguṇaḥ*—the quality of mystic power.

TRANSLATION

The son of Kṛtavīrya was Arjuna. He [Kārtavīryārjuna] became the emperor of the entire world, consisting of seven islands, and received mystic power from Dattātreya, the incarnation of the Supreme Personality of Godhead. Thus he obtained the mystic perfections known as aṣṭa-siddhi.

TEXT 25

न नूनं कार्तवीर्यस्य गतिं यास्यन्ति पार्थिवाः ।
यज्ञदानतपोयोगैः श्रुतवीर्यदयादिभिः ॥२५॥

na nūnaṁ kārtavīryasya
gatiṁ yāsyanti pārthivāḥ
yajña-dāna-tapo-yogaiḥ
śruta-vīrya-dayādibhiḥ

na—not; *nūnam*—indeed; *kārtavīryasya*—of Emperor Kārtavīrya; *gatim*—the activities; *yāsyanti*—could understand or achieve; *pārthivāḥ*—everyone on the earth; *yajña*—sacrifices; *dāna*—charity;

tapaḥ—austerities; *yogaiḥ*—mystic powers; *śruta*—education; *vīrya*—strength; *dayā*—mercy; *ādibhiḥ*—by all these qualities.

TRANSLATION

No other king in this world could equal Kārtavīryārjuna in sacrifices, charity, austerity, mystic power, education, strength or mercy.

TEXT 26

पञ्चाशीतिसहस्राणि ह्यव्याहतबलः समाः ।
अनष्टवित्तस्मरणो बुभुजेऽक्षय्यषड्वसु ॥२६॥

pañcāśīti sahasrāṇi
hy avyāhata-balaḥ samāḥ
anaṣṭa-vitta-smaraṇo
bubhuje 'kṣayya-ṣaḍ-vasu

pañcāśīti—eighty-five; *sahasrāṇi*—thousands; *hi*—indeed; *avyāhata*—inexhaustible; *balaḥ*—the strength of whom; *samāḥ*—years; *anaṣṭa*—without deterioration; *vitta*—material opulences; *smaraṇaḥ*—and memory; *bubhuje*—enjoyed; *akṣayya*—without deterioration; *ṣaṭ-vasu*—six kinds of enjoyable material opulence.

TRANSLATION

For eighty-five thousand years, Kārtavīryārjuna continuously enjoyed material opulences with full bodily strength and unimpaired memory. In other words, he enjoyed inexhaustible material opulences with his six senses.

TEXT 27

तस्य पुत्रसहस्रेषु पञ्चैवोर्वरिता मृधे ।
जयध्वजः शूरसेनो वृषभो मधुरूर्जितः ॥२७॥

tasya putra-sahasreṣu
pañcaivorvaritā mṛdhe

jayadhvajaḥ śūraseno
vṛṣabho madhur ūrjitaḥ

tasya—of him (Kārtavīryārjuna); *putra-sahasreṣu*—among the one thousand sons; *pañca*—five; *eva*—only; *urvaritāḥ*—remained alive; *mṛdhe*—in a fight (with Paraśurāma); *jayadhvajaḥ*—Jayadhvaja; *śūrasenaḥ*—Śūrasena; *vṛṣabhaḥ*—Vṛṣabha; *madhuḥ*—Madhu; *ūrjitaḥ*—and Ūrjita.

TRANSLATION

Of the one thousand sons of Kārtavīryārjuna, only five remained alive after the fight with Paraśurāma. Their names were Jayadhvaja, Śūrasena, Vṛṣabha, Madhu and Ūrjita.

TEXT 28

जयध्वजात् तालजङ्घस्तस्य पुत्रशतं त्वभूत् ।
क्षत्रं यत् तालजङ्घाख्यमौर्वतेजोपसंहृतम् ॥२८॥

jayadhvajāt tālajaṅghas
tasya putra-śataṁ tv abhūt
kṣatraṁ yat tālajaṅghākhyam
aurva-tejopasaṁhṛtam

jayadhvajāt—of Jayadhvaja; *tālajaṅghaḥ*—a son named Tālajaṅgha; *tasya*—of him (Tālajaṅgha); *putra-śatam*—one hundred sons; *tu*—indeed; *abhūt*—were born; *kṣatram*—a dynasty of *kṣatriyas; yat*—which; *tālajaṅgha-ākhyam*—were known as the Tālajaṅghas; *aurva-tejaḥ*—being very powerful; *upasaṁhṛtam*—were killed by Mahārāja Sagara.

TRANSLATION

Jayadhvaja had a son named Tālajaṅgha, who had one hundred sons. All the kṣatriyas in that dynasty, known as Tālajaṅgha, were annihilated by the great power received by Mahārāja Sagara from Aurva Ṛṣi.

TEXT 29

तेषां ज्येष्ठो वीतिहोत्रो वृष्णिः पुत्रो मधोः स्मृतः ।
तस्य पुत्रशतं त्वासीद् वृष्णिज्येष्ठं यतः कुलम् ॥२९॥

teṣāṁ jyeṣṭho vītihotro
vṛṣṇiḥ putro madhoḥ smṛtaḥ
tasya putra-śataṁ tv āsīd
vṛṣṇi-jyeṣṭhaṁ yataḥ kulam

teṣām—of all of them; *jyeṣṭhaḥ*—the eldest son; *vītihotraḥ*—a son named Vītihotra; *vṛṣṇiḥ*—Vṛṣṇi; *putraḥ*—the son; *madhoḥ*—of Madhu; *smṛtaḥ*—was well known; *tasya*—of him (Vṛṣṇi); *putra-śatam*—one hundred sons; *āsīt*—there were; *vṛṣṇi*—Vṛṣṇi; *jyeṣṭham*—the eldest; *yataḥ*—from him; *kulam*—the dynasty.

TRANSLATION

Of the sons of Tālajaṅgha, Vītihotra was the eldest. The son of Vītihotra named Madhu had a celebrated son named Vṛṣṇi. Madhu had one hundred sons, of whom Vṛṣṇi was the eldest. The dynasties known as Yādava, Mādhava and Vṛṣṇi had their origin from Yadu, Madhu and Vṛṣṇi.

TEXTS 30–31

माधवा वृष्णयो राजन् यादवाश्चेति संज्ञिताः ।
यदुपुत्रस्य च क्रोष्टोः पुत्रो वृजिनवांस्ततः ॥३०॥
स्वाहितोऽतो विषद्गुर्वै तस्य चित्ररथस्ततः ।
शशबिन्दुर्महायोगी महाभागो महानभूत् ।
चतुर्दशमहारत्नश्चक्रवर्त्यपराजितः ॥३१॥

mādhavā vṛṣṇayo rājan
yādavāś ceti saṁjñitāḥ
yadu-putrasya ca kroṣṭoḥ
putro vṛjinavāṁs tataḥ

svāhito 'to viṣadgur vai
tasya citrarathas tataḥ
śaśabindur mahā-yogī
mahā-bhāgo mahān abhūt
caturdaśa-mahāratnaś
cakravarty aparājitaḥ

mādhavāḥ—the dynasty beginning from Madhu; *vṛṣṇayaḥ*—the dynasty beginning from Vṛṣṇi; *rājan*—O King (Mahārāja Parīkṣit); *yādavāḥ*—the dynasty beginning from Yadu; *ca*—and; *iti*—thus; *saṁjñitāḥ*—are so-called because of those different persons; *yadu-putrasya*—of the son of Yadu; *ca*—also; *kroṣṭoḥ*—of Kroṣṭā; *putraḥ*—the son; *vṛjinavān*—his name was Vṛjinavān; *tataḥ*—from him (Vṛjinavān); *svāhitaḥ*—Svāhita; *ataḥ*—thereafter; *viṣadguḥ*—a son named Viṣadgu; *vai*—indeed; *tasya*—of him; *citrarathaḥ*—Citraratha; *tataḥ*—from him; *śaśabinduḥ*—Śaśabindu; *mahā-yogī*—a great mystic; *mahā-bhāgaḥ*—most fortunate; *mahān*—a great personality; *abhūt*—he became; *caturdaśa-mahāratnaḥ*—fourteen kinds of great opulences; *cakravartī*—he possessed as the emperor; *aparājitaḥ*—not defeated by anyone else.

TRANSLATION

O Mahārāja Parīkṣit, because Yadu, Madhu and Vṛṣṇi each inaugurated a dynasty, their dynasties are known as Yādava, Mādhava and Vṛṣṇi. The son of Yadu named Kroṣṭā had a son named Vṛjinavān. The son of Vṛjinavān was Svāhita; the son of Svāhita, Viṣadgu; the son of Viṣadgu, Citraratha; and the son of Citraratha, Śaśabindu. The greatly fortunate Śaśabindu, who was a great mystic, possessed fourteen opulences and was the owner of fourteen great jewels. Thus he became the emperor of the world.

PURPORT

In the *Mārkaṇḍeya Purāṇa* the fourteen kinds of great jewels are described as follows: (1) an elephant, (2) a horse, (3) a chariot, (4) a wife, (5) arrows, (6) a reservoir of wealth, (7) a garland, (8) valuable costumes, (9) trees, (10) a spear, (11) a noose, (12) jewels, (13) an umbrella, and (14) regulative principles. To be the emperor, one must possess all fourteen of these opulences. Śaśabindu possessed them all.

TEXT 32

तस्य पत्नीसहस्राणां दशानां सुमहायशाः ।
दशलक्षसहस्राणि पुत्राणां तास्वजीजनत् ॥३२॥

tasya patnī-sahasrāṇāṁ
daśānāṁ sumahā-yaśāḥ
daśa-lakṣa-sahasrāṇi
putrāṇāṁ tāsv ajījanat

tasya—of Śaśabindu; *patnī*—wives; *sahasrāṇām*—of thousands; *daśānām*—ten; *su-mahā-yaśāḥ*—greatly famous; *daśa*—ten; *lakṣa*—*lakhs* (one *lakh* equals one hundred thousand); *sahasrāṇi*—thousands; *putrāṇām*—of sons; *tāsu*—in them; *ajījanat*—he begot.

TRANSLATION

The famous Śaśabindu had ten thousand wives, and by each he begot a lakh of sons. Therefore the number of his sons was ten thousand lakhs.

TEXT 33

तेषां तु षट्प्रधानानां पृथुश्रवस आत्मजः ।
धर्मो नामोशना तस्य हयमेधशतस्य याट् ॥३३॥

teṣāṁ tu ṣaṭ pradhānānāṁ
pṛthuśravasa ātmajaḥ
dharmo nāmośanā tasya
hayamedha-śatasya yāṭ

teṣām—out of so many sons; *tu*—but; *ṣaṭ pradhānānām*—of whom there were six foremost sons; *pṛthuśravasaḥ*—of Pṛthuśravā; *ātmajaḥ*—the son; *dharmaḥ*—Dharma; *nāma*—by the name; *uśanā*—Uśanā; *tasya*—his; *hayamedha-śatasya*—of one hundred *aśvamedha* sacrifices; *yāṭ*—he was the performer.

TRANSLATION

Among these many sons, six were the foremost, such as Pṛthuśravā and Pṛthukīrti. The son of Pṛthuśravā was known as Dharma, and his son was known as Uśanā. Uśanā was the performer of one hundred horse sacrifices.

TEXT 34

तत्सुतो रुचकस्तस्य पञ्चासन्नात्मजाः शृणु ।
पुरुजिद्रुक्मरुक्मेषुपृथुज्यामघसंज्ञिताः ॥३४॥

tat-suto rucakas tasya
pañcāsann ātmajāḥ śṛṇu
purujid-rukma-rukmeṣu-
pṛthu-jyāmagha-saṁjñitāḥ

tat-sutaḥ—the son of Uśanā; *rucakaḥ*—Rucaka; *tasya*—of him; *pañca*—five; *āsan*—there were; *ātmajāḥ*—sons; *śṛṇu*—please hear (their names); *purujit*—Purujit; *rukma*—Rukma; *rukmeṣu*—Rukmeṣu; *pṛthu*—Pṛthu; *jyāmagha*—Jyāmagha; *saṁjñitāḥ*—these five sons were named.

TRANSLATION

The son of Uśanā was Rucaka, who had five sons—Purujit, Rukma, Rukmeṣu, Pṛthu and Jyāmagha. Please hear of these sons from me.

TEXTS 35–36

ज्यामघस्त्वप्रजोऽप्यन्यां भार्यां शैब्यापतिर्भयात् ।
नाविन्दच्छत्रुभवनाद् भोज्यां कन्यामहारषीत् ।
रथस्थां तां निरीक्ष्याह शैब्या पतिममर्षिता ॥३५॥
केयं कुहक मत्स्थानं रथमारोपितेति वै ।
स्नुषा तवेत्यभिहिते स्मयन्ती पतिमब्रवीत् ॥३६॥

jyāmaghas tv aprajo 'py anyāṁ
bhāryāṁ śaibyā-patir bhayāt

nāvindac chatru-bhavanād
bhojyāṁ kanyām ahāraṣīt
ratha-sthāṁ tāṁ nirīkṣyāha
śaibyā patim amarṣitā

keyaṁ kuhaka mat-sthānaṁ
ratham āropiteti vai
snuṣā tavety abhihite
smayantī patim abravīt

jyāmaghaḥ—King Jyāmagha; *tu*—indeed; *aprajaḥ api*—although issueless; *anyām*—another; *bhāryām*—wife; *śaibyā-patiḥ*—because he was the husband of Śaibyā; *bhayāt*—out of fear; *na avindat*—did not accept; *śatru-bhavanāt*—from the enemy's camp; *bhojyām*—a prostitute used for sense gratification; *kanyām*—girl; *ahāraṣīt*—brought; *ratha-sthām*—who was seated on the chariot; *tām*—her; *nirīkṣya*—seeing; *āha*—said; *śaibyā*—Śaibyā, the wife of Jyāmagha; *patim*—unto her husband; *amarṣitā*—being very angry; *kā iyam*—who is this; *kuhaka*—you cheater; *mat-sthānam*—my place; *ratham*—on the chariot; *aropitā*—has been allowed to sit; *iti*—thus; *vai*—indeed; *snuṣā*—daughter-in-law; *tava*—your; *iti*—thus; *abhihite*—being informed; *smayantī*—smilingly; *patim*—unto her husband; *abravīt*—said.

TRANSLATION

Jyāmagha had no sons, but because he was fearful of his wife, Śaibyā, he could not accept another wife. Jyāmagha once took from the house of some royal enemy a girl who was a prostitute, but upon seeing her Śaibyā was very angry and said to her husband, "My husband, you cheater, who is this girl sitting upon my seat on the chariot?" Jyāmagha then replied, "This girl will be your daughter-in-law." Upon hearing these joking words, Śaibyā smilingly replied.

TEXT 37

अहं बन्ध्यासपत्नी च स्नुषा मे युज्यते कथम् ।
जनयिष्यसि यं राज्ञि तस्येयमुपयुज्यते ॥३७॥

ahaṁ bandhyāsapatnī ca
snuṣā me yujyate katham
janayiṣyasi yaṁ rājñi
tasyeyam upayujyate

aham—I am; *bandhyā*—sterile; *asa-patnī*—I have no co-wife; *ca*—also; *snuṣā*—daughter-in-law; *me*—my; *yujyate*—could be; *katham*—how; *janayiṣyasi*—you will give birth to; *yam*—which son; *rājñi*—O my dear Queen; *tasya*—for him; *iyam*—this girl; *upayujyate*—will be very suitable.

TRANSLATION

Śaibyā said, "I am sterile and have no co-wife. How can this girl be my daughter-in-law? Please tell me." Jyāmagha replied, "My dear Queen, I shall see that you indeed have a son and that this girl will be your daughter-in-law."

TEXT 38

अन्वमोदन्त तद्विश्वेदेवाः पितर एव च ।
शैब्या गर्भमधात् काले कुमारं सुषुवे शुभम् ।
स विदर्भ इति प्रोक्त उपयेमे स्नुषां सतीम् ॥३८॥

anvamodanta tad viśve-
devāḥ pitara eva ca
śaibyā garbham adhāt kāle
kumāraṁ suṣuve śubham
sa vidarbha iti prokta
upayeme snuṣāṁ satīm

anvamodanta—accepted; *tat*—that statement predicting the birth of a son; *viśvedevāḥ*—the Viśvedeva demigods; *pitaraḥ*—the Pitās or forefathers; *eva*—indeed; *ca*—also; *śaibyā*—the wife of Jyāmagha; *garbham*—pregnancy; *adhāt*—conceived; *kāle*—in due course of time; *kumāram*—a son; *suṣuve*—gave birth to; *śubham*—very auspicious; *saḥ*—that son; *vidarbhaḥ*—Vidarbha; *iti*—thus; *proktaḥ*—was well known; *upayeme*—later married; *snuṣām*—who was accepted as daughter-in-law; *satīm*—very chaste girl.

TRANSLATION

Long, long ago, Jyāmagha had satisfied the demigods and Pitās by worshiping them. Now, by their mercy, Jyāmagha's words came true. Although Śaibyā was barren, by the grace of the demigods she became pregnant and in due course of time gave birth to a child named Vidarbha. Before the child's birth, the girl had been accepted as a daughter-in-law, and therefore Vidarbha actually married her when he grew up.

Thus end the Bhaktivedanta purports of the Ninth Canto, Twenty-third Chapter, of the Śrīmad-Bhāgavatam, *entitled "The Dynasties of the Sons of Yayāti."*

CHAPTER TWENTY-FOUR

Kṛṣṇa, the Supreme Personality of Godhead

Vidarbha had three sons, named Kuśa, Kratha and Romapāda. Of these three, Romapāda expanded his dynasty by the sons and grandsons named Babhru, Kṛti, Uśika, Cedi and Caidya, all of whom later became kings. From the son of Vidarbha named Kratha came a son named Kunti, from whose dynasty came the descendants named Vṛṣṇi, Nirvṛti, Daśārha, Vyoma, Jīmūta, Vikṛti, Bhīmaratha, Navaratha, Daśaratha, Śakuni, Karambhi, Devarāta, Devakṣatra, Madhu, Kuruvaśa, Anu, Puruhotra, Ayu and Sātvata. Sātvata had seven sons. One of them was Devāvṛdha, whose son was Babhru. Another son of Sātvata was Mahābhoja, by whom the Bhoja dynasty was inaugurated. Another was Vṛṣṇi, who had a son named Yudhājit. From Yudhājit came Anamitra and Śini, and from Anamitra came Nighna and another Śini. The descendants in succession from Śini were Satyaka, Yuyudhāna, Jaya, Kuṇi and Yugandhara. Another son of Anamitra was Vṛṣṇi. From Vṛṣṇi came Śvaphalka, by whom Akrūra and twelve other sons were generated. From Akrūra came two sons, named Devavān and Upadeva. The son of Andhaka named Kukura was the origin of the descendants known as Vahni, Vilomā, Kapotaromā, Anu, Andhaka, Dundubhi, Avidyota, Punarvasu and Āhuka. Āhuka had two sons, named Devaka and Ugrasena. The four sons of Devaka were known as Devavān, Upadeva, Sudeva and Devavardhana, and his seven daughters were Dhṛtadevā, Śāntidevā, Upadevā, Śrīdevā, Devarakṣitā, Sahadevā and Devakī. Vasudeva married all seven daughters of Devaka. Ugrasena had nine sons named Kaṁsa, Sunāmā, Nyagrodha, Kaṅka, Śaṅku, Suhū, Rāṣṭrapāla, Dhṛṣṭi and Tuṣṭimān, and he had five daughters named Kaṁsā, Kaṁsavatī, Kaṅkā, Śūrabhū and Rāṣṭrapālikā. The younger brothers of Vasudeva married all the daughters of Ugrasena.

Vidūratha, the son of Citraratha, had a son named Śūra, who had ten other sons, of whom Vasudeva was the chief. Śūra gave one of his five daughters, Pṛthā, to his friend Kunti, and therefore she was also named

Kuntī. In her maiden state she gave birth to a child named Karṇa, and later she married Mahārāja Pāṇḍu.

Vṛddhaśarmā married the daughter of Śūra named Śrutadevā, from whose womb Dantavakra was born. Dhṛṣṭaketu married Śūra's daughter named Śrutakīrti, who had five sons. Jayasena married Śūra's daughter named Rājādhidevī. The king of Cedi-deśa, Damaghoṣa, married the daughter of Śūra named Śrutaśravā, from whom Śiśupāla was born.

Devabhāga, through the womb of Kaṁsā, begot Citraketu and Bṛhadbala; and Devaśravā, through the womb of Kaṁsavatī, begot Suvīra and Iṣumān. From Kaṅka, through the womb of Kaṅkā, came Baka, Satyajit and Purujit, and from Sṛñjaya, through the womb of Rāṣṭrapālikā, came Vṛṣa and Durmarṣaṇa. Śyāmaka, through the womb of Śūrabhūmi, begot Harikeśa and Hiraṇyākṣa. Vatsaka, through the womb of Miśrakeśī, begot Vṛka, who begot the sons named Takṣa, Puṣkara and Śāla. From Samīka came Sumitra and Arjunapāla, and from Ānaka came Ṛtadhāmā and Jaya.

Vasudeva had many wives, of whom Devakī and Rohiṇī were the most important. From the womb of Rohiṇī, Baladeva was born, along with Gada, Sāraṇa, Durmada, Vipula, Dhruva, Kṛta and others. Vasudeva had many other sons by his other wives, and the eighth son to appear from the womb of Devakī was the Supreme Personality of Godhead, who delivered the entire world from the burden of demons. This chapter ends by glorifying the Supreme Personality of Godhead Vāsudeva.

TEXT 1

श्रीशुक उवाच

तस्यां विदर्भोऽजनयत् पुत्रौ नाम्ना कुशक्रथौ ।
तृतीयं रोमपादं च विदर्भकुलनन्दनम् ॥ १ ॥

śrī-śuka uvāca
tasyāṁ vidarbho 'janayat
putrau nāmnā kuśa-krathau
tṛtīyaṁ romapādaṁ ca
vidarbha-kula-nandanam

śrī-śukaḥ uvāca—Śrī Śukadeva Gosvāmī said; *tasyām*—in that girl; *vidarbhaḥ*—the son born of Śaibyā named Vidarbha; *ajanayat*—gave birth; *putrau*—to two sons; *nāmnā*—by the name; *kuśa-krathau*—Kuśa and Kratha; *tṛtīyam*—and a third son; *romapādam ca*—Romapāda also; *vidarbha-kula-nandanam*—the favorite in the dynasty of Vidarbha.

TRANSLATION

Śukadeva Gosvāmī said: By the womb of the girl brought by his father, Vidarbha begot three sons, named Kuśa, Kratha and Romapāda. Romapāda was the favorite in the dynasty of Vidarbha.

TEXT 2

रोमपादसुतो बभ्रुर्बभ्रोः कृतिरजायत ।
उशिकस्तत्सुतस्तस्माच्चेदिश्चैद्यादयो नृपाः ॥ २ ॥

romapāda-suto babhrur
babhroḥ kṛtir ajāyata
uśikas tat-sutas tasmāc
cediś caidyādayo nṛpāḥ

romapāda-sutaḥ—the son of Romapāda; *babhruḥ*—Babhru; *babhroḥ*—from Babhru; *kṛtiḥ*—Kṛti; *ajāyata*—was born; *uśikaḥ*—Uśika; *tat-sutaḥ*—the son of Kṛti; *tasmāt*—from him (Uśika); *cediḥ*—Cedi; *caidya*—Caidya (Damaghoṣa); *ādayaḥ*—and others; *nṛpāḥ*—kings.

TRANSLATION

The son of Romapāda was Babhru, from whom there came a son named Kṛti. The son of Kṛti was Uśika, and the son of Uśika was Cedi. From Cedi was born the king known as Caidya and others.

TEXTS 3–4

क्रथस्य कुन्तिः पुत्रोऽभूद् वृष्णिस्तस्याथ निर्वृतिः ।
ततो दशार्हो नाम्नाभूत् तस्य व्योमः सुतस्ततः ॥ ३ ॥

जीमूतो विकृतिस्तस्य यस्य भीमरथः सुतः ।
ततो नवरथः पुत्रो जातो दशरथस्ततः ॥ ४ ॥

krathasya kuntiḥ putro 'bhūd
vṛṣṇis tasyātha nirvṛtiḥ
tato daśārho nāmnābhūt
tasya vyomaḥ sutas tataḥ

jīmūto vikṛtis tasya
yasya bhīmarathaḥ sutaḥ
tato navarathaḥ putro
jāto daśarathas tataḥ

krathasya—of Kratha; *kuntiḥ*—Kunti; *putraḥ*—a son; *abhūt*—was born; *vṛṣṇiḥ*—Vṛṣṇi; *tasya*—his; *atha*—then; *nirvṛtiḥ*—Nirvṛti; *tataḥ*—from him; *daśārhaḥ*—Daśārha; *nāmnā*—by name; *abhūt*—was born; *tasya*—of him; *vyomaḥ*—Vyoma; *sutaḥ*—a son; *tataḥ*—from him; *jīmūtaḥ*—Jīmūta; *vikṛtiḥ*—Vikṛti; *tasya*—his (Jīmūta's son); *yasya*—of whom (Vikṛti); *bhīmarathaḥ*—Bhīmaratha; *sutaḥ*—a son; *tataḥ*—from him (Bhīmaratha); *navarathaḥ*—Navaratha; *putraḥ*—a son; *jātaḥ*—was born; *daśarathaḥ*—Daśaratha; *tataḥ*—from him.

TRANSLATION

The son of Kratha was Kunti; the son of Kunti, Vṛṣṇi; the son of Vṛṣṇi, Nirvṛti; and the son of Nirvṛti, Daśārha. From Daśārha came Vyoma; from Vyoma came Jīmūta; from Jīmūta, Vikṛti; from Vikṛti, Bhīmaratha; from Bhīmaratha, Navaratha; and from Navaratha, Daśaratha.

TEXT 5

करम्भिः शकुनेः पुत्रो देवरातस्तदात्मजः ।
देवक्षत्रस्ततस्तस्य मधुः कुरुवशादनुः ॥ ५ ॥

karambhiḥ śakuneḥ putro
devarātas tad-ātmajaḥ

devakṣatras tatas tasya
madhuḥ kuruvaśād anuḥ

karambhiḥ—Karambhi; *śakuneḥ*—from Śakuni; *putraḥ*—a son; *devarātaḥ*—Devarāta; *tat-ātmajaḥ*—the son of him (Karambhi); *devakṣatraḥ*—Devakṣatra; *tataḥ*—thereafter; *tasya*—from him (Devakṣatra); *madhuḥ*—Madhu; *kuruvaśāt*—from Kuruvaśa, the son of Madhu; *anuḥ*—Anu.

TRANSLATION

From Daśaratha came a son named Śakuni and from Śakuni a son named Karambhi. The son of Karambhi was Devarāta, and his son was Devakṣatra. The son of Devakṣatra was Madhu, and his son was Kuruvaśa, from whom there came a son named Anu.

TEXTS 6–8

पुरुहोत्रस्त्वनोः पुत्रस्तस्यायुः सात्वतस्ततः ।
भजमानो भजिर्दिव्यो वृष्णिर्देवावृधोऽन्धकः ॥ ६ ॥
सात्वतस्य सुताः सप्त महाभोजश्च मारिष ।
भजमानस्य निम्लोचिः किङ्कणो धृष्टिरेव च ॥ ७ ॥
एकस्यामात्मजाः पत्न्यामन्यस्यां च त्रयः सुताः ।
शताजिच्च सहस्राजिदयुताजिदिति प्रभो ॥ ८ ॥

puruhotras tv anoḥ putras
tasyāyuḥ sātvatas tataḥ
bhajamāno bhajir divyo
vṛṣṇir devāvṛdho 'ndhakaḥ

sātvatasya sutāḥ sapta
mahābhojaś ca māriṣa
bhajamānasya nimlociḥ
kiṅkaṇo dhṛṣṭir eva ca

ekasyām ātmajāḥ patnyām
anyasyāṁ ca trayaḥ sutāḥ

śatājic ca sahasrājid
ayutājid iti prabho

puruhotraḥ—Puruhotra; *tu*—indeed; *anoḥ*—of Anu; *putraḥ*—the son; *tasya*—of him (Puruhotra); *ayuḥ*—Ayu; *sātvataḥ*—Sātvata; *tataḥ*—from him (Ayu); *bhajamānaḥ*—Bhajamāna; *bhajiḥ*—Bhaji; *divyaḥ*—Divya; *vṛṣṇiḥ*—Vṛṣṇi; *devāvṛdhaḥ*—Devāvṛdha; *andhakaḥ*—Andhaka; *sātvatasya*—of Sātvata; *sutāḥ*—sons; *sapta*—seven; *mahābhojaḥ ca*—as well as Mahābhoja; *māriṣa*—O great King; *bhajamānasya*—of Bhajamāna; *nimlociḥ*—Nimloci; *kiṅkaṇaḥ*—Kiṅkaṇa; *dhṛṣṭiḥ*—Dhṛṣṭi; *eva*—indeed; *ca*—also; *ekasyām*—born from one wife; *ātmajāḥ*—sons; *patnyām*—by a wife; *anyasyām*—another; *ca*—also; *trayaḥ*—three; *sutāḥ*—sons; *śatājit*—Śatājit; *ca*—also; *sahasrājit*—Sahasrājit; *ayutājit*—Ayutājit; *iti*—thus; *prabho*—O King.

TRANSLATION

The son of Anu was Puruhotra, the son of Puruhotra was Ayu, and the son of Ayu was Sātvata. O great Aryan King, Sātvata had seven sons, named Bhajamāna, Bhaji, Divya, Vṛṣṇi, Devāvṛdha, Andhaka and Mahābhoja. From Bhajamāna by one wife came three sons—Nimloci, Kiṅkaṇa and Dhṛṣṭi. And from his other wife came three other sons—Śatājit, Sahasrājit and Ayutājit.

TEXT 9

बभ्रुर्देवावृधसुतस्तयोः श्लोकौ पठन्त्यमू ।
यथैव शृणुमो दूरात् सम्पश्यामस्तथान्तिकात् ॥ ९ ॥

babhrur devāvṛdha-sutas
tayoḥ ślokau paṭhanty amū
yathaiva śṛṇumo dūrāt
sampaśyāmas tathāntikāt

babhruḥ—Babhru; *devāvṛdha*—of Devāvṛdha; *sutaḥ*—the son; *tayoḥ*—of them; *ślokau*—two verses; *paṭhanti*—all the members of the old generation recite; *amū*—those; *yathā*—as; *eva*—indeed;

śṛṇumaḥ—we have heard; *dūrāt*—from a distance; *sampaśyāmaḥ*—are actually seeing; *tathā*—similarly; *antikāt*—presently also.

TRANSLATION

The son of Devāvṛdha was Babhru. Concerning Devāvṛdha and Babhru there are two famous songs of prayer, which were sung by our predecessors and which we have heard from a distance. Even now I hear the same prayers about their qualities [because that which was heard before is still sung continuously].

TEXTS 10–11

बभ्रुः श्रेष्ठो मनुष्याणां देवैर्देवावृधः समः ।
पुरुषाः पञ्चषष्टिश्च षट् सहस्राणि चाष्ट च ॥१०॥
येऽमृतत्वमनुप्राप्ता बभ्रोर्देवावृधादपि ।
महाभोजोऽतिधर्मात्मा भोजा आसंस्तदन्वये ॥११॥

babhruḥ śreṣṭho manuṣyāṇāṁ
devair devāvṛdhaḥ samaḥ
puruṣāḥ pañca-ṣaṣṭiś ca
ṣaṭ-sahasrāṇi cāṣṭa ca

ye 'mṛtatvam anuprāptā
babhror devāvṛdhād api
mahābhojo 'tidharmātmā
bhojā āsaṁs tad-anvaye

babhruḥ—King Babhru; *śreṣṭhaḥ*—the best of all kings; *manuṣyāṇām*—of all human beings; *devaiḥ*—with the demigods; *devāvṛdhaḥ*—King Devāvṛdha; *samaḥ*—equally situated; *puruṣāḥ*—persons; *pañca-ṣaṣṭiḥ*—sixty-five; *ca*—also; *ṣaṭ-sahasrāṇi*—six thousand; *ca*—also; *aṣṭa*—eight thousand; *ca*—also; *ye*—all of them who; *amṛtatvam*—liberation from material bondage; *anuprāptāḥ*—achieved; *babhroḥ*—because of association with Babhru; *devāvṛdhāt*—and because of association with Devāvṛdha; *api*—indeed; *mahābhojaḥ*—King Mahābhoja; *ati-dharma-ātmā*—exceedingly religious; *bhojāḥ*—the kings known as Bhoja; *āsan*—existed; *tat-anvaye*—in the dynasty of him (Mahābhoja).

TRANSLATION

"It has been decided that among human beings Babhru is the best and that Devāvṛdha is equal to the demigods. Because of the association of Babhru and Devāvṛdha, all of their descendants, numbering 14,065, achieved liberation." In the dynasty of King Mahābhoja, who was exceedingly religious, there appeared the Bhoja kings.

TEXT 12

वृष्णेः सुमित्रः पुत्रोऽभूद् युधाजिच्च परंतप ।
शिनिस्तस्यानमित्रश्च निघ्नोऽभूदनमित्रतः ॥१२॥

vṛṣṇeḥ sumitraḥ putro 'bhūd
yudhājic ca parantapa
śinis tasyānamitraś ca
nighno 'bhūd anamitrataḥ

vṛṣṇeḥ—of Vṛṣṇi, the son of Sātvata; *sumitraḥ*—Sumitra; *putraḥ*—a son; *abhūt*—appeared; *yudhājit*—Yudhājit; *ca*—also; *param-tapa*—O king who can suppress enemies; *śiniḥ*—Śini; *tasya*—his; *ana-mitraḥ*—Anamitra; *ca*—and; *nighnaḥ*—Nighna; *abhūt*—appeared; *anamitrataḥ*—from Anamitra.

TRANSLATION

O King, Mahārāja Parīkṣit, who can suppress your enemies, the sons of Vṛṣṇi were Sumitra and Yudhājit. From Yudhājit came Śini and Anamitra, and from Anamitra came a son named Nighna.

TEXT 13

सत्राजितः प्रसेनश्च निघ्नस्याथासतुः सुतौ ।
अनमित्रसुतो योऽन्यः शिनिस्तस्य च सत्यकः ॥१३॥

satrājitaḥ prasenaś ca
nighnasyāthāsatuḥ sutau
anamitra-suto yo 'nyaḥ
śinis tasya ca satyakaḥ

satrājitaḥ—Satrājita; *prasenaḥ ca*—Prasena also; *nighnasya*—the sons of Nighna; *atha*—thus; *asatuḥ*—existed; *sutau*—two sons; *anamitra-sutaḥ*—the son of Anamitra; *yaḥ*—one who; *anyaḥ*—another; *śiniḥ*—Śini; *tasya*—his; *ca*—also; *satyakaḥ*—the son named Satyaka.

TRANSLATION

The two sons of Nighna were Satrājita and Prasena. Another son of Anamitra was another Śini, and his son was Satyaka.

TEXT 14

युयुधानः सात्यकिर्वै जयस्तस्य कुणिस्ततः ।
युगन्धरोऽनमित्रस्य वृष्णिः पुत्रोऽपरस्ततः ॥१४॥

yuyudhānaḥ sātyakir vai
jayas tasya kuṇis tataḥ
yugandharo 'namitrasya
vṛṣṇiḥ putro 'paras tataḥ

yuyudhānaḥ—Yuyudhāna; *sātyakiḥ*—the son of Satyaka; *vai*—indeed; *jayaḥ*—Jaya; *tasya*—of him (Yuyudhāna); *kuṇiḥ*—Kuṇi; *tataḥ*—from him (Jaya); *yugandharaḥ*—Yugandhara; *anamitrasya*—a son of Anamitra; *vṛṣṇiḥ*—Vṛṣṇi; *putraḥ*—a son; *aparaḥ*—other; *tataḥ*—from him.

TRANSLATION

The son of Satyaka was Yuyudhāna, whose son was Jaya. From Jaya came a son named Kuṇi and from Kuṇi a son named Yugandhara. Another son of Anamitra was Vṛṣṇi.

TEXT 15

श्वफल्कश्चित्ररथश्च गान्दिन्यां च श्वफल्कतः ।
अक्रूरप्रमुखा आसन् पुत्रा द्वादश विश्रुताः ॥१५॥

śvaphalkaś citrarathaś ca
gāndinyāṁ ca śvaphalkataḥ
akrūra-pramukhā āsan
putrā dvādaśa viśrutāḥ

śvaphalkaḥ—Śvaphalka; *citrarathaḥ ca*—and Citraratha; *gāndinyām*—through the wife named Gāndinī; *ca*—and; *śvaphalkataḥ*—from Śvaphalka; *akrūra*—Akrūra; *pramukhāḥ*—headed by; *āsan*—there were; *putrāḥ*—sons; *dvādaśa*—twelve; *viśrutāḥ*—most celebrated.

TRANSLATION

From Vṛṣṇi came the sons named Śvaphalka and Citraratha. From Śvaphalka by his wife Gāndinī came Akrūra. Akrūra was the eldest, but there were twelve other sons, all of whom were most celebrated.

TEXTS 16–18

आसङ्गः सारमेयश्च मृदुरो मृदुविद् गिरिः ।
धर्मवृद्धः सुकर्मा च क्षेत्रोपेक्षोऽरिमर्दनः ॥१६॥
शत्रुघ्नो गन्धमादश्च प्रतिबाहुश्च द्वादश ।
तेषां स्वसा सुचाराख्या द्वावक्रूरसुतावपि ॥१७॥
देववानुपदेवश्च तथा चित्ररथात्मजाः ।
पृथुर्विदूरथाद्याश्च बहवो वृष्णिनन्दनाः ॥१८॥

āsaṅgaḥ sārameyaś ca
mṛduro mṛduvid giriḥ
dharmavṛddhaḥ sukarmā ca
kṣetropekṣo 'rimardanaḥ

śatrughno gandhamādaś ca
pratibāhuś ca dvādaśa
teṣāṁ svasā sucārākhyā
dvāv akrūra-sutāv api

devavān upadevaś ca
tathā citrarathātmajāḥ
pṛthur vidūrathādyāś ca
bahavo vṛṣṇi-nandanāḥ

āsaṅgaḥ—Āsaṅga; *sārameyaḥ*—Sārameya; *ca*—also; *mṛduraḥ*—Mṛdura; *mṛduvit*—Mṛduvit; *giriḥ*—Giri; *dharmavṛddhaḥ*—Dharmavṛddha; *sukarmā*—Sukarmā; *ca*—also; *kṣetropekṣaḥ*—Kṣetropekṣa; *arimardanaḥ*—Arimardana; *śatrughnaḥ*—Śatrughna; *gandhamādaḥ*—Gandhamāda; *ca*—and; *pratibāhuḥ*—Pratibāhu; *ca*—and; *dvādaśa*—twelve; *teṣām*—of them; *svasā*—sister; *sucārā*—Sucārā; *ākhyā*—well known; *dvau*—two; *akrūra*—of Akrūra; *sutau*—sons; *api*—also; *devavān*—Devavān; *upadevaḥ ca*—and Upadeva; *tathā*—thereafter; *citraratha-ātmajāḥ*—the sons of Citraratha; *pṛthuḥ vidūratha*—Pṛthu and Vidūratha; *ādyāḥ*—beginning with; *ca*—also; *bahavaḥ*—many; *vṛṣṇi-nandanāḥ*—the sons of Vṛṣṇi.

TRANSLATION

The names of these twelve were Āsaṅga, Sārameya, Mṛdura, Mṛduvit, Giri, Dharmavṛddha, Sukarmā, Kṣetropekṣa, Arimardana, Śatrughna, Gandhamāda and Pratibāhu. These brothers also had a sister named Sucārā. From Akrūra came two sons, named Devavān and Upadeva. Citraratha had many sons, headed by Pṛthu and Vidūratha, all of whom were known as belonging to the dynasty of Vṛṣṇi.

TEXT 19

कुकुरो भजमानश्च शुचिः कम्बलबर्हिषः ।
कुकुरस्य सुतो वह्निर्विलोमा तनयस्ततः ॥१९॥

kukuro bhajamānaś ca
śuciḥ kambalabarhiṣaḥ
kukurasya suto vahnir
vilomā tanayas tataḥ

kukuraḥ—Kukura; *bhajamānaḥ*—Bhajamāna; *ca*—also; *śuciḥ*—Śuci; *kambalabarhiṣaḥ*—Kambalabarhiṣa; *kukurasya*—of Kukura; *sutaḥ*—a son; *vahniḥ*—Vahni; *vilomā*—Vilomā; *tanayaḥ*—son; *tataḥ*—from him (Vahni).

TRANSLATION

Kukura, Bhajamāna, Śuci and Kambalabarhiṣa were the four sons of Andhaka. The son of Kukura was Vahni, and his son was Vilomā.

TEXT 20

कपोतरोमा तस्यानुः सखा यस्य च तुम्बुरुः ।
अन्धकाद् दुन्दुभिस्तस्मादविद्योतः पुनर्वसुः ॥२०॥

kapotaromā tasyānuḥ
sakhā yasya ca tumburuḥ
andhakād dundubhis tasmād
avidyotaḥ punarvasuḥ

kapotaromā—Kapotaromā; *tasya*—his (son); *anuḥ*—Anu; *sakhā*—friend; *yasya*—whose; *ca*—also; *tumburuḥ*—Tumburu; *andhakāt*—of Andhaka, the son of Anu; *dundubhiḥ*—a son named Dundubhi; *tasmāt*—from him (Dundubhi); *avidyotaḥ*—a son named Avidyota; *punarvasuḥ*—a son named Punarvasu.

TRANSLATION

The son of Vilomā was Kapotaromā, and his son was Anu, whose friend was Tumburu. From Anu came Andhaka; from Andhaka, Dundubhi; and from Dundubhi, Avidyota. From Avidyota came a son named Punarvasu.

TEXTS 21–23

तस्याहुकश्चाहुकी च कन्या चैवाहुकात्मजौ ।
देवकश्चोग्रसेनश्च चत्वारो देवकात्मजाः ॥२१॥
देववानुपदेवश्च सुदेवो देववर्धनः ।
तेषां स्वसारः सप्तासन् धृतदेवादयो नृप ॥२२॥
शान्तिदेवोपदेवा च श्रीदेवा देवरक्षिता ।
सहदेवा देवकी च वसुदेव उवाह ताः ॥२३॥

tasyāhukaś cāhukī ca
kanyā caivāhukātmajau
devakaś cograsenaś ca
catvāro devakātmajāḥ

devavān upadevaś ca
sudevo devavardhanaḥ
teṣāṁ svasāraḥ saptāsan
dhṛtadevādayo nṛpa

śāntidevopadevā ca
śrīdevā devarakṣitā
sahadevā devakī ca
vasudeva uvāha tāḥ

tasya—from him (Punarvasu); *āhukaḥ*—Āhuka; *ca*—and; *āhukī*—Āhukī; *ca*—also; *kanyā*—a daughter; *ca*—also; *eva*—indeed; *āhuka*—of Āhuka; *ātmajau*—two sons; *devakaḥ*—Devaka; *ca*—and; *ugrasenaḥ*—Ugrasena; *ca*—also; *catvāraḥ*—four; *devaka-ātmajāḥ*—sons of Devaka; *devavān*—Devavān; *upadevaḥ*—Upadeva; *ca*—and; *sudevaḥ*—Sudeva; *devavardhanaḥ*—Devavardhana; *teṣām*—of all of them; *svasāraḥ*—sisters; *sapta*—seven; *āsan*—existed; *dhṛtadevā-ādayaḥ*—headed by Dhṛtadevā; *nṛpa*—O King (Mahārāja Parīkṣit); *śāntidevā*—Śāntidevā; *upadevā*—Upadevā; *ca*—also; *śrīdevā*—Śrīdevā; *devarakṣitā*—Devarakṣitā; *sahadevā*—Sahadevā; *devakī*—Devakī; *ca*—and; *vasudevaḥ*—Śrī Vasudeva, the father of Kṛṣṇa; *uvāha*—married; *tāḥ*—them.

TRANSLATION

Punarvasu had a son and a daughter, named Āhuka and Āhukī respectively, and Āhuka had two sons, named Devaka and Ugrasena. Devaka had four sons, named Devavān, Upadeva, Sudeva and Devavardhana, and he also had seven daughters, named Śāntidevā, Upadevā, Śrīdevā, Devarakṣitā, Sahadevā, Devakī and Dhṛtadevā. Dhṛtadevā was the eldest. Vasudeva, the father of Kṛṣṇa, married all these sisters.

TEXT 24

कंसः सुनामा न्यग्रोधः कङ्कः शङ्कुः सुहूस्तथा ।
राष्ट्रपालोऽथ धृष्टिश्च तुष्टिमानौग्रसेनयः ॥२४॥

kaṁsaḥ sunāmā nyagrodhaḥ
kaṅkaḥ śaṅkuḥ suhūs tathā
rāṣṭrapālo 'tha dhṛṣṭiś ca
tuṣṭimān augrasenayaḥ

kaṁsaḥ—Kaṁsa; *sunāmā*—Sunāmā; *nyagrodhaḥ*—Nyagrodha; *kaṅkaḥ*—Kaṅka; *śaṅkuḥ*—Śaṅku; *suhūḥ*—Suhū; *tathā*—as well as; *rāṣṭrapālaḥ*—Rāṣṭrapāla; *atha*—thereafter; *dhṛṣṭiḥ*—Dhṛṣṭi; *ca*—also; *tuṣṭimān*—Tuṣṭimān; *augrasenayaḥ*—the sons of Ugrasena.

TRANSLATION

Kaṁsa, Sunāmā, Nyagrodha, Kaṅka, Śaṅku, Suhū, Rāṣṭrapāla, Dhṛṣṭi and Tuṣṭimān were the sons of Ugrasena.

TEXT 25

कंसा कंसवती कङ्का शूरभू राष्ट्रपालिका ।
उग्रसेनदुहितरो वसुदेवानुजस्त्रियः ॥२५॥

kaṁsā kaṁsavatī kaṅkā
śūrabhū rāṣṭrapālikā
ugrasena-duhitaro
vasudevānuja-striyaḥ

kaṁsā—Kaṁsā; *kaṁsavatī*—Kaṁsavatī; *kaṅkā*—Kaṅkā; *śūrabhū*—Śūrabhū; *rāṣṭrapālikā*—Rāṣṭrapālikā; *ugrasena-duhitaraḥ*—the daughters of Ugrasena; *vasudeva-anuja*—of the younger brothers of Vasudeva; *striyaḥ*—the wives.

TRANSLATION

Kaṁsā, Kaṁsavatī, Kaṅkā, Śūrabhū and Rāṣṭrapālikā were the daughters of Ugrasena. They became the wives of Vasudeva's younger brothers.

TEXT 26

शूरो विदूरथादासीद् भजमानस्तु तत्सुतः ।
शिनिस्तस्मात् स्वयम्भोजो हृदिकस्तत्सुतो मतः॥२६॥

śūro vidūrathād āsīd
bhajamānas tu tat-sutaḥ
śinis tasmāt svayam bhojo
hṛdikas tat-suto mataḥ

śūraḥ—Śūra; *vidūrathāt*—from Vidūratha, the son of Citraratha; *āsīt*—was born; *bhajamānaḥ*—Bhajamāna; *tu*—and; *tat-sutaḥ*—the son of him (Śūra); *śiniḥ*—Śini; *tasmāt*—from him; *svayam*—personally; *bhojaḥ*—the famous King Bhoja; *hṛdikaḥ*—Hṛdika; *tat-sutaḥ*—the son of him (Bhoja); *mataḥ*—is celebrated.

TRANSLATION

The son of Citraratha was Vidūratha, the son of Vidūratha was Śūra, and his son was Bhajamāna. The son of Bhajamāna was Śini, the son of Śini was Bhoja, and the son of Bhoja was Hṛdika.

TEXT 27

देवमीढः शतधनुः कृतवर्मेति तत्सुताः ।
देवमीढस्य शूरस्य मारिषा नाम पत्न्यभूत् ॥२७॥

devamīḍhaḥ śatadhanuḥ
kṛtavarmeti tat-sutāḥ

devamīḍhasya śūrasya
māriṣā nāma patny abhūt

devamīḍhaḥ—Devamīḍha; *śatadhanuḥ*—Śatadhanu; *kṛtavarmā*—Kṛtavarmā; *iti*—thus; *tat-sutāḥ*—the sons of him (Hṛdika); *deva-mīḍhasya*—of Devamīḍha; *śūrasya*—of Śūra; *māriṣā*—Māriṣā; *nāma*—named; *patnī*—wife; *abhūt*—there was.

TRANSLATION

The three sons of Hṛdika were Devamīḍha, Śatadhanu and Kṛtavarmā. The son of Devamīḍha was Śūra, whose wife was named Māriṣā.

TEXTS 28–31

तस्यां स जनयामास दश पुत्रानकल्मषान् ।
वसुदेवं देवभागं देवश्रवसमानकम् ॥२८॥
सृञ्जयं श्यामकं कङ्कं शमीकं वत्सकं वृकम् ।
देवदुन्दुभयो नेदुरानका यस्य जन्मनि ॥२९॥
वसुदेवं हरेः स्थानं वदन्त्यानकदुन्दुभिम् ।
पृथा च श्रुतदेवा च श्रुतकीर्तिः श्रुतश्रवाः ॥३०॥
राजाधिदेवी चैतेषां भगिन्यः पञ्च कन्यकाः ।
कुन्तेः सख्युः पिता शूरो ह्यपुत्रस्य पृथामदात् ॥३१॥

tasyāṁ sa janayām āsa
daśa putrān akalmaṣān
vasudevaṁ devabhāgaṁ
devaśravasam ānakam

sṛñjayaṁ śyāmakaṁ kaṅkaṁ
śamīkaṁ vatsakaṁ vṛkam
deva-dundubhayo nedur
ānakā yasya janmani

vasudevaṁ hareḥ sthānaṁ
vadanty ānakadundubhim
pṛthā ca śrutadevā ca
śrutakīrtiḥ śrutaśravāḥ

rājādhidevī caiteṣāṁ
bhaginyaḥ pañca kanyakāḥ
kunteḥ sakhyuḥ pitā śūro
hy aputrasya pṛthām adāt

tasyām—in her (Māriṣā); *saḥ*—he (Śūra); *janayām āsa*—begot; *daśa*—ten; *putrān*—sons; *akalmaṣān*—spotless; *vasudevam*—Vasudeva; *devabhāgam*—Devabhāga; *devaśravasam*—Devaśravā; *ānakam*—Ānaka; *sṛñjayam*—Sṛñjaya; *śyāmakam*—Śyāmaka; *kaṅkam*—Kaṅka; *śamīkam*—Śamīka; *vatsakam*—Vatsaka; *vṛkam*—Vṛka; *devadundubhayaḥ*—kettledrums sounded by the demigods; *neduḥ*—were beaten; *ānakāḥ*—a kind of kettledrum; *yasya*—whose; *janmani*—at the time of birth; *vasudevam*—unto Vasudeva; *hareḥ*—of the Supreme Personality of Godhead; *sthānam*—that place; *vadanti*—they call; *ānakadundubhim*—Ānakadundubhi; *pṛthā*—Pṛthā; *ca*—and; *śrutadevā*—Śrutadevā; *ca*—also; *śrutakīrtiḥ*—Śrutakīrti; *śrutaśravāḥ*—Śrutaśravā; *rājādhidevī*—Rājādhidevī; *ca*—also; *eteṣām*—of all these; *bhaginyaḥ*—sisters; *pañca*—five; *kanyakāḥ*—daughters (of Śūra); *kunteḥ*—of Kunti; *sakhyuḥ*—a friend; *pitā*—father; *śūraḥ*—Śūra; *hi*—indeed; *aputrasya*—(of Kunti) who was sonless; *pṛthām*—Pṛthā; *adāt*—delivered.

TRANSLATION

Through Māriṣā, King Śūra begot Vasudeva, Devabhāga, Devaśravā, Ānaka, Sṛñjaya, Śyāmaka, Kaṅka, Śamīka, Vatsaka and Vṛka. These ten sons were spotlessly pious personalities. When Vasudeva was born, the demigods from the heavenly kingdom sounded kettledrums. Therefore Vasudeva, who provided the proper place for the appearance of the Supreme Personality of Godhead, Kṛṣṇa, was also known as Ānakadundubhi. The five daughters of King Śūra, named Pṛthā, Śrutadevā, Śrutakīrti,

Śrutaśravā and Rājādhidevī, were Vasudeva's sisters. Śūra gave Pṛthā to his friend Kunti, who had no issue, and therefore another name of Pṛthā was Kuntī.

TEXT 32

साप दुर्वाससो विद्यां देवहूतीं प्रतोषितात् ।
तस्या वीर्यपरीक्षार्थमाजुहाव रविं शुचिः ॥३२॥

sāpa durvāsaso vidyāṁ
deva-hūtīṁ pratoṣitāt
tasyā vīrya-parīkṣārtham
ājuhāva raviṁ śuciḥ

sā—she (Kuntī, or Pṛthā); *āpa*—achieved; *durvāsasaḥ*—from the great sage Durvāsā; *vidyām*—mystic power; *deva-hūtīm*—calling any demigod; *pratoṣitāt*—who was satisfied; *tasyāḥ*—with that (particular mystic power); *vīrya*—potency; *parīkṣa-artham*—just to examine; *ājuhāva*—called for; *ravim*—the sun-god; *śuciḥ*—the pious (Pṛthā).

TRANSLATION

Once when Durvāsā was a guest at the house of Pṛthā's father, Kunti, Pṛthā satisfied Durvāsā by rendering service. Therefore she received a mystic power by which she could call any demigod. To examine the potency of this mystic power, the pious Kuntī immediately called for the sun-god.

TEXT 33

तदैवोपागतं देवं वीक्ष्य विस्मितमानसा ।
प्रत्ययार्थं प्रयुक्ता मे याहि देव क्षमस्व मे ॥३३॥

tadaivopāgataṁ devaṁ
vīkṣya vismita-mānasā
pratyayārthaṁ prayuktā me
yāhi deva kṣamasva me

tadā—at that time; *eva*—indeed; *upāgatam*—appeared (before her); *devam*—the sun-god; *vīkṣya*—seeing; *vismita-mānasā*—very much surprised; *pratyaya-artham*—just to see the potency of the mystic power; *prayuktā*—I have used it; *me*—me; *yāhi*—please return; *deva*—O demigod; *kṣamasva*—forgive; *me*—me.

TRANSLATION

As soon as Kuntī called for the demigod of the sun, he immediately appeared before her, and she was very much surprised. She told the sun-god, "I was simply examining the effectiveness of this mystic power. I am sorry I have called you unnecessarily. Please return and excuse me."

TEXT 34

अमोघं देवसंदर्शमादधे त्वयि चात्मजम् ।
योनिर्यथा न दुष्येत कर्ताहं ते सुमध्यमे ॥३४॥

amoghaṁ deva-sandarśam
ādadhe tvayi cātmajam
yonir yathā na duṣyeta
kartāhaṁ te sumadhyame

amogham—without failure; *deva-sandarśam*—meeting with the demigods; *ādadhe*—I shall give (my semen); *tvayi*—unto you; *ca*—also; *ātmajam*—a son; *yoniḥ*—the source of birth; *yathā*—as; *na*—not; *duṣyeta*—becomes polluted; *kartā*—shall arrange; *aham*—I; *te*—unto you; *sumadhyame*—O beautiful girl.

TRANSLATION

The sun-god said: O beautiful Pṛthā, your meeting with the demigods cannot be fruitless. Therefore, let me place my seed in your womb so that you may bear a son. I shall arrange to keep your virginity intact, since you are still an unmarried girl.

PURPORT

According to Vedic civilization, if a girl gives birth to a child before she is married, no one will marry her. Therefore although the sun-god, after appearing before Pṛthā, wanted to give her a child, Pṛthā hesitated because she was still unmarried. To keep her virginity undisturbed, the sun-god arranged to give her a child that came from her ear, and therefore the child was known as Karṇa. The custom is that a girl should be married *akṣata-yoni*, that is, with her virginity undisturbed. A girl should never bear a child before her marriage.

TEXT 35

इति तस्यां स आधाय गर्भं सूर्यो दिवं गतः ।
सद्यः कुमारः संजज्ञे द्वितीय इव भास्करः ॥३५॥

iti tasyāṁ sa ādhāya
garbhaṁ sūryo divaṁ gataḥ
sadyaḥ kumāraḥ sañjajñe
dvitīya iva bhāskaraḥ

iti—in this way; *tasyām*—unto her (Pṛthā); *saḥ*—he (the sun-god); *ādhāya*—discharging semen; *garbham*—pregnancy; *sūryaḥ*—the sun-god; *divam*—in the celestial planets; *gataḥ*—returned; *sadyaḥ*—immediately; *kumāraḥ*—a child; *sañjajñe*—was born; *dvitīyaḥ*—second; *iva*—like; *bhāskaraḥ*—the sun-god.

TRANSLATION

After saying this, the sun-god discharged his semen into the womb of Pṛthā and then returned to the celestial kingdom. Immediately thereafter, from Kuntī a child was born, who was like a second sun-god.

TEXT 36

तं सात्यजन्नदीतोये कृच्छ्राल्लोकस्य बिभ्यती ।
प्रपितामहस्तामुवाह पाण्डुर्वै सत्यविक्रमः ॥३६॥

taṁ sātyajan nadī-toye
kṛcchrāl lokasya bibhyatī
prapitāmahas tām uvāha
pāṇḍur vai satya-vikramaḥ

tam—that child; *sā*—she (Kuntī); *atyajat*—gave up; *nadī-toye*—in the water of the river; *kṛcchrāt*—with great repentance; *lokasya*—of the people in general; *bibhyatī*—fearing; *prapitāmahaḥ*—(your) great-grandfather; *tām*—her (Kuntī); *uvāha*—married; *pāṇḍuḥ*—the king known as Pāṇḍu; *vai*—indeed; *satya-vikramaḥ*—very pious and chivalrous.

TRANSLATION

Because Kuntī feared people's criticisms, with great difficulty she had to give up her affection for her child. Unwillingly, she packed the child in a basket and let it float down the waters of the river. O Mahārāja Parīkṣit, your great-grandfather the pious and chivalrous King Pāṇḍu later married Kuntī.

TEXT 37

श्रुतदेवां तु कारूषो वृद्धशर्मा समग्रहीत् ।
यस्यामभूद् दन्तवक्र ऋषिशप्तो दितेः सुतः ॥३७॥

śrutadevāṁ tu kārūṣo
vṛddhaśarmā samagrahīt
yasyām abhūd dantavakra
ṛṣi-śapto diteḥ sutaḥ

śrutadevām—unto Śrutadevā, a sister of Kuntī's; *tu*—but; *kārūṣaḥ*—the King of Karūṣa; *vṛddhaśarmā*—Vṛddhaśarmā; *samagrahīt*—married; *yasyām*—through whom; *abhūt*—was born; *dantavakraḥ*—Dantavakra; *ṛṣi-śaptaḥ*—was formerly cursed by the sages Sanaka and Sanātana; *diteḥ*—of Diti; *sutaḥ*—son.

TRANSLATION

Vṛddhaśarmā, the King of Karūṣa, married Kuntī's sister Śrutadevā, and from her womb Dantavakra was born. Having been cursed by the sages headed by Sanaka, Dantavakra had formerly been born as the son of Diti named Hiraṇyākṣa.

TEXT 38

कैकेयो धृष्टकेतुश्च श्रुतकीर्तिमविन्दत ।
सन्तर्दनादयस्तस्यां पञ्चासन् कैकयाः सुताः ॥३८॥

kaikeyo dhṛṣṭaketuś ca
śrutakīrtim avindata
santardanādayas tasyāṁ
pañcāsan kaikayāḥ sutāḥ

kaikeyaḥ—the King of Kekaya; *dhṛṣṭaketuḥ*—Dhṛṣṭaketu; *ca*—also; *śrutakīrtim*—a sister of Kuntī's named Śrutakīrti; *avindata*—married; *santardana-ādayaḥ*—headed by Santardana; *tasyām*—through her (Śrutakīrti); *pañca*—five; *āsan*—there were; *kaikayāḥ*—the sons of the King of Kekaya; *sutāḥ*—sons.

TRANSLATION

King Dhṛṣṭaketu, the King of Kekaya, married Śrutakīrti, another sister of Kuntī's. Śrutakīrti had five sons, headed by Santardana.

TEXT 39

राजाधिदेव्यामावन्त्यौ जयसेनोऽजनिष्ट ह ।
दमघोषश्चेदिराजः श्रुतश्रवसमग्रहीत् ॥३९॥

rājādhidevyām āvantyau
jayaseno 'janiṣṭa ha
damaghoṣaś cedi-rājaḥ
śrutaśravasam agrahīt

rājādhidevyām—through Rājādhidevī, another sister of Kuntī's; *āvantyau*—the sons (named Vinda and Anuvinda); *jayasenaḥ*—King Jayasena; *ajaniṣṭa*—gave birth to; *ha*—in the past; *damaghoṣaḥ*—Damaghoṣa; *cedi-rājaḥ*—the king of the state of Cedi; *śrutaśravasam*—Śrutaśravā, another sister; *agrahīt*—married.

TRANSLATION

Through the womb of Rājādhidevī, another sister of Kuntī's, Jayasena begot two sons, named Vinda and Anuvinda. Similarly, the king of the Cedi state married Śrutaśravā. This king's name was Damaghoṣa.

TEXT 40

शिशुपालः सुतस्तस्याः कथितस्तस्य सम्भवः ।
देवभागस्य कंसायां चित्रकेतुबृहद्बलौ ॥४०॥

śiśupālaḥ sutas tasyāḥ
kathitas tasya sambhavaḥ
devabhāgasya kaṁsāyāṁ
citraketu-bṛhadbalau

śiśupālaḥ—Śiśupāla; *sutaḥ*—the son; *tasyāḥ*—of her (Śrutaśravā); *kathitaḥ*—already described (in the Seventh Canto); *tasya*—his; *sambhavaḥ*—birth; *devabhāgasya*—from Devabhāga, a brother of Vasudeva's; *kaṁsāyām*—in the womb of Kaṁsā, his wife; *citraketu*—Citraketu; *bṛhadbalau*—and Bṛhadbala.

TRANSLATION

The son of Śrutaśravā was Śiśupāla, whose birth has already been described [in the Seventh Canto of Śrīmad-Bhāgavatam]. Vasudeva's brother named Devabhāga had two sons born of his wife, Kaṁsā. These two sons were Citraketu and Bṛhadbala.

TEXT 41

कंसवत्यां देवश्रवसः सुवीर इषुमांस्तथा ।
बकः कङ्कात् तु कङ्कायां सत्यजित् पुरुजित् तथा ॥४१॥

kaṁsavatyāṁ devaśravasaḥ
suvīra iṣumāṁs tathā
bakaḥ kaṅkāt tu kaṅkāyāṁ
satyajit purujit tathā

kaṁsavatyām—in the womb of Kaṁsavatī; *devaśravasaḥ*—from Devaśravā, a brother of Vasudeva's; *suvīraḥ*—Suvīra; *iṣumān*—Iṣumān; *tathā*—as well as; *bakaḥ*—Baka; *kaṅkāt*—from Kaṅka; *tu*—indeed; *kaṅkāyām*—in his wife, named Kaṅkā; *satyajit*—Satyajit; *purujit*—Purujit; *tathā*—as well as.

TRANSLATION

Vasudeva's brother named Devaśravā married Kaṁsavatī, by whom he begot two sons, named Suvīra and Iṣumān. Kaṅka, by his wife Kaṅkā, begot three sons, named Baka, Satyajit and Purujit.

TEXT 42

सृञ्जयो राष्ट्रपाल्यां च वृषदुर्मर्षणादिकान् ।
हरिकेशहिरण्याक्षौ शूरभूम्यां च श्यामकः ॥४२॥

sṛñjayo rāṣṭrapālyāṁ ca
vṛṣa-durmarṣaṇādikān
harikeśa-hiraṇyākṣau
śūrabhūmyāṁ ca śyāmakaḥ

sṛñjayaḥ—Sṛñjaya; *rāṣṭrapālyām*—through his wife, Rāṣṭrapālikā; *ca*—and; *vṛṣa-durmarṣaṇa-ādikān*—begot sons headed by Vṛṣa and Durmarṣaṇa; *harikeśa*—Harikeśa; *hiraṇyākṣau*—and Hiraṇyākṣa; *śūrabhūmyām*—in the womb of Śūrabhūmi; *ca*—and; *śyāmakaḥ*—King Śyāmaka.

TRANSLATION

King Sṛñjaya, by his wife, Rāṣṭrapālikā, begot sons headed by Vṛṣa and Durmarṣaṇa. King Śyāmaka, by his wife, Śūrabhūmi, begot two sons, named Harikeśa and Hiraṇyākṣa.

TEXT 43

मिश्रकेश्यामप्सरसि वृकादीन् वत्सकस्तथा ।
तक्षपुष्करशालादीन् दुर्वाक्ष्यां वृक आदधे ॥४३॥

miśrakeśyām apsarasi
vṛkādīn vatsakas tathā
takṣa-puṣkara-śālādīn
durvākṣyāṁ vṛka ādadhe

miśrakeśyām—in the womb of Miśrakeśī; *apsarasi*—who belonged to the Apsarā group; *vṛka-ādīn*—Vṛka and other sons; *vatsakaḥ*—Vatsaka; *tathā*—as well; *takṣa-puṣkara-śāla-ādīn*—sons headed by Takṣa, Puṣkara and Śāla; *durvākṣyām*—in the womb of his wife, Durvākṣī; *vṛkaḥ*—Vṛka; *ādadhe*—begot.

TRANSLATION

Thereafter, King Vatsaka, by the womb of his wife, Miśrakeśī, who was an Apsarā, begot sons headed by Vṛka. Vṛka, by his wife, Durvākṣī, begot Takṣa, Puṣkara, Śāla and so on.

TEXT 44

सुमित्रार्जुनपालादीन् समीकात्तु सुदामनी ।
आनकः कर्णिकायां वै ऋतधामाजयावपि ॥४४॥

sumitrārjunapālādīn
samīkāt tu sudāmanī
ānakaḥ karṇikāyāṁ vai
ṛtadhāmā-jayāv api

sumitra—Sumitra; *arjunapāla*—Arjunapāla; *ādīn*—headed by; *samīkāt*—from King Samīka; *tu*—indeed; *sudāmanī*—in the womb of Sudāmanī, his wife; *ānakaḥ*—King Ānaka; *karṇikāyām*—in the womb of his wife Karṇikā; *vai*—indeed; *ṛtadhāmā*—Ṛtadhāmā; *jayau*—and Jaya; *api*—indeed.

TRANSLATION

From Samīka, by the womb of his wife, Sudāmanī, came Sumitra, Arjunapāla and other sons. King Ānaka, by his wife, Karṇikā, begot two sons, namely Ṛtadhāmā and Jaya.

TEXT 45

पौरवी रोहिणी भद्रा मदिरा रोचना इला ।
देवकीप्रमुखाश्चासन् पत्न्य आनकदुन्दुभेः ॥४५॥

pauravī rohiṇī bhadrā
madirā rocanā ilā
devakī-pramukhāś cāsan
patnya ānakadundubheḥ

pauravī—Pauravī; *rohiṇī*—Rohiṇī; *bhadrā*—Bhadrā; *madirā*—Madirā; *rocanā*—Rocanā; *ilā*—Ilā; *devakī*—Devakī; *pramukhāḥ*—headed by; *ca*—and; *āsan*—existed; *patnyaḥ*—wives; *ānaka-dundubheḥ*—of Vasudeva, who was known as Ānakadundubhi.

TRANSLATION

Devakī, Pauravī, Rohiṇī, Bhadrā, Madirā, Rocanā, Ilā and others were all wives of Ānakadundubhi [Vasudeva]. Among them all, Devakī was the chief.

TEXT 46

बलं गदं सारणं च दुर्मदं विपुलं ध्रुवम् ।
वसुदेवस्तु रोहिण्यां कृतादीनुदपादयत् ॥४६॥

balaṁ gadaṁ sāraṇaṁ ca
durmadaṁ vipulaṁ dhruvam
vasudevas tu rohiṇyāṁ
kṛtādīn udapādayat

balam—Bala; *gadam*—Gada; *sāraṇam*—Sāraṇa; *ca*—also; *durmadam*—Durmada; *vipulam*—Vipula; *dhruvam*—Dhruva; *vasudevaḥ*—Vasudeva (the father of Kṛṣṇa); *tu*—indeed; *rohiṇyām*—in the wife named Rohiṇī; *kṛta-ādīn*—the sons headed by Kṛta; *udapādayat*—begot.

TRANSLATION

Vasudeva, by the womb of his wife Rohiṇī, begot sons such as Bala, Gada, Sāraṇa, Durmada, Vipula, Dhruva, Kṛta and others.

TEXTS 47–48

सुभद्रो भद्रबाहुश्च दुर्मदो भद्र एव च ।
पौरव्यास्तनया ह्येते भूताद्या द्वादशाभवन् ॥४७॥
नन्दोपनन्दकृतकशूराद्या मदिरात्मजाः ।
कौशल्या केशिनं त्वेकमसूत कुलनन्दनम् ॥४८॥

subhadro bhadrabāhuś ca
durmado bhadra eva ca
pauravyās tanayā hy ete
bhūtādyā dvādaśābhavan

nandopananda-kṛtaka-
śūrādyā madirātmajāḥ
kauśalyā keśinaṁ tv ekam
asūta kula-nandanam

subhadraḥ—Subhadra; *bhadrabāhuḥ*—Bhadrabāhu; *ca*—and; *durmadaḥ*—Durmada; *bhadraḥ*—Bhadra; *eva*—indeed; *ca*—also; *pauravyāḥ*—of the wife named Pauravī; *tanayāḥ*—sons; *hi*—indeed; *ete*—all of them; *bhūta-ādyāḥ*—headed by Bhūta; *dvādaśa*—twelve; *abhavan*—were born; *nanda-upananda-kṛtaka-śūra-ādyāḥ*—Nanda, Upananda, Kṛtaka, Śūra and others; *madirā-ātmajāḥ*—the sons of Madirā; *kauśalyā*—Kauśalyā; *keśinam*—a son named Keśī; *tu ekam*—only one; *asūta*—gave birth to; *kula-nandanam*—a son.

TRANSLATION

From the womb of Pauravī came twelve sons, including Bhūta, Subhadra, Bhadrabāhu, Durmada and Bhadra. Nanda, Upananda, Kṛtaka, Śūra and others were born from the womb of Madirā. Bhadrā [Kauśalyā] gave birth to only one son, named Keśī.

TEXT 49

रोचनायामतो जाता हस्तहेमाङ्गदादयः ।
इलायामुरुवल्कादीन् यदुमुख्यानजीजनत् ॥४९॥

rocanāyām ato jātā
hasta-hemāṅgadādayaḥ
ilāyām uruvalkādīn
yadu-mukhyān ajījanat

rocanāyām—in another wife, whose name was Rocanā; *ataḥ*—thereafter; *jātāḥ*—were born; *hasta*—Hasta; *hemāṅgada*—Hemāṅgada; *ādayaḥ*—and others; *ilāyām*—in another wife, named Ilā; *uruvalka-ādīn*—sons headed by Uruvalka; *yadu-mukhyān*—principal personalities in the Yadu dynasty; *ajījanat*—he begot.

TRANSLATION

Vasudeva, by another of his wives, whose name was Rocanā, begot Hasta, Hemāṅgada and other sons. And by his wife named Ilā he begot sons headed by Uruvalka, all of whom were chief personalities in the dynasty of Yadu.

TEXT 50

विपृष्टो धृतदेवायामेक आनकदुन्दुभेः ।
शान्तिदेवात्मजा राजन् प्रशमप्रसितादयः ॥५०॥

vipṛṣṭho dhṛtadevāyām
eka ānakadundubheḥ
śāntidevātmajā rājan
praśama-prasitādayaḥ

vipṛṣṭhaḥ—Vipṛṣṭha; *dhṛtadevāyām*—in the womb of the wife named Dhṛtadevā; *ekaḥ*—one son; *ānakadundubheḥ*—of Ānakadundubhi, Vasudeva; *śāntidevā-ātmajāḥ*—the sons of another wife, named Śāntidevā; *rājan*—O Mahārāja Parīkṣit; *praśama-prasita-ādayaḥ*—Praśama, Prasita and other sons.

TRANSLATION

From the womb of Dhṛtadevā, one of the wives of Ānakadundubhi [Vasudeva], came a son named Vipṛṣṭha. The sons of

Śāntidevā, another wife of Vasudeva, were Praśama, Prasita and others.

TEXT 51

राजन्यकल्पवर्षाद्या उपदेवासुता दश ।
वसुहंससुवंशाद्याः श्रीदेवायास्तु षट् सुताः ॥५१॥

rājanya-kalpa-varṣādyā
upadevā-sutā daśa
vasu-haṁsa-suvaṁśādyāḥ
śrīdevāyās tu ṣaṭ sutāḥ

rājanya—Rājanya; *kalpa*—Kalpa; *varṣa-ādyāḥ*—Varṣa and others; *upadevā-sutāḥ*—sons of Upadevā, another wife of Vasudeva's; *daśa*—ten; *vasu*—Vasu; *haṁsa*—Haṁsa; *suvaṁśa*—Suvaṁśa; *ādyāḥ*—and others; *śrīdevāyāḥ*—born of another wife, named Śrīdevā; *tu*—but; *ṣaṭ*—six; *sutāḥ*—sons.

TRANSLATION

Vasudeva also had a wife named Upadevā, from whom came ten sons, headed by Rājanya, Kalpa and Varṣa. From Śrīdevā, another wife, came six sons, such as Vasu, Haṁsa and Suvaṁśa.

TEXT 52

देवरक्षितया लब्धा नव चात्र गदादयः ।
वसुदेवः सुतानष्टावादधे सहदेवया ॥५२॥

devarakṣitayā labdhā
nava cātra gadādayaḥ
vasudevaḥ sutān aṣṭāv
ādadhe sahadevayā

devarakṣitayā—by the wife named Devarakṣitā; *labdhāḥ*—achieved; *nava*—nine; *ca*—also; *atra*—here; *gadā-ādayaḥ*—sons headed by Gadā; *vasudevaḥ*—Śrīla Vasudeva; *sutān*—sons; *aṣṭau*—eight; *ā-dadhe*—begot; *sahadevayā*—in the wife named Sahadevā.

TRANSLATION

By the semen of Vasudeva in the womb of Devarakṣitā, nine sons were born, headed by Gadā. Vasudeva, who was religion personified, also had a wife named Sahadevā, by whose womb he begot eight sons, headed by Śruta and Pravara.

TEXTS 53–55

प्रवरश्रुतमुख्यांश्च साक्षाद् धर्मो वसूनिव ।
वसुदेवस्तु देवक्यामष्ट पुत्रानजीजनत् ॥५३॥
कीर्तिमन्तं सुषेणं च भद्रसेनमुदारधीः ।
ऋजुं सम्मर्दनं भद्रं संकर्षणमहीश्वरम् ॥५४॥
अष्टमस्तु तयोरासीत् स्वयमेव हरिः किल ।
सुभद्रा च महाभागा तव राजन् पितामही ॥५५॥

pravara-śruta-mukhyāṁś ca
sākṣād dharmo vasūn iva
vasudevas tu devakyām
aṣṭa putrān ajījanat

kīrtimantaṁ suṣeṇaṁ ca
bhadrasenam udāra-dhīḥ
ṛjuṁ sammardanaṁ bhadraṁ
saṅkarṣaṇam ahīśvaram

aṣṭamas tu tayor āsīt
svayam eva hariḥ kila
subhadrā ca mahābhāgā
tava rājan pitāmahī

pravara—Pravara (in some readings, Pauvara); *śruta*—Śruta; *mukhyān*—headed by; *ca*—and; *sākṣāt*—directly; *dharmaḥ*—religion personified; *vasūn iva*—exactly like the chief Vasus in the heavenly planets; *vasudevaḥ*—Śrīla Vasudeva, the father of Kṛṣṇa; *tu*—indeed; *devakyām*—in the womb of Devakī; *aṣṭa*—eight; *putrān*—sons;

ajījanat—begot; *kīrtimantam*—Kīrtimān; *suṣeṇam ca*—and Suṣeṇa; *bhadrasenam*—Bhadrasena; *udāra-dhīḥ*—all fully qualified; *ṛjum*—Ṛju; *sammardanam*—Sammardana; *bhadram*—Bhadra; *saṅkarṣaṇam*—Saṅkarṣaṇa; *ahi-īśvaram*—the supreme controller and serpent incarnation; *aṣṭamaḥ*—the eighth one; *tu*—but; *tayoḥ*—of both (Devakī and Vasudeva); *āsīt*—appeared; *svayam eva*—directly, personally; *hariḥ*—the Supreme Personality of Godhead; *kila*—what to speak of; *subhadrā*—a sister, Subhadrā; *ca*—and; *mahābhāgā*—highly fortunate; *tava*—your; *rājan*—O Mahārāja Parīkṣit; *pitāmahī*—grandmother.

TRANSLATION

The eight sons born of Sahadevā such as Pravara and Śruta, were exact incarnations of the eight Vasus in the heavenly planets. Vasudeva also begot eight highly qualified sons through the womb of Devakī. These included Kīrtimān, Suṣeṇa, Bhadrasena, Ṛju, Sammardana, Bhadra and Saṅkarṣaṇa, the controller and serpent incarnation. The eighth son was the Supreme Personality of Godhead Himself—Kṛṣṇa. The highly fortunate Subhadrā, the one daughter, was your grandmother.

PURPORT

The fifty-fifth verse says, *svayam eva hariḥ kila*, indicating that Kṛṣṇa, the eighth son of Devakī, is the Supreme Personality of Godhead. Kṛṣṇa is not an incarnation. Although there is no difference between the Supreme Personality of Godhead Hari and His incarnation, Kṛṣṇa is the original Supreme Person, the complete Godhead. Incarnations exhibit only a certain percentage of the potencies of Godhead; the complete Godhead is Kṛṣṇa Himself, who appeared as the eighth son of Devakī.

TEXT 56

यदा यदा हि धर्मस्य क्षयो वृद्धिश्च पाप्मनः ।
तदा तु भगवानीश आत्मानं सृजते हरिः ॥५६॥

yadā yadā hi dharmasya
kṣayo vṛddhiś ca pāpmanaḥ

tadā tu bhagavān īśa
ātmānaṁ sṛjate hariḥ

yadā—whenever; *yadā*—whenever; *hi*—indeed; *dharmasya*—of the principles of religion; *kṣayaḥ*—deterioration; *vṛddhiḥ*—increasing; *ca*—and; *pāpmanaḥ*—of sinful activities; *tadā*—at that time; *tu*—indeed; *bhagavān*—the Supreme Personality of Godhead; *īśaḥ*—the supreme controller; *ātmānam*—personally; *sṛjate*—descends; *hariḥ*—the Supreme Personality of Godhead.

TRANSLATION

Whenever the principles of religion deteriorate and the principles of irreligion increase, the supreme controller, the Personality of Godhead Śrī Hari, appears by His own will.

PURPORT

The principles by which an incarnation of the Supreme Personality of Godhead descends upon earth are explained in this verse. The same principles are also explained in *Bhagavad-gītā* (4.7) by the Lord Himself:

yadā yadā hi dharmasya
glānir bhavati bhārata
abhyutthānam adharmasya
tadātmānaṁ sṛjāmy aham

"Whenever and wherever there is a decline in religious practice, O descendant of Bharata, and a predominant rise of irreligion—at that time I descend Myself."

In the present age, the Supreme Personality of Godhead has appeared as Śrī Caitanya Mahāprabhu to inaugurate the Hare Kṛṣṇa movement. At the present time, in Kali-yuga, people are extremely sinful and bad (*manda*). They have no idea of spiritual life and are misusing the benefits of the human form to live like cats and dogs. Under these circumstances Śrī Caitanya Mahāprabhu has inaugurated the Hare Kṛṣṇa movement, which is not different from Kṛṣṇa, the Supreme Personality of Godhead. If one associates with this movement, he directly associates with the Supreme Personality of Godhead. People should take advantage of the chanting of the Hare Kṛṣṇa *mantra* and thus gain relief from all the problems created in this age of Kali.

TEXT 57

न ह्यस्य जन्मनो हेतुः कर्मणो वा महीपते ।
आत्ममायां विनेशस्य परस्य द्रष्टुरात्मनः ॥५७॥

na hy asya janmano hetuḥ
karmaṇo vā mahīpate
ātma-māyāṁ vineśasya
parasya draṣṭur ātmanaḥ

na—not; *hi*—indeed; *asya*—of Him (the Supreme Personality of Godhead); *janmanaḥ*—of the appearance, or taking birth; *hetuḥ*—there is any cause; *karmaṇaḥ*—or for acting; *vā*—either; *mahīpate*—O King (Mahārāja Parīkṣit); *ātma-māyām*—His supreme compassion for the fallen souls; *vinā*—without; *īśasya*—of the supreme controller; *parasya*—of the Personality of Godhead, who is beyond the material world; *draṣṭuḥ*—of the Supersoul, who witnesses everyone's activities; *ātmanaḥ*—of the Supersoul of everyone.

TRANSLATION

O King, Mahārāja Parīkṣit, but for the Lord's personal desire, there is no cause for His appearance, disappearance or activities. As the Supersoul, He knows everything. Consequently there is no cause that affects Him, not even the results of fruitive activities.

PURPORT

This verse points out the difference between the Supreme Personality of Godhead and an ordinary living being. An ordinary living being receives a particular type of body according to his past activities (*karmaṇā daiva-netreṇa jantur dehopapattaye*). A living being is never independent and can never appear independently. Rather, one is forced to accept a body imposed upon him by *māyā* according to his past *karma.*

As explained in *Bhagavad-gītā* (18.61), *yantrārūḍhāni māyayā*. The body is a kind of machine created and offered to the living entity by the material energy under the direction of the Supreme Personality of Godhead. Therefore the living entity must accept a particular type of body awarded to him by *māyā*, the material energy, according to his *karma*. One cannot independently say, "Give me a body like this" or "Give me a body like that." One must accept whatever body is offered by the material energy. This is the position of the ordinary living being.

When Kṛṣṇa descends, however, He does so out of His merciful compassion for the fallen souls. As the Lord says in *Bhagavad-gītā* (4.8):

paritrāṇāya sādhūnāṁ
vināśāya ca duṣkṛtām
dharma-saṁsthāpanārthāya
sambhavāmi yuge yuge

"To deliver the pious and to annihilate the miscreants, as well as to reestablish the principles of religion, I advent Myself millennium after millennium." The Supreme Lord is not forced to appear. Indeed, no one can subject Him to force, for He is the Supreme Personality of Godhead. Everyone is under His control, and He is not under the control of anyone else. Foolish people who because of a poor fund of knowledge think that one can equal Kṛṣṇa or become Kṛṣṇa are condemned in every way. No one can equal or surpass Kṛṣṇa, who is therefore described as *asamaurdhva*. According to the *Viśva-kośa* dictionary, the word *māyā* is used in the sense of "false pride" and also in the sense of "compassion." For an ordinary living being, the body in which he appears is his punishment. As the Lord says in *Bhagavad-gītā* (7.14), *daivī hy eṣā guṇamayī mama māyā duratyayā:* "This divine energy of Mine, consisting of the three modes of material nature, is difficult to overcome." But when Kṛṣṇa comes the word *māyā* refers to His compassion or mercy upon the devotees and fallen souls. By His potency, the Lord can deliver everyone, whether sinful or pious.

TEXT 58

यन्मायाचेष्टितं पुंसः स्थित्युत्पत्त्यप्ययाय हि ।
अनुग्रहस्तन्निवृत्तेरात्मलाभाय चेष्यते ॥५८॥

yan māyā-ceṣṭitaṁ puṁsaḥ
sthity-utpatty-apyayāya hi
anugrahas tan-nivṛtter
ātma-lābhāya ceṣyate

yat—whatever; *māyā-ceṣṭitam*—the laws of material nature enacted by the Supreme Personality of Godhead; *puṁsaḥ*—of the living entities; *sthiti*—duration of life; *utpatti*—birth; *apyayāya*—annihilation; *hi*—indeed; *anugrahaḥ*—compassion; *tat-nivṛtteḥ*—the creation and manifestation of cosmic energy to stop the repetition of birth and death; *ātma-lābhāya*—thus going home, back to Godhead; *ca*—indeed; *iṣyate*—for this purpose the creation is there.

TRANSLATION

The Supreme Personality of Godhead acts through His material energy in the creation, maintenance and annihilation of this cosmic manifestation just to deliver the living entity by His compassion and stop the living entity's birth, death and duration of materialistic life. Thus He enables the living being to return home, back to Godhead.

PURPORT

Materialistic men sometimes ask why God has created the material world for the suffering of the living entities. The material creation is certainly meant for the suffering of the conditioned souls, who are part of the Supreme Personality of Godhead, as confirmed by the Lord Himself in *Bhagavad-gītā* (15.7):

mamaivāṁśo jīva-loke
jīva-bhūtaḥ sanātanaḥ
manaḥ ṣaṣṭhānīndriyāṇi
prakṛti-sthāni karṣati

"The living entities in this conditioned world are My eternal, fragmental parts. Due to conditioned life, they are struggling very hard with the six senses, which include the mind." All the living entities are part and parcel of the Supreme Personality of Godhead and are as good as the

Lord qualitatively, but quantitatively there is a great difference between them, for the Lord is unlimited whereas the living entities are limited. Thus the Lord possesses unlimited potency for pleasure, and the living entities have a limited pleasure potency. *Ānandamayo 'bhyāsāt* (*Vedānta-sūtra* 1.1.12). Both the Lord and the living entity, being qualitatively spirit soul, have the tendency for peaceful enjoyment, but when the part of the Supreme Personality of Godhead unfortunately wants to enjoy independently, without Kṛṣṇa, he is put into the material world, where he begins his life as Brahmā and is gradually degraded to the status of an ant or a worm in stool. This is called *manaḥ ṣaṣṭhānīndriyāṇi prakṛti-sthāni karṣati.* There is a great struggle for existence because the living entity conditioned by material nature is under nature's full control (*prakṛteḥ kriyamāṇāni guṇaiḥ karmāṇi sarvaśaḥ*). Because of his limited knowledge, however, the living entity thinks he is enjoying in this material world. *Manaḥ ṣaṣṭhānīndriyāṇi prakṛti-sthāni karṣati.* He is actually under the full control of material nature, but still he thinks himself independent (*ahaṅkāra-vimūḍhātmā kartāham iti manyate*). Even when he is elevated by speculative knowledge and tries to merge into the existence of Brahman, the same disease continues. *Āruhya kṛcchreṇa paraṁ padaṁ tataḥ patanty adhaḥ* (*Bhāg.* 10.2.32). Even having attained that *paraṁ padam,* having merged into the impersonal Brahman, he falls again to the material world.

In this way, the conditioned soul undergoes a great struggle for existence in this material world, and therefore the Lord, out of compassion for him, appears in this world and instructs him. Thus the Lord says in *Bhagavad-gītā* (4.7):

yadā yadā hi dharmasya
glānir bhavati bhārata
abhyutthānam adharmasya
tadātmānaṁ sṛjāmy aham

"Whenever and wherever there is a decline in religious practice, O descendant of Bharata, and a predominant rise of irreligion—at that time I descend Myself." The real *dharma* is to surrender unto Kṛṣṇa, but the rebellious living entity, instead of surrendering to Kṛṣṇa, engages in *adharma*, in a struggle for existence to become like Kṛṣṇa. Therefore out of compassion Kṛṣṇa creates this material world to give the living entity a chance to understand his real position. *Bhagavad-gītā* and similar Vedic literatures are presented so that the living being may understand his relationship with Kṛṣṇa. *Vedaiś ca sarvair aham eva vedyaḥ* (Bg. 15.15). All these Vedic literatures are meant to enable the human being to understand what he is, what his actual position is, and what his relationship is with the Supreme Personality of Godhead. This is called *brahma-jijñāsā*. Every conditioned soul is struggling, but human life provides the best chance for him to understand his position. Therefore this verse says, *anugrahas tan-nivṛtteḥ*, indicating that the false life of repeated birth and death must be stopped and the conditioned soul should be educated. This is the purpose of the creation.

The creation does not arise whimsically, as atheistic men think.

asatyam apratiṣṭhaṁ te
jagad āhur anīśvaram
aparaspara-sambhūtaṁ
kim anyat kāma-haitukam

"They say that this world is unreal, that there is no foundation and that there is no God in control. It is produced of sex desire and has no cause other than lust." (Bg. 16.8) Atheistic rascals think that there is no God and that the creation has taken place by chance, just as a man and woman meet by chance and the woman becomes pregnant and gives birth to a child. Actually, however, this is not the fact. The fact is that there is a purpose for this creation: to give the conditioned soul a chance to return to his original consciousness, Kṛṣṇa consciousness, and then return home, back to Godhead, and be completely happy in the spiritual world. In the material world the conditioned soul is given a chance to satisfy his senses, but at the same time he is informed by Vedic knowledge that this material world is not his actual place for happiness. *Janma-mṛtyu-jarā-vyādhi-duḥkha-doṣānudarśanam* (Bg. 13.9). One must stop the repetition of birth and death. Every human being, therefore, should take advantage of this creation by understanding Kṛṣṇa and his relationship with Kṛṣṇa and in this way return home, back to Godhead.

TEXT 59

अक्षौहिणीनां पतिभिरसुरैर्नृपलाञ्छनैः ।
भुव आक्रम्यमाणाया अभाराय कृतोद्यमः ॥५९॥

akṣauhiṇīnāṁ patibhir
asurair nṛpa-lāñchanaiḥ
bhuva ākramyamāṇāyā
abhārāya kṛtodyamaḥ

akṣauhiṇīnām—of kings possessing great military power; *patibhiḥ*—by such kings or government; *asuraiḥ*—actually demons (because they do not need such military power but create it unnecessarily); *nṛpa-lāñchanaiḥ*—who are actually unfit to be kings (although they have somehow taken possession of the government); *bhuvaḥ*—on the surface of the earth; *ākramyamāṇāyāḥ*—aiming at attacking one another; *abhārāya*—paving the way for diminishing the number of demons on the surface of the earth; *kṛta-udyamaḥ*—enthusiastic (they spend all the revenue of the state to increase military power).

TRANSLATION

Although the demons who take possession of the government are dressed like men of government, they do not know the duty of the government. Consequently, by the arrangement of God, such demons, who possess great military strength, fight with one another, and thus the great burden of demons on the surface of the earth is reduced. The demons increase their military power by the will of the Supreme, so that their numbers will be diminished and the devotees will have a chance to advance in Kṛṣṇa consciousness.

PURPORT

As stated in *Bhagavad-gītā* (4.8), *paritrāṇāya sādhūnāṁ vināśāya ca duṣkṛtām.* The *sādhus*, the devotees of the Lord, are always eager to advance the cause of Kṛṣṇa consciousness so that the conditioned souls may be released from the bondage of birth and death. But the *asuras*, the demons, impede the advancement of the Kṛṣṇa consciousness movement, and therefore Kṛṣṇa arranges occasional fights between different *asuras* who are very much interested in increasing their military power. The duty of the government or king is not to increase military power unnecessarily; the real duty of the government is to see that the people of the state advance in Kṛṣṇa consciousness. For this purpose, Kṛṣṇa says in *Bhagavad-gītā* (4.13), *cātur-varṇyaṁ mayā sṛṣṭaṁ guṇa-karma-vibhāgaśaḥ:* "According to the three modes of material nature and the work ascribed to them, the four divisions of human society were created by Me." There should be an ideal class of men who are bona fide *brāhmaṇas,* and they should be given all protection. *Namo brahmaṇya-devāya go-brāhmaṇa-hitāya ca.* Kṛṣṇa is very fond of *brāhmaṇas* and cows. The *brāhmaṇas* promulgate the cause of advancement in Kṛṣṇa consciousness, and the cows give enough milk to maintain the body in the mode of goodness. The *kṣatriyas* and the government should be advised by the *brāhmaṇas.* Next, the *vaiśyas* should produce enough foodstuffs, and the *śūdras,* who cannot do anything beneficial on their own, should serve the three higher classes (the *brāhmaṇas, kṣatriyas* and *vaiśyas*). This is the arrangement of the Supreme Personality of Godhead so that the conditioned souls will be released from the material condition and return home, back to Godhead. This is the purpose of Kṛṣṇa's descent on the surface of the earth (*paritrāṇāya sādhūnāṁ vināśāya ca duṣkṛtām*).

Everyone must understand Kṛṣṇa's activities (*janma karma ca me divyam*). If one understands the purpose of Kṛṣṇa's coming to this earth and performing His activities, one is immediately liberated. This liberation is the purpose of the creation and Kṛṣṇa's descent upon the surface of the earth. Demons are very much interested in advancing a plan by which people will labor hard like cats, dogs and hogs, but Kṛṣṇa's devotees want to teach Kṛṣṇa consciousness so that people will be satisfied with plain living and Kṛṣṇa conscious advancement. Although demons have created many plans for industry and hard labor so that people will work day and night like animals, this is not the purpose of civilization. Such endeavors are *jagato 'hitaḥ;* that is, they are meant for the misfortune of the people in general. *Kṣayāya:* such activities lead to annihilation. One who understands the purpose of Kṛṣṇa, the Supreme

Personality of Godhead, should seriously understand the importance of the Kṛṣṇa consciousness movement and seriously take part in it. One should not endeavor for *ugra-karma*, or unnecessary work for sense gratification. *Nūnaṁ pramattaḥ kurute vikarma yad indriya-prītaya āpṛṇoti* (*Bhāg.* 5.5.4). Simply for sense gratification, people make plans for material happiness. *Māyā-sukhāya bharam udvahato vimūḍhān* (*Bhāg.* 7.9.43). They do this because they are all *vimūḍhas*, rascals. For flickering happiness, people waste their human energy, not understanding the importance of the Kṛṣṇa consciousness movement but instead accusing the simple devotees of brainwashing. Demons may falsely accuse the preachers of the Kṛṣṇa consciousness movement, but Kṛṣṇa will arrange a fight between the demons in which all their military power will be engaged and both parties of demons will be annihilated.

TEXT 60

कर्माण्यपरिमेयाणि मनसापि सुरेश्वरैः ।
सहसंकर्षणश्चक्रे भगवान् मधुसूदनः ॥६०॥

karmāṇy aparimeyāṇi
manasāpi sureśvaraiḥ
saha-saṅkarṣaṇaś cakre
bhagavān madhusūdanaḥ

karmāṇi—activities; *aparimeyāṇi*—immeasurable, unlimited; *manasā api*—even by such plans perceived within the mind; *sura-īśvaraiḥ*—by the controllers of the universe like Brahmā and Śiva; *saha-saṅkarṣaṇaḥ*—along with Saṅkarṣaṇa (Baladeva); *cakre*—performed; *bhagavān*—the Supreme Personality of Godhead; *madhu-sūdanaḥ*—the killer of the Madhu demon.

TRANSLATION

The Supreme Personality of Godhead, Kṛṣṇa, with the cooperation of Saṅkarṣaṇa, Balarāma, performed activities beyond the mental comprehension of even such personalities as Lord Brahmā

and Lord Śiva. [For instance, Kṛṣṇa arranged the Battle of Kurukṣetra to kill many demons for the relief of the entire world.]

TEXT 61

कलौ जनिष्यमाणानां दुःखशोकतमोनुदम् ।
अनुग्रहाय भक्तानां सुपुण्यं व्यतनोद् यशः ॥६१॥

kalau janiṣyamāṇānāṁ
duḥkha-śoka-tamo-nudam
anugrahāya bhaktānāṁ
supuṇyaṁ vyatanod yaśaḥ

kalau—in this age of Kali; *janiṣyamāṇānām*—of the conditioned souls who will take birth in the future; *duḥkha-śoka-tamaḥ-nudam*—to minimize their unlimited unhappiness and lamentation, which are caused by ignorance; *anugrahāya*—just to show mercy; *bhaktānām*—to the devotees; *su-puṇyam*—very pious, transcendental activities; *vyatanot*—expanded; *yaśaḥ*—His glories or reputation.

TRANSLATION

To show causeless mercy to the devotees who would take birth in the future in this age of Kali, the Supreme Personality of Godhead, Kṛṣṇa, acted in such a way that simply by remembering Him one will be freed from all the lamentation and unhappiness of material existence. [In other words, He acted so that all future devotees, by accepting the instructions of Kṛṣṇa consciousness stated in Bhagavad-gītā, could be relieved from the pangs of material existence.]

PURPORT

The Lord's activities of saving the devotees and killing the demons (*paritrāṇāya sādhūnāṁ vināśāya ca duṣkṛtām*) take place side by side. Kṛṣṇa actually appears for the deliverance of the *sādhus*, or *bhaktas*, but by killing the demons He shows them mercy also, for anyone killed by Kṛṣṇa is liberated. Whether the Lord kills or gives protection, He is kind to both the demons and the devotees.

TEXT 62

यस्मिन् सत्कर्णपीयूषे यशस्तीर्थवरे सकृत् ।
श्रोत्राञ्जलिरुपस्पृश्य धुनुते कर्मवासनाम् ॥६२॥

yasmin sat-karṇa-pīyuṣe
yaśas-tīrtha-vare sakṛt
śrotrāñjalir upaspṛśya
dhunute karma-vāsanām

yasmin—in the history of the transcendental activities of Kṛṣṇa upon the surface of the earth; *sat-karṇa-pīyuṣe*—who pleases the demands of the transcendental, purified ears; *yaśaḥ-tīrtha-vare*—keeping oneself in the best of holy places by hearing the transcendental activities of the Lord; *sakṛt*—once only, immediately; *śrotra-añjaliḥ*—in the form of hearing the transcendental message; *upaspṛśya*—touching (exactly like the water of the Ganges); *dhunute*—destroys; *karma-vāsanām*—the strong desire for fruitive activities.

TRANSLATION

Simply by receiving the glories of the Lord through purified transcendental ears, the devotees of the Lord are immediately freed from strong material desires and engagement in fruitive activities.

PURPORT

When the devotees aurally receive the activities of the Supreme Personality of Godhead as enacted in *Bhagavad-gītā* and *Śrīmad-Bhāgavatam*, they immediately achieve a transcendental vision in which they are no longer interested in materialistic activities. Thus they achieve freedom from the material world. For sense gratification practically everyone is engaged in materialistic activities, which prolong the process of *janma-mṛtyu-jarā-vyādhi*—birth, death, old age and disease—but the devotee, simply by hearing the message of *Bhagavad-gītā* and further relishing the narrations of *Śrīmad-Bhāgavatam*, becomes so pure that he no longer takes interest in materialistic activities. At the moment, devotees in the Western countries are being attracted by Kṛṣṇa consciousness and becoming uninterested in materialistic activities, and therefore people are trying to oppose this movement. But they cannot possibly check this movement or stop the activities of the devotees in Europe and America by their artificial impositions. Here the words *śrotrāñjalir upaspṛśya* indicate that simply by hearing the transcendental activities of the Lord the devotees become so pure that they are immediately immune to the contamination of materialistic fruitive activities. *Anyābhilāṣitā-śūnyam.* Materialistic activities are unnecessary for the soul, and therefore the devotees are freed from such activities. The devotees are situated in liberation (*brahma-bhūyāya kalpate*), and therefore they cannot be called back to their material homes and materialistic activities.

TEXTS 63–64

भोजवृष्ण्यन्धकमधुशूरसेनदशार्हकैः ।
श्लाघनीयेहितः शश्वत् कुरुसृञ्जयपाण्डुभिः ॥६३॥
स्निग्धस्मितेक्षितोदारैर्वाक्यैर्विक्रमलीलया ।
नृलोकं रमयामास मूर्त्या सर्वाङ्गरम्यया ॥६४॥

bhoja-vṛṣṇy-andhaka-madhu-
śūrasena-daśārhakaiḥ
ślāghanīyehitaḥ śaśvat
kuru-sṛñjaya-pāṇḍubhiḥ

snigdha-smitekṣitodārair
vākyair vikrama-līlayā
nṛlokaṁ ramayām āsa
mūrtyā sarvāṅga-ramyayā

bhoja—assisted by the Bhoja dynasty; *vṛṣṇi*—and by the Vṛṣṇis; *andhaka*—and by the Andhakas; *madhu*—and by the Madhus; *śūrasena*—and by the Śūrasenas; *daśārhakaiḥ*—and by the Daśārhakas; *ślāghanīya*—by the praiseworthy; *īhitaḥ*—endeavoring; *śaśvat*—always; *kuru-sṛñjaya-pāṇḍubhiḥ*—assisted by the Pāṇḍavas, Kurus and Sṛñjayas; *snigdha*—affectionate; *smita*—smiling; *īkṣita*—being regarded as; *udāraiḥ*—magnanimous; *vākyaiḥ*—the instructions;

vikrama-līlayā—the pastimes of heroism; *nṛ-lokam*—human society; *ramayām āsa*—pleased; *mūrtyā*—by His personal form; *sarva-aṅga-ramyayā*—the form that pleases everyone by all parts of the body.

TRANSLATION

Assisted by the descendants of Bhoja, Vṛṣṇi, Andhaka, Madhu, Śūrasena, Daśārha, Kuru, Sṛñjaya and Pāṇḍu, Lord Kṛṣṇa performed various activities. By His pleasing smiles, His affectionate behavior, His instructions and His uncommon pastimes like raising Govardhana Hill, the Lord, appearing in His transcendental body, pleased all of human society.

PURPORT

The words *nṛlokaṁ ramayām āsa mūrtyā sarvāṅga-ramyayā* are significant. Kṛṣṇa is the original form. Bhagavān, the Supreme Personality of Godhead, is therefore described here by the word *mūrtyā*. The word *mūrti* means "form." Kṛṣṇa, or God, is never impersonal; the impersonal feature is but a manifestation of His transcendental body (*yasya prabhā prabhavato jagad-aṇḍa-koṭi*). The Lord is *narākṛti*, exactly resembling the form of a human being, but His form is different from ours. Therefore the word *sarvāṅga-ramyayā* informs us that every part of His body is pleasing for everyone to see. Apart from His smiling face, every part of His body—His hands, His legs, His chest—is pleasing to the devotees, who cannot at any time stop seeing the beautiful form of the Lord.

TEXT 65

यस्याननं मकरकुण्डलचारुकर्ण-
भ्राजत्कपोलसुभगं सविलासहासम् ।
नित्योत्सवं न ततृपुर्दृषिभिः पिबन्त्यो
नार्यो नराश्च मुदिताः कुपिता निमेश्च ॥६५॥

yasyānanaṁ makara-kuṇḍala-cāru-karṇa-
bhrājat-kapola-subhagaṁ savilāsa-hāsam

nityotsavaṁ na tatṛpur dṛśibhiḥ pibantyo
nāryo narāś ca muditāḥ kupitā nimeś ca

yasya—whose; *ānanam*—face; *makara-kuṇḍala-cāru-karṇa*—decorated by earrings resembling sharks and by beautiful ears; *bhrājat*—brilliantly decorated; *kapola*—forehead; *subhagam*—declaring all opulences; *sa-vilāsa-hāsam*—with smiles of enjoyment; *nitya-utsavam*—whenever one sees Him, one feels festive; *na tatṛpuḥ*—they could not be satisfied; *dṛśibhiḥ*—by seeing the form of the Lord; *pibantyaḥ*—as if drinking through the eyes; *nāryaḥ*—all the women of Vṛndāvana; *narāḥ*—all the male devotees; *ca*—also; *muditāḥ*—fully satisfied; *kupitāḥ*—angry; *nimeḥ*—the moment they are disturbed by the blinking of the eyes; *ca*—also.

TRANSLATION

Kṛṣṇa's face is decorated with ornaments, such as earrings resembling sharks. His ears are beautiful, His cheeks brilliant, and His smiling attractive to everyone. Whoever sees Lord Kṛṣṇa sees a festival. His face and body are fully satisfying for everyone to see, but the devotees are angry at the creator for the disturbance caused by the momentary blinking of their eyes.

PURPORT

As stated by the Lord Himself in the *Bhagavad-gītā* (7.3):

manuṣyāṇāṁ sahasreṣu
kaścid yatati siddhaye
yatatām api siddhānāṁ
kaścin māṁ vetti tattvataḥ

"Out of many thousands among men, one may endeavor for perfection, and of those who have achieved perfection, hardly one knows Me in truth." Unless one is qualified to understand Kṛṣṇa, one cannot appreciate the presence of Kṛṣṇa on earth. Among the Bhojas, Vṛṣṇis, Andhakas, Pāṇḍavas and many other kings intimately related with Kṛṣṇa, the intimate relationship between Kṛṣṇa and the inhabitants of

Vṛndāvana is especially to be noted. That relationship is described in this verse by the words *nityotsavaṁ na tatṛpur dṛśibhiḥ pibantyaḥ*. The inhabitants of Vṛndāvana especially, such as the cowherd boys, the cows, the calves, the *gopīs* and Kṛṣṇa's father and mother, were never fully satisfied, although they saw Kṛṣṇa's beautiful features constantly. Seeing Kṛṣṇa is described here as *nitya-utsava*, a daily festival. The inhabitants of Vṛndāvana saw Kṛṣṇa almost every moment, but when Kṛṣṇa left the village for the pasturing grounds, where He tended the cows and calves, the *gopīs* were very much afflicted because they saw Kṛṣṇa walking on the sand and thought that Kṛṣṇa's lotus feet, which they dared not place on their breasts because they thought their breasts not soft enough, were being pierced by broken chips of stone. By even thinking of this, the *gopīs* were affected, and they cried at home. These *gopīs*, who were therefore the exalted friends of Kṛṣṇa, saw Kṛṣṇa constantly, but because their eyelids disturbed their vision of Kṛṣṇa, the *gopīs* condemned the creator, Lord Brahmā. Therefore the beauty of Kṛṣṇa, especially the beauty of His face, is described here. At the end of the Ninth Canto, in the Twenty-fourth Chapter, we find a hint of Kṛṣṇa's beauty. Now we are proceeding to the Tenth Canto, which is considered Kṛṣṇa's head. The entire *Śrīmad-Bhāgavata Purāṇa* is the embodiment of Kṛṣṇa's form, and the Tenth Canto is His face. This verse gives a hint of how beautiful His face is. Kṛṣṇa's smiling face, with His cheeks, His lips, the ornaments in His ears, His chewing of betel nuts—all this was minutely observed by the *gopīs*, who thus enjoyed transcendental bliss, so much so that they were never fully satisfied to see Kṛṣṇa's face, but instead condemned the creator of the body for making eyelids that obstructed their vision. The beauty of Kṛṣṇa's face was therefore much more appreciated by the *gopīs* than by His friends the cowherd boys or even by Yaśodā Mātā, who was also interested in decorating the face of Kṛṣṇa.

TEXT 66

जातो गतः पितृगृहाद् व्रजमेधितार्थो
हत्वा रिपून् सुतशतानि कृतोरुदारः ।
उत्पाद्य तेषु पुरुषः क्रतुभिः समीजे
आत्मानमात्मनिगमं प्रथयञ्जनेषु ॥६६॥

jāto gataḥ pitṛ-gṛhād vrajam edhitārtho
hatvā ripūn suta-śatāni kṛtorudāraḥ
utpādya teṣu puruṣaḥ kratubhiḥ samīje
ātmānam ātma-nigamaṁ prathayañ janeṣu

jātaḥ—after taking birth as the son of Vasudeva; *gataḥ*—went away; *pitṛ-gṛhāt*—from the houses of His father; *vrajam*—to Vṛndāvana; *edhita-arthaḥ*—to exalt the position (of Vṛndāvana); *hatvā*—killing there; *ripūn*—many demons; *suta-śatāni*—hundreds of sons; *kṛta-uru-dāraḥ*—accepting many thousands of wives, the best of women; *utpādya*—begot; *teṣu*—in them; *puruṣaḥ*—the Supreme Person, who exactly resembles a human being; *kratubhiḥ*—by many sacrifices; *samīje*—worshiped; *ātmānam*—Himself (because He is the person worshiped by all sacrifices); *ātma-nigamam*—exactly according to the ritualistic ceremonies of the *Vedas; prathayan*—expanding the Vedic principles; *janeṣu*—among the people in general.

TRANSLATION

The Supreme Personality of Godhead, Śrī Kṛṣṇa, known as līlā-puruṣottama, appeared as the son of Vasudeva but immediately left His father's home and went to Vṛndāvana to expand His loving relationship with His confidential devotees. In Vṛndāvana the Lord killed many demons, and afterwards He returned to Dvārakā, where according to Vedic principles He married many wives who were the best of women, begot through them hundreds of sons, and performed sacrifices for His own worship to establish the principles of householder life.

PURPORT

As stated in *Bhagavad-gītā* (15.15), *vedaiś ca sarvair aham eva vedyaḥ:* by all the *Vedas,* it is Kṛṣṇa who is to be known. Lord Śrī Kṛṣṇa, setting an example by His own behavior, performed many ritualistic ceremonies described in the *Vedas* and established the principles of *gṛhastha* life by marrying many wives and begetting many children just to show people in general how to be happy by living according to Vedic principles. The center of Vedic sacrifice is Kṛṣṇa (*vedaiś ca sarvair aham eva vedyaḥ*). To advance in human life, human society must follow the Vedic principles personally demonstrated by Lord Kṛṣṇa in His householder life. The real purpose of Kṛṣṇa's appearance, however, was to manifest how one can take part in loving affairs with the Supreme Personality of Godhead. Reciprocations of loving affairs in ecstasy are possible only in Vṛndāvana. Therefore just after His appearance as the son of Vasudeva, the Lord immediately left for Vṛndāvana. In Vṛndāvana, the Lord not only took part in loving affairs with His father and mother, the *gopīs* and the cowherd boys, but also gave liberation to many demons by killing them. As stated in *Bhagavad-gītā* (4.8), *paritrāṇāya sādhūnāṁ vināśāya ca duṣkṛtām:* the Lord appears in order to protect the devotees and kill the demons. This was fully exhibited by His personal behavior. In *Bhagavad-gītā* the Lord is understood by Arjuna to be *puruṣaṁ śāśvataṁ divyam*—the eternal, transcendental Supreme Person. Here also we find the words *utpādya teṣu puruṣaḥ*. Therefore it is to be concluded that the Absolute Truth is *puruṣa*, a person. The impersonal feature is but one of the features of His personality. Ultimately, He is a person; He is not impersonal. And not only is He *puruṣa*, a person, but He is the *līlā-puruṣottama*, the best of all persons.

TEXT 67

पृथ्व्याः स वै गुरुभरं क्षपयन् कुरूणा-
मन्तःसमुत्थकलिना युधि भूपचम्वः ।
दृष्ट्या विधूय विजये जयमुद्विघोष्य
प्रोच्योद्धवाय च परं समगात् स्वधाम ॥६७॥

pṛthvyāḥ sa vai guru-bharaṁ kṣapayan kurūṇām
antaḥ-samuttha-kalinā yudhi bhūpa-camvaḥ
dṛṣṭyā vidhūya vijaye jayam udvighoṣya
procyoddhavāya ca paraṁ samagāt sva-dhāma

pṛthvyāḥ—on the earth; *saḥ*—He (Lord Kṛṣṇa); *vai*—indeed; *guru-bharam*—a great burden; *kṣapayan*—completely finishing; *kurūṇām*—of the personalities born in the Kuru dynasty; *antaḥ-samuttha-kalinā*—by creating enmity between the brothers by disagreement; *yudhi*—in the Battle of Kurukṣetra; *bhūpa-camvaḥ*—all the demoniac kings; *dṛṣṭyā*—

by His glance; *vidhūya*—cleansing their sinful activities; *vijaye*—in victory; *jayam*—victory; *udvighoṣya*—declaring (the victory for Arjuna); *procya*—giving instructions; *uddhavāya*—unto Uddhava; *ca*—also; *param*—transcendental; *samagāt*—returned; *sva-dhāma*—to His own place.

TRANSLATION

Thereafter, Lord Śrī Kṛṣṇa created a misunderstanding between family members just to diminish the burden of the world. Simply by His glance, He annihilated all the demoniac kings on the Battlefield of Kurukṣetra and declared victory for Arjuna. Finally, He instructed Uddhava about transcendental life and devotion and then returned to His abode in His original form.

PURPORT

Paritrāṇāya sādhūnāṁ vināśāya ca duṣkṛtām. The mission of Lord Kṛṣṇa was performed on the Battlefield of Kurukṣetra, for by the Lord's mercy Arjuna was victorious due to being a great devotee whereas the others were killed simply by the Lord's glance, which cleansed them of all sinful activities and enabled them to attain *sārūpya.* Finally, Lord Kṛṣṇa instructed Uddhava about the transcendental life of devotional service, and then, in due course of time, He returned to His abode. The Lord's instructions in the form of *Bhagavad-gītā* are full of *jñāna* and *vairāgya,* knowledge and renunciation. In the human form of life, one must learn these two things—how to become detached from the material world and how to acquire full knowledge in spiritual life. This is the Lord's mission (*paritrāṇāya sādhūnāṁ vināśāya ca duṣkṛtām*). After executing His complete mission, the Lord returned to His home, Goloka Vṛndāvana.

Thus end the Bhaktivedanta purports of the Ninth Canto, Twenty-fourth Chapter, of the Śrīmad-Bhāgavatam, *entitled "Kṛṣṇa, the Supreme Personality of Godhead."*

—Completed in Bhuvaneśvara, India, on the occasion of establishing a Kṛṣṇa-Balarāma temple.

END OF THE NINTH CANTO

Appendixes

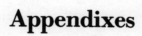

The Author

His Divine Grace A. C. Bhaktivedanta Swami Prabhupāda appeared in this world in 1896 in Calcutta, India. He first met his spiritual master, Śrīla Bhaktisiddhānta Sarasvatī Gosvāmī, in Calcutta in 1922. Bhaktisiddhānta Sarasvatī, a prominent devotional scholar and the founder of sixty-four Gauḍīya Maṭhas (Vedic institutes), liked this educated young man and convinced him to dedicate his life to teaching Vedic knowledge. Śrīla Prabhupāda became his student, and eleven years later (1933) at Allahabad he became his formally initiated disciple.

At their first meeting, in 1922, Śrīla Bhaktisiddhānta Sarasvatī Ṭhākura requested Śrīla Prabhupāda to broadcast Vedic knowledge through the English language. In the years that followed, Śrīla Prabhupāda wrote a commentary on the *Bhagavad-gītā*, assisted the Gauḍīya Maṭha in its work and, in 1944, without assistance, started an English fortnightly magazine, edited it, typed the manuscripts and checked the galley proofs. He even distributed the individual copies freely and struggled to maintain the publication. Once begun, the magazine never stopped; it is now being continued by his disciples in the West.

Recognizing Śrīla Prabhupāda's philosophical learning and devotion, the Gauḍīya Vaiṣṇava Society honored him in 1947 with the title "Bhaktivedanta." In 1950, at the age of fifty-four, Śrīla Prabhupāda retired from married life, and four years later he adopted the *vānaprastha* (retired) order to devote more time to his studies and writing. Śrīla Prabhupāda traveled to the holy city of Vṛndāvana, where he lived in very humble circumstances in the historic medieval temple of Rādhā-Dāmodara. There he engaged for several years in deep study and writing. He accepted the renounced order of life (*sannyāsa*) in 1959. At Rādhā-Dāmodara, Śrīla Prabhupāda began work on his life's masterpiece: a multivolume translation and commentary on the eighteen thousand verse *Śrīmad-Bhāgavatam* (*Bhāgavata Purāṇa*). He also wrote *Easy Journey to Other Planets.*

After publishing three volumes of *Bhāgavatam*, Śrīla Prabhupāda came to the United States, in 1965, to fulfill the mission of his spiritual master. Since that time, His Divine Grace has written over forty volumes of authoritative translations, commentaries and summary studies of the philosophical and religious classics of India.

In 1965, when he first arrived by freighter in New York City, Śrīla Prabhupāda was practically penniless. It was after almost a year of great difficulty that he established the International Society for Krishna Consciousness in July of 1966. Under his careful guidance, the Society has grown within a decade to a worldwide confederation of almost one hundred *āśramas*, schools, temples, institutes and farm communities.

In 1968, Śrīla Prabhupāda created New Vṛndāvana, an experimental Vedic community in the hills of West Virginia. Inspired by the success of New Vṛndāvana, now a thriving farm community of more than one thousand acres, his students have since founded several similar communities in the United States and abroad.

In 1972, His Divine Grace introduced the Vedic system of primary and secondary education in the West by founding the Gurukula school in Dallas, Texas. The school began with 3 children in 1972, and by the beginning of 1975 the enrollment had grown to 150.

Śrīla Prabhupāda has also inspired the construction of a large international center at Śrīdhāma Māyāpur in West Bengal, India, which is also the site for a planned Institute of Vedic Studies. A similar project is the magnificent Kṛṣṇa-Balarāma Temple and International Guest House in Vṛndāvana, India. These are centers where Westerners can live to gain firsthand experience of Vedic culture.

Śrīla Prabhupāda's most significant contribution, however, is his books. Highly respected by the academic community for their authoritativeness, depth and clarity, they are used as standard textbooks in numerous college courses. His writings have been translated into eleven languages. The Bhaktivedanta Book Trust, established in 1972 exclusively to publish the works of His Divine Grace, has thus become the world's largest publisher of books in the field of Indian religion and philosophy. Its latest project is the publishing of Śrīla Prabhupāda's most recent work: a seventeen-volume translation and commentary—completed by Śrīla Prabhupāda in only eighteen months—on the Bengali religious classic *Śrī Caitanya-caritāmṛta.*

In the past ten years, in spite of his advanced age, Śrīla Prabhupāda has circled the globe twelve times on lecture tours that have taken him to six continents. In spite of such a vigorous schedule, Śrīla Prabhupāda continues to write prolifically. His writings constitute a veritable library of Vedic philosophy, religion, literature and culture.

References

The purports of *Śrīmad-Bhāgavatam* are all confirmed by standard Vedic authorities. The following authentic scriptures are specifically cited in this volume:

Bhagavad-gītā, 36, 41, 42–43, 50–51, 65, 74, 76, 88, 102, 103, 105, 107, 124, 132, 133, 134–135, 137, 191, 192, 236, 238, 239, 240, 241, 242, 243, 249, 251, 252

Brahma-vaivarta Purāṇa, 107, 163

Mārkaṇḍeya Purāṇa, 198–199

Śrīmad-Bhāgavatam, 15, 29, 68, 79, 81, 82, 85, 108, 191, 240, 244

Vedānta-sūtra, 240

GENEALOGICAL TABLE

The Descendants of Purūravā

This genealogical chart delineates the Yadu and Pūru dynasties, as well as other descendants of King Purūravā. Kṛṣṇa, the Supreme Personality of Godhead, appeared in the Yadu dynasty as the eighth son of Vasudeva and Devakī.

Note: a vertical arrow summarizes a line of descendants.

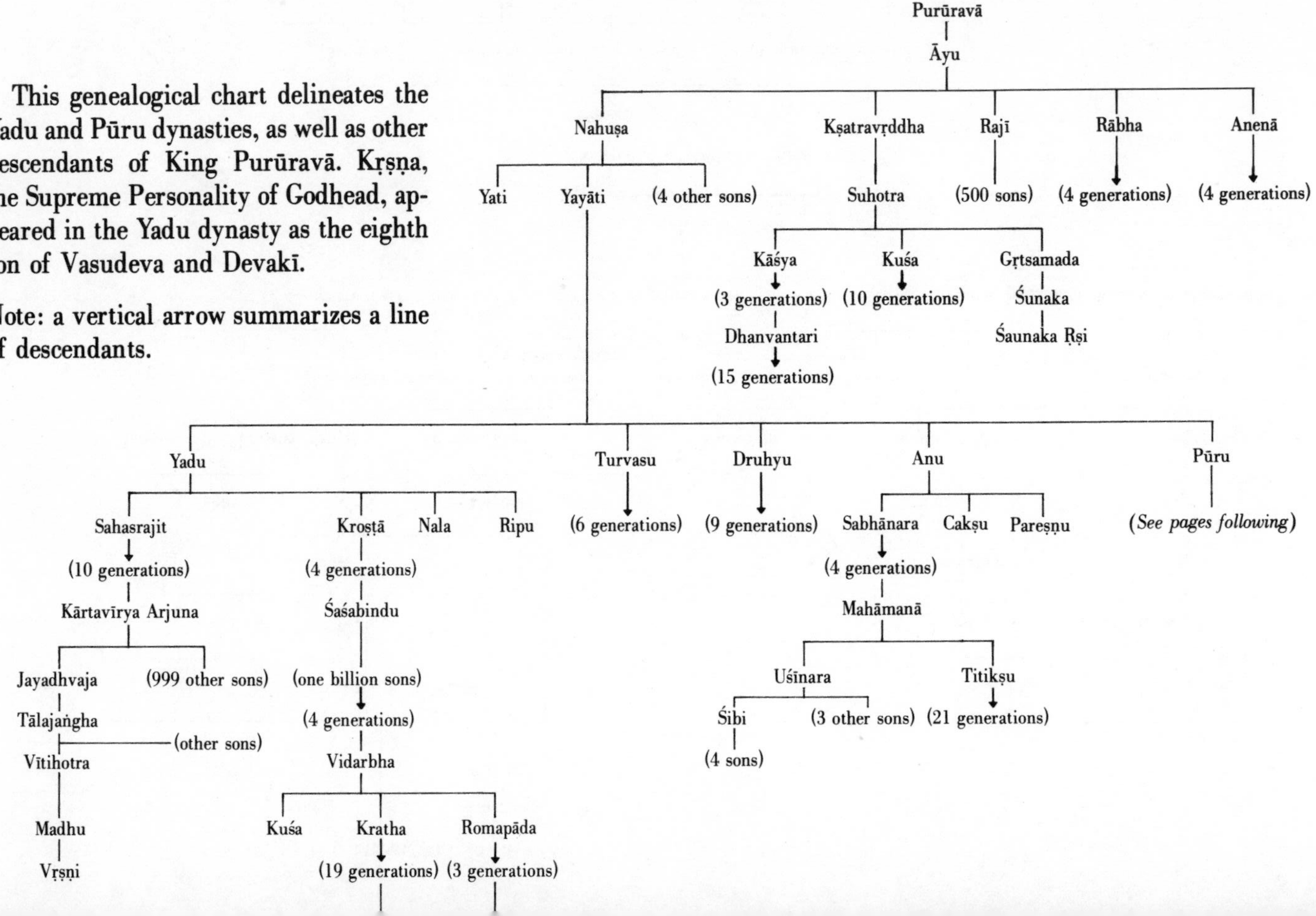

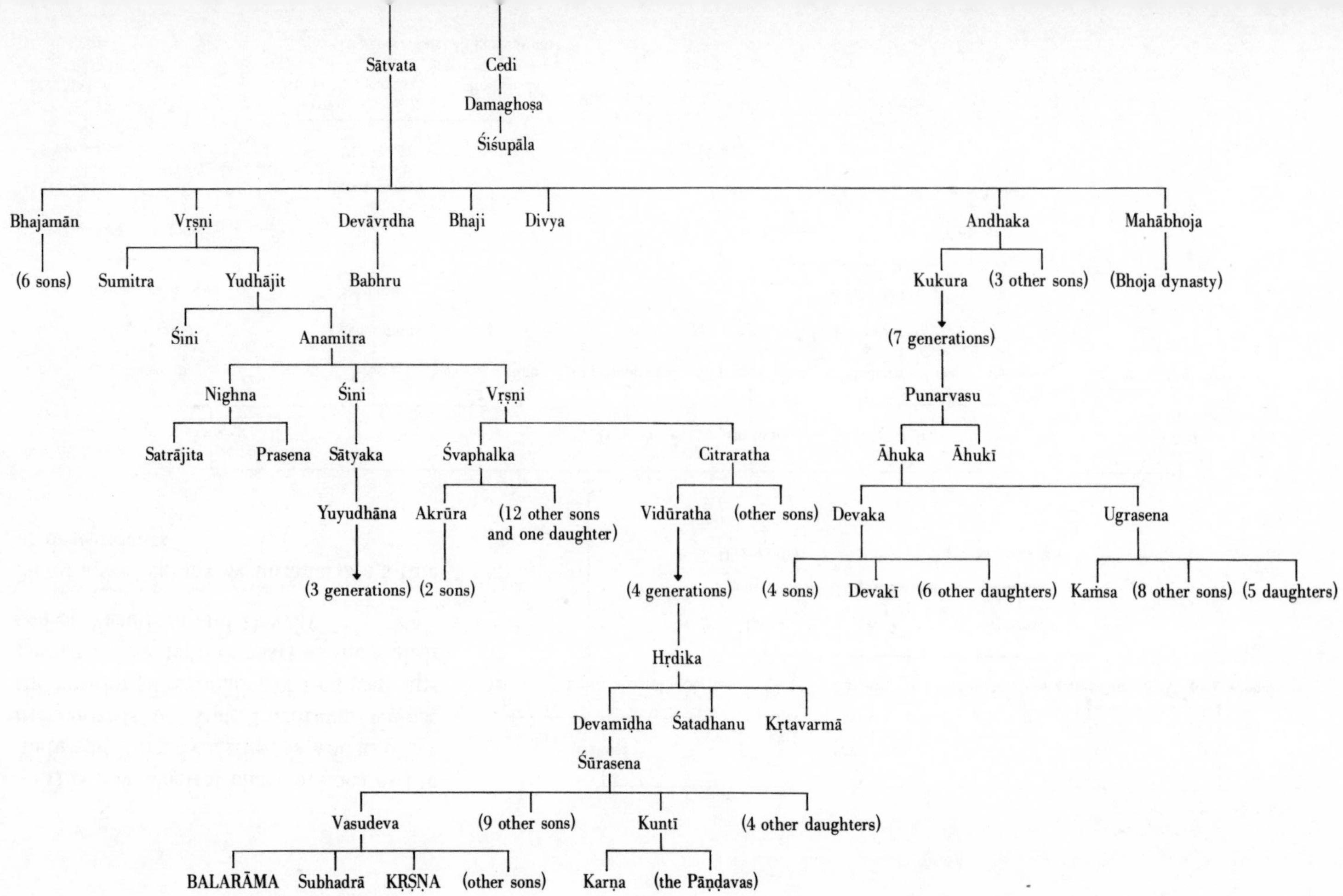

Sātvata
Cedi
Damaghoṣa
Śiśupāla
Bhajamān
Vṛṣṇi
Devāvṛdha
Bhaji
Divya
Andhaka
Mahābhoja
(6 sons)
Sumitra
Yudhājit
Babhru
Kukura
(3 other sons)
(Bhoja dynasty)
Śini
Anamitra
(7 generations)
Nighna
Śini
Vṛṣṇi
Punarvasu
Satrājita
Prasena
Sātyaka
Śvaphalka
Citraratha
Āhuka
Āhukī
Yuyudhāna
Akrūra
(12 other sons
and one daughter)
Vidūratha
(other sons)
Devaka
Ugrasena
(3 generations)
(2 sons)
(4 generations)
(4 sons)
Devakī
(6 other daughters)
Kaṁsa
(8 other sons)
(5 daughters)
Hṛdika
Devamīḍha
Śatadhanu
Kṛtavarmā
Śūrasena
Vasudeva
(9 other sons)
Kuntī
(4 other daughters)
BALARĀMA
Subhadrā
KṚṢṆA
(other sons)
Karṇa
(the Pāṇḍavas)

The Descendants of Purūravā (cont.)
(The Dynasty of Pūru)

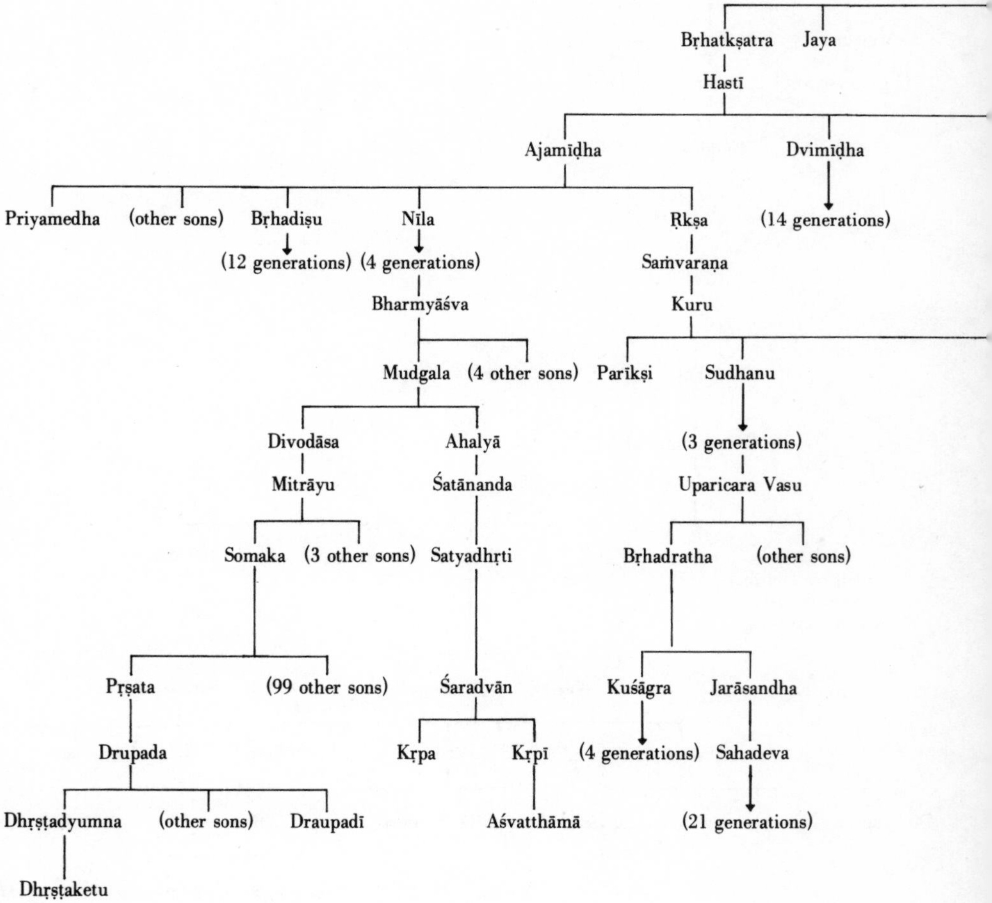

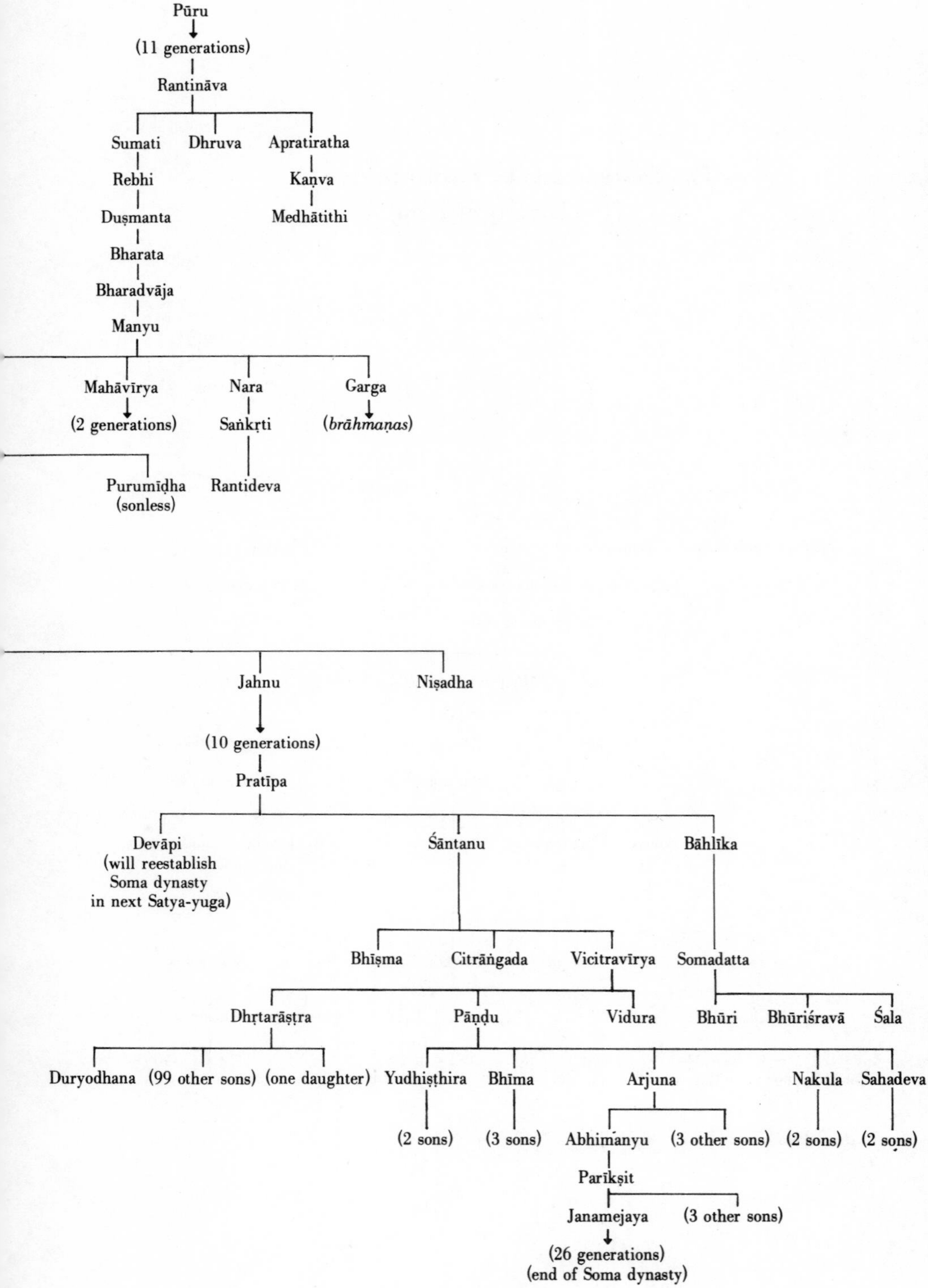

Pūru
(11 generations)
Rantināva
Sumati
Dhruva
Apratiratha
Rebhi
Kaṇva
Duṣmanta
Medhātithi
Bharata
Bharadvāja
Manyu
Mahāvīrya
Nara
Garga
(2 generations)
Saṅkṛti
(*brāhmaṇas*)
Purumīḍha
(sonless)
Rantideva
Jahnu
Niṣadha
(10 generations)
Pratīpa
Devāpi
(will reestablish
Soma dynasty
in next Satya-yuga)
Śāntanu
Bāhlīka
Bhīṣma
Citrāṅgada
Vicitravīrya
Somadatta
Dhṛtarāṣṭra
Pāṇḍu
Vidura
Bhūri
Bhūriśravā
Śala
Duryodhana
(99 other sons)
(one daughter)
Yudhiṣṭhira
Bhīma
Arjuna
Nakula
Sahadeva
(2 sons)
(3 sons)
Abhimanyu
(3 other sons)
(2 sons)
(2 sons)
Parīkṣit
Janamejaya
(3 other sons)
(26 generations)
(end of Soma dynasty)

Glossary

A

Ācārya—a spiritual master who teaches by example.

Agnihotra-yajña—a sacrificial ceremony in which a sacred fire is kindled.

Apsarā—beautiful female demigoddesses residing on the heavenly planet Apsaroloka.

Ārati—a ceremony for greeting the Lord with offerings of food, lamps, fans, flowers and incense.

Arcanā—the devotional process of Deity worship.

Āśrama—the four spiritual orders of life: celibate student, householder, retired life and renounced life.

Aṣṭa-siddhi—the powers attainable by mystic *yogīs.*

Asuras—atheistic demons.

Avatāra—a descent of the Supreme Lord.

B

Bhagavad-gītā—the basic directions for spiritual life spoken by the Lord Himself.

Bhakta—a devotee.

Bhakti-yoga—linking with the Supreme Lord by devotional service.

Brahmacarya—celibate student life; the first order of Vedic spiritual life.

Brahman—the Absolute Truth; especially the impersonal aspect of the Absolute.

Brāhmaṇa—one wise in the *Vedas* who can guide society; the first Vedic social order.

Brahmāstra—a nuclear weapon produced by chanting *mantras.*

C

Caṇḍāla—a lowborn person accustomed to filthy habits such as dog-eating.

D

Deva-gaṇa—a type of demigod.

Dharma—eternal occupational duty; religious principles.

E

Ekādaśī—a special fast day for increased remembrance of Kṛṣṇa, which comes on the eleventh day of both the waxing and waning moon.

G

Goloka (Kṛṣṇaloka)—the highest spiritual planet, containing Kṛṣṇa's personal abodes, Dvārakā, Mathurā and Vṛndāvana.

Gopīs—Kṛṣṇa's cowherd girl friends, His most confidential servitors.

Gṛhastha—regulated householder life; the second order of Vedic spiritual life.

Guru—a spiritual master.

H

Hare Kṛṣṇa mantra—*See: Mahā-mantra*

J

Jāta-karma—a purificatory ceremony performed at the birth of a child.

Jīva-tattva—the living entities, atomic parts of the Lord.

K

Kali-yuga (Age of Kali)—the present age, characterized by quarrel; it is last in the cycle of four and began five thousand years ago.

Karatālas—hand cymbals used in *kīrtana.*

Karma—fruitive action, for which there is always reaction, good or bad.

Karmī—a person satisfied with working hard for flickering sense gratification.

Kīrtana—chanting the glories of the Supreme Lord.

Kṛṣṇaloka—*See:* Goloka

Kṣatriyas—a warrior or administrator; the second Vedic social order.

M

Mahā-mantra—the great chanting for deliverance:

Hare Kṛṣṇa, Hare Kṛṣṇa, Kṛṣṇa Kṛṣṇa, Hare Hare
Hare Rāma, Hare Rāma, Rāma Rāma, Hare Hare.

Mahātmās—self-realized souls.

Mantra—a sound vibration that can deliver the mind from illusion.

Manuṣya-gaṇa—mankind.

Mathurā—Lord Kṛṣṇa's abode, surrounding Vṛndāvana, where He took birth and later returned to after performing His Vṛndāvana pastimes.

Māyā—illusion; forgetfulness of one's relationship with Kṛṣṇa.

Māyāvādīs—impersonal philosophers who say that the Lord cannot have a transcendental body.

Mṛdaṅga—a clay drum used for congregational chanting.

P

Paramparā—the chain of spiritual masters in disciplic succession.

Parivrājakācārya—the third stage of the *sannyāsa* order; the *parivrājakācārya* constantly travels throughout the world, preaching the glories of the Lord.

Prasāda—food spiritualized by being offered to the Lord.

R

Rakṣasa-gaṇa—man-eating demons.

S

Sac-cid-ānanda-vigraha—the Lord's transcendental form, which is eternal, full of knowledge and bliss.

Saṅkīrtana—public chanting of the names of God, the approved *yoga* process for this age.

Sannyāsa—renounced life; the fourth order of Vedic spiritual life.

Śara grass—a whitish reed.

Sārūpya—the liberation of having a form similar to the Lord's.

Śāstras—revealed scriptures.

Śravaṇaṁ kīrtanaṁ viṣṇoḥ—the devotional processes of hearing and chanting about Lord Viṣṇu.

Śūdra—a laborer; the fourth of the Vedic social orders.

Svāmī—one who controls his mind and senses; title of one in the renounced order of life.

T

Tapasya—austerity; accepting some voluntary inconvenience for a higher purpose.

Tilaka—auspicious clay marks that sanctify a devotee's body as a temple of the Lord.

V

Vaikuṇṭha—the spiritual world.

Vaiṣṇava—a devotee of Lord Viṣṇu, Kṛṣṇa.

Vaiśyas—farmers and merchants; the third Vedic social order.

Vānaprastha—one who has retired from family life; the third order of Vedic spiritual life.

Varṇa—the four occupational divisions of society: the intellectual class, the administrative class, the mercantile class, and the laborer class.

Varṇāśrama—the Vedic social system of four social and four spiritual orders.

Vedas—the original revealed scriptures, first spoken by the Lord Himself.

Virāṭ-rūpa—the conception likening the physical form of the universe to the Lord's bodily form.

Viṣṇu, Lord—Kṛṣṇa's expansion for the creation and maintenance of the material universes.

Vṛndāvana—Kṛṣṇa's personal abode, where He fully manifests His quality of sweetness.

Vyāsadeva—Kṛṣṇa's incarnation, at the end of Dvāpara-yuga, for compiling the *Vedas.*

Y

Yajña—an activity performed to satisfy either Lord Viṣṇu or the demigods.

Yogī—a transcendentalist who, in one way or another, is striving for union with the Supreme.

Yugas—ages in the life of a universe, occurring in a repeated cycle of four.

Sanskrit Pronunciation Guide

Vowels

अ a आ ā इ i ई ī उ u ऊ ū ऋ ṛ ॠ ṝ

ऌ ḷ ए e ऐ ai ओ o औ au

ं ṁ *(anusvāra)* ः ḥ *(visarga)*

Consonants

Gutturals:	क ka	ख kha	ग ga	घ gha	ङ ṅa
Palatals:	च ca	छ cha	ज ja	झ jha	ञ ña
Cerebrals:	ट ṭa	ठ ṭha	ड ḍa	ढ ḍha	ण ṇa
Dentals:	त ta	थ tha	द da	ध dha	न na
Labials:	प pa	फ pha	ब ba	भ bha	म ma
Semivowels:	य ya	र ra	ल la	व va	
Sibilants:	श śa	ष ṣa	स sa		
Aspirate:	ह ha	ऽ ' *(avagraha)* – the apostrophe			

The numerals are: ० -0 १-1 २-2 ३-3 ४-4 ५-5 ६-6 ७-7 ८-8 ९-9

The vowels above should be pronounced as follows:

a – like the *a* in org*a*n or the *u* in b*u*t.
ā – like the *a* in f*a*r but held twice as long as short *a*.
i – like the *i* in p*i*n.
ī – like the *i* in p*i*que but held twice as long as short *i*.

u – like the *u* in p*u*sh.
ū – like the *u* in r*u*le but held twice as long as short *u*.
ṛ – like the *ri* in *ri*m.
ṝ – like *ree* in *ree*d.
ḷ – like *l* followed by *ṛ* (*lṛ*).
e – like the *e* in th*ey*.
ai – like the *ai* in *ai*sle.
o – like the *o* in g*o*.
au – like the *ow* in h*ow*.
ṁ (*anusvāra*) – a resonant nasal like the *n* in the French word *bon*.
ḥ (*visarga*) – a final *h*-sound: *aḥ* is pronounced like *aha; iḥ* like *ihi*.

The vowels are written as follows after a consonant:

ा ā ि i ी ī ु u ू ū ृ ṛ ॄ ṝ े e ै ai ो o ौ au

For example: क ka का kā कि ki की kī कु ku कू kū

कृ kṛ कॄ kṝ के ke कै kai को ko कौ kau

The vowel "a" is implied after a consonant with no vowel symbol.

The symbol virāma (्) indicates that there is no final vowel: क्

The consonants are pronounced as follows:

k – as in *k*ite
kh – as in Ec*kh*art
g – as in *g*ive
gh – as in di*g-h*ard
ṅ – as in si*ng*
c – as in *ch*air
ch – as in staun*ch-h*eart
j – as in *j*oy
jh – as in he*dgeh*og
ñ – as in ca*ny*on
ṭ – as in *t*ub
ṭh – as in ligh*t-h*eart
ḍ – as in *d*ove
ḍha- as in re*d-h*ot
ṇ – as r*na* (prepare to say the *r* and say *na*).

Cerebrals are pronounced with tongue to roof of mouth, but the following dentals are pronounced with tongue against teeth:

t – as in *t*ub but with tongue against teeth.
th – as in ligh*t-h*eart but with tongue against teeth.

d – as in *d*ove but with tongue against teeth.
dh – as in re*d-h*ot but with tongue against teeth.
n – as in *n*ut but with tongue between teeth.
p – as in *p*ine
ph – as in u*ph*ill (not *f*)
b – as in *b*ird
bh – as in ru*b-h*ard
m – as in *m*other
y – as in *y*es
r – as in *r*un
l – as in *l*ight
v – as in *v*ine
ś (palatal) – as in the *s* in the German word *sprechen*
ṣ (cerebral) – as the *sh* in *sh*ine
s – as in *s*un
h – as in *h*ome

Generally two or more consonants in conjunction are written together in a special form, as for example: क्ष kṣa त्र tra

There is no strong accentuation of syllables in Sanskrit, or pausing between words in a line, only a flowing of short and long (twice as long as the short) syllables. A long syllable is one whose vowel is long (ā, ī, ū, e, ai, o, au), or whose short vowel is followed by more than one consonant (including anusvāra and visarga). Aspirated consonants (such as kha and gha) count as only single consonants.

Index of Sanskrit Verses

This index constitutes a complete listing of the first and third lines of each of the Sanskrit poetry verses of this volume of *Śrīmad-Bhāgavatam,* arranged in English alphabetical order. The first column gives the Sanskrit transliteration, and the second and third columns, respectively, list the chapter-verse reference and page number for each verse.

U

V

General Index

Numerals in boldface type indicate references to translations of the verses of *Śrīmad-Bhāgavatam.*

A

Abhimanyu, **168**
Abhyutthānam adharmasya
verse quoted, 236, 240
Ābrahma-bhuvanāl lokāḥ
quoted, 76
Absolute Truth
aspects of, three listed, 191–192
Lord as, 51
as person, 252
as rarely realized, 191–192
See also: Supreme Lord
Ācārya defined, 64
Activities
of Lord, 243, **244–245,** 246, 247, **248,** 250, **251,** 252, **253**
of Lord & living entity contrasted, 237–238
material, devotees free of, **246,** 247
sinful, 108
See also: Karma
Adharma defined, 240–241
Adharma-jña defined, 44
Adhiratha, **186, 187**
Administrators. *See:* King; *Kṣatriya(s);* Leaders, government
Affection. *See:* Attachment; Love; Lust
Agastya, **16**
Age (time of life)
of retirement from family life, 57, 67, 74
See also: Old age
Age of Kali. *See:* Kali-yuga
Agnihotra-yajña, 157
Ahalyā, **145**
Ahaṁ bīja-pradaḥ pitā
quoted, 102
Ahaṁ tvāṁ sarva-pāpebhyo
quoted, 79
Ahaṁyāti, **90**
Ahaṅkāra-vimūḍhātmā
quoted, 82, 240
Aho gṛha-kṣetra-sutapta-vittair
quoted, 59
Āhuka, **218**
Āhukī, **218**
Ajamīḍha, **137, 138, 143, 151**
Akriya, **7**
Akrodhana, **155**
Akrūra, **214, 215**
Akṣata-yoni defined, 224
Alarka, **5, 6**
Ambā, 160
Ambālikā, 160, **162, 163**
Ambikā, 160, **162, 163**
Amṛta defined, 128
Ānaka, **221, 229**
Analogies
bird and surrendered soul, 79
butter fire and lusty desire, **68**–69
dark well and family life, 57, 66
goats and materialists, 61, 64
ghost and lust, **61**
heart disease and lust, 68
Anamitra, **212, 213**
Ānandamayo 'bhyāsāt
quoted, 240
Andhaka, son of Anu, **216**
Andhaka, son of Sātvata, **210, 216**
Anenā, **3, 7**
Aṅga, **182, 183**
Anger of Devayānī & Śarmiṣṭhā, **20–24, 37**
Animals
humans contrasted to, 46

D

E

N

O

P

Q

R

T

W

Y

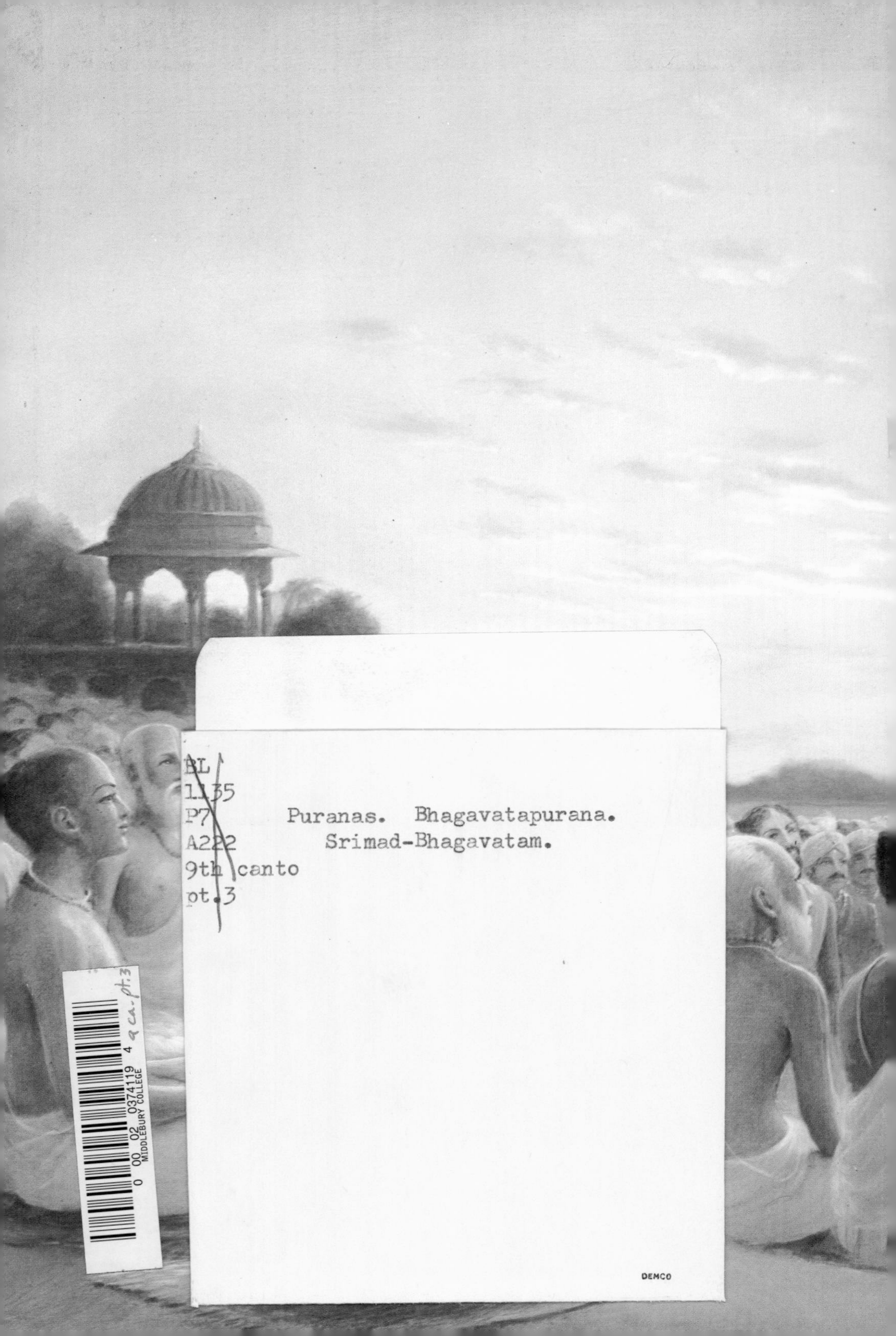